# CHIRON

## Abandonment

# 1985
# A REVIEW OF JUNGIAN ANALYSIS

### *Chiron's* policy on capitalizing the term "Self"

Jung's understanding of the Self is significantly different from how this term is often used in other contemporary psychoanalytic literature. The difference hinges primarily on the understanding of archetypes: The Jungian conceptualization of the Self sees it as rooted in the transpersonal dimension. Hence the frequent capitalization of this term. Since the clinical concern with the Self often relates more narrowly to the sphere of ego-consciousness, however, it can be more mystifying than edifying always to allude to the archetypal level in the literature. Consequently the editors of *Chiron* have chosen to allow authors to exercise an option on the question of capitalization. They may choose to capitalize Self and thereby to emphasize its transpersonal, archetypal base; or, they may choose to employ the lower case, signifying by this that they are discussing issues that have to do principally with ego-identity and the personal relation to this central factor of psychic life, which may be less precisely articulated by reference to the archetypal substratum.

# Editors' Preface

*Chiron* has been established, with the co-sponsorship of the Chicago and Inter-Regional Societies of Jungian Analysts, to encourage the further development of a clinical literature in the field of analytical psychology. The adjective "clinical" is broadly interpreted and has wide-ranging connotations, but for our purposes all of them can be collected under the rubric "practical therapeutic application" of analytical psychology and Jungian theory. While papers without specific reference to analytical work may have great value for culture, the future of a field devoted primarily to working in psychotherapy from a Jungian perspective will be best served by keeping the therapeutic interaction directly in focus. The editors will prefer, therefore, to publish papers that have a direct relation to analytical practice.

It is hoped that *Chiron* will be a carrier of the further clinical extensions of the wisdom contained in Jung's works and in the field of analytical psychology. The editors recognize that the approaches of other psychoanalytic schools are useful and can be employed fruitfully to amplify and to extend Jung's ideas. Papers that reflect an awareness of the developments in these schools of thought and have a bearing on the Jungian approach are therefore invited to be submitted for publication in *Chiron*. While *Chiron* will attempt to bridge Jungian and non-Jungian perspectives on therapy and theory, its basic intention is to further the field of analytical psychology as a clinically vital approach to psychological treatment.

The journal is named after a mythical figure, Chiron, a teacher of many Greek heroes and of the healer Aesclepius. Descended from an ancient race, half-human and half-beast, centaurs were liminal figures who linked the instinctual and spiritual dimensions of human existence. Figures like Chiron symbolize a link between the wisdom of the body and newer forms of human consciousness. *Chiron* is dedicated to this spirit of linking the body of past achievements to new directions.

*Nathan Schwartz-Salant*
*Murray Stein*

# Abandonment in Infancy

## Michael Fordham

Babies, children, lovers, husbands, and wives can be aban-doned; so can friends or dying soldiers on the battlefield. The consequences for these victims can vary according to their inner resources: Starvation and death apart, abandonment can lead to renewal through pain and suffering, a theme which Jung took up in his essay, "The Psychology of the Child Archetype" (1969a).

In that essay, a companion piece to Kerenyi's "The Primordial Child in Primordial Times" (1949), Jung singles out abandonment for special consideration. His account is puzzling in a number of ways because he almost seems to understand growing up as a sequence of abandonment episodes. Just who is abandoned is not specified. Is it the mother, is it the child, or is it the unconscious from which separation is required? But is it justifiable to provide such a favorable view of a seemingly destructive process? The last part of his essay, where he works out stages in the individuation

**Michael Fordham,** M.D., is a member of The Society of Analytical Psychology, London. He is co-editor of *The Collected Works of C. G. Jung* and author of numerous papers and books in analytical psychology, including *Jungian Psychotherapy, The Self and Autism* and *Explorations into the Self* (forthcoming). Dr. Fordham is the founder of the C. G. Jung Clinic in London.

process, makes it rather more clear. First there is the stage of personal infantilism, which

> presents the picture of an "abandoned" or "misunderstood" child with overweening pretentions. The epiphany of the hero (the second identification) shows itself in a corresponding inflation . . . and conscious inferiority. . . . Once the reef of the second identification has been successfully circumnavigated, conscious processes can be clearly separated from the unconscious and the latter observed objectively (Jung 1969a, p. 180),

thus leading to individuation in which the symbolic image of the child reveals the self transcending the conflict of opposites. That, in my view, presupposes the resolution of the essentially destructive act. I shall maintain that Jung's conclusion is too optimistic.

Jung's essay should be read in conjunction with Kerenyi's, in which the phenomenon of the child archetype is given in dramatic records of myths. These depict predominantly violent emotion, in which abandonment either of the child itself, the mother, or both is graphically shown. Reading Jung alone, one gets a too decorous view of abandonment. His part of the volume has, however, the virtue that it considers abandonment in its psychological aspects. Yet abandonment cannot be considered only as a myth. We need to think of it in relation to outer conditions and inner resources. It was to the latter that Jung paid attention, not to the former.

I shall focus attention on infancy. One might ask if infancy is important, or relevant, to a Jungian. Since Jung himself contributed to the psychology of mature persons, it might be argued that we ought to be furthering that, not delving into the first weeks and months of an individual's extrauterine life; that infancy is long since over and done with. We should get on with more serious matters. For many years I have argued against that proposition and have built on another one: that infant and child mentality is a permanent feature of the development of anyone who is alive and growing.

I had worked on child development since 1933 and had come to the conclusion that, contrary to the views of Frances Wickes and Jung (at that time), archetypal images were relatively common in childhood and functioned in much the same way as in adult life (Fordham 1944, 1969). In this I gained much support from the work of Melanie Klein (1932) who, first amongst psychoanalysts, opened up the inner world of childhood and infancy just as Jung had done for adults. I next found symbolic images of the self in mandala form and in the omnipotent fantasies of children (cf. Fordham 1957, p. 144). That, at the time, shocking discovery led me to speculate about small children and even infants, but I did not then develop the theoretical consequences.

Concurrently I studied the theory of archetypes (Fordham 1957), transference, countertransference, and technique and began to think about whether the self was basic to infancy. My ideas developed gradually, but they seemed at the time too revolutionary to expand without further data about infancy, which I did not have available. I was, however, getting massive experience to show that the current idea of a child as being so much part of the parents—mother more than father—and having virtually no coherent mental structure was a considerable overstatement, if not grossly wrong. Jung in various places had also suggested, however, that this thesis could be turned upside down and that parents could be considered the creation of the child. Nevertheless, my view that a child is not all that different in his mental structures from an adult and that the difference is basically quantitative rather than qualitative was treated with disbelief. The idea that the treatment of children was best conducted through the parents was brought under more and more serious question, indeed it seemed that child analysis was in many cases the treatment of choice (cf. Fordham 1980).

In 1947 I published my tentative ideas, which ran as follows: An infant is primarily an integrated whole, and the primary self and its integrity are essential elements in development. The self preserves continuity of being and the infant's individuality. I also reflected that if this were so, then the self, being a closed system, must have another characteristic: It must deintegrate to bring the baby into relation with the mother. There could also follow a rhythm of integration, deintegration, integration. The hypothesis then hung fire, as far as infancy was concerned, because I had no data by which to test it. It was not until I came to hear of the work of the Tavistock Clinic on infant-mother observations that the necessary data began to emerge. Infant-mother observation seminars were started at the S.A.P. (Society of Analytical Psychology in London) and Gianna Henry was lent to us to lead them. I did not myself make observations, but I listened to the students' reports with fascination and considerable emotion. Here, it seemed, was my hypothesis being enacted graphically and often dramatically. One could listen to detailed accounts of how a baby and its mother interacted with each other. It was clear that the idea of primitive identity simply did not apply and that babies were quite different from each other, even within the same family. They had recognizable individuality and reacted to their mothers not only in a physical way; they seemed able to adapt to and to know in some way about their mother's emotional states. Thus one could speak of a "helpful baby" or a "sparing one"—one who did not make demands—phrases in use to represent the baby's personality.

The integrative-deintegrative sequences stared me in the face. It was only necessary to observe a good feeding to see the baby unpacking, as it were, itself, approaching the breast and feeding until satisfied, and after which returning to an integrative sleep. That almost ideal pattern has numerous variants, with passages of violent emotion and crisis which, when well enough handled, can be negotiated, but, which could even happen when a mother's responses were apparently quite inadequate. Klein spoke of splitting, whereby she suggested that a baby, in the course of development, splits up in such a way that wholeness is violated. Deintegration, by contrast, means that the quality of wholeness permeates the baby's actions. The difference between these two hypotheses may be thought about as follows. Early on in extrauterine life, a baby experiences one breast as good and another one as bad, depending on the degree of satisfaction or frustration experienced in the feeding. It is believed that a baby does not know that both breasts are the same; that awareness comes later as cognitive and emotional development proceed. One can say that the two breasts are the consequence of splitting, or that deintegrates become classed as good or bad because emotional development has not reached the stage of being able to grasp that the two experiences emanate from the same source. Whether one or the other of the hypotheses be correct, the distinction becomes important in emotional development.

In either case the subjects of consciousness and the ego must inevitably arise. I would conceive the deintegrates as providing the groundwork for developing ego nuclei, but early on in infant development I do not find the dichotomy of conscious-unconscious useful. Those conceptions become relevant as the structuralization of systems takes place.

The main body of this article will be occupied with a description of an infant interacting with its mother. In the course of the baby's development an episode occurred in which the infant depic-ted the emotional state of being abandoned even though, on the surface, reasonable provision had been made by his mother for her temporary absence.

The account I provide is taken from observations made on mothers and infants in interviews that took place in the home setting for one hour once a week; they continued for the first two years of extrauterine life. Where possible, parents are seen before the birth of the baby to try and initiate good enough relationships between the observer and the family for the study to be pursued without serious interruption. At this interview, it will also be possible to convey to parents the nature of the exercise, especially that the observations aim to be objective and that the student is there to learn and not to give advice or to initiate anything like therapy. (The last objective is not always possible to implement, and this intro-duces sometimes fruitful and interesting complications.) Finally, though any part of the infant's life will be of interest, feeding, diapering, and bathing activities will be of special value. During the interviews, care is taken not to elicit information about, for instance, the parents' life; nevertheless, any information given without prob-ing is accepted gratefully.

The observers were students of the Child Analytic Training conducted at the S.A.P. They had not attended many, if any, seminars and so were theoretically unsophisticated. None of them had ana-lyzed a child. Each had had, however, considerable experience with children either as teachers or as workers in the field of infant or child care.

Each report, which comprises three or more typescript pages for each interview, is as objective and detailed as can be. Three or more interviews are reported at the monthly seminar. Copies of the interview are distributed to the seminar leader and other students, about six in number. Besides the observer's reporting the findings, a second person (always the same) is deputed to summarize the previous seminar discussion, thereby maintaining continuity. After the full reports have been read, they are discussed under the lead-ership of an experienced child analyst who has acquired special knowledge of mothers and infants.

It is apparent that these procedures differ from those adopted by such researchers as Gesel or Piaget. Both of them investigated infants and children in relative isolation so that developmental stages could be determined. They were at pains to exclude emotion, whereas we placed emotion in the center of the stage.

My procedure is at variance with the usual one of giving the history, including a sketch of the parents' personalities and any possible psychopathology. Those who proceed in that fashion tend to be looking for causes and not the meaning of an event to the infant.

Let me illustrate what I mean by a rather stark example. One baby after birth refused to feed from the bottle his mother presented. Some members of the seminar almost immediately demanded to know about his mother's psychopathology. That avoided the fact that the baby had refused the bottle and furthermore that two skilled nurses had also failed, resulting in the baby's having to go into intensive care. My conclusion was that once you start looking for causes the facts fly out of the window. I do not want, therefore, to provide the opportunity for denying the facts. After that, the reader who wants to can, I hope, gain sufficient satisfaction for speculation if I outline what seemed to be important in the infant's relation with his mother from birth to one year and three weeks.

I will now detail this child's experience on an occasion when his mother had temporarily departed, then I will give two other descriptions of her leaving. I will not give information either about the home situation or the infant's history. I do this because I want to describe the meaning, to the infant, of his mother's departure. That is the important feature to underline. Here is what the observer witnessed.

"I [the observer] knocked on the door and Pop, an elderly friend of F [the mother], let me in, explaining that F was out and had left me a note. I could hear loud cries and sobs from the bedroom and caught a glimpse of N [the baby] standing up in his crib, crying miserably, looking out to where we were standing in the hall. I went into the kitchen and read F's note. She had forgotten I had arranged to come on Tuesdays from now on, and she had made other plans and had gone out; she apologized in the note and said she would see me next week.

"Pop and I went into the bedroom to see N. His little face was flushed and stained with tears, his eyes were brimming over, and his nose was running. He was too upset to pay much attention to my greeting [he had regularly greeted the observer warmly before], and, after looking at me through his tears, clung to Pop's stomach and, with his arms outstretched, pulled and tugged at Pop's sweater in an attempt to be lifted up. Pop smiled and talked to him a little, and then holding N's bottle attempted to put the nipple into N's mouth. N shook his head and waved his hand in a discarding motion and continued to cry and pull at Pop in great distress and unhappiness.

"Finally Pop lifted him up, and N stopped crying, although he looked terribly unhappy. He was clearly not consoled very much by being held and a moment later slithered to the floor. His face cleared and he sat on his bottom in front of a chest of drawers. He immediately pulled out the bottom drawer and looked inside. A few moments later he shut it and crawled quickly out of the bedroom into the hall, his lip trembling and his expression anxious. He immediately went to the front door, and with tears splashing down his cheeks and in great distress he pulled and scratched at the door, reaching for the letter slot and hitting it in a confused, despairing way, looking back at Pop and me. I knelt beside him and stroked him, trying to comfort him. It was very painful to watch his distress. Finally I picked him up in an effort to soothe him. His loud cries stopped, and he then seemed to cry silently. He reached out slightly toward Pop, so I handed N to him. N sat sadly in his arms rubbing his ears and face and being clearly very tired.

"Pop said he would try putting him down again. He put him into the crib, and N relaxed and, for a moment, I thought he was going to start smiling. However, he wouldn't lie down and without making any noise stood up by the rails, reaching out to Pop, with tears still streaming down his face and very distressed. Pop stood nearby, sympathetic but not too concerned. He put a huge soft, cuddly pink elephant into N's crib, which barely left any room for N.

"Soon after, Pop went into the kitchen and I stayed with N. He stayed standing by the rail, his arms half outstretched to me, pulling to get out and his face still visibly working. I was quite distressed also, knowing he would not be soothed by my picking him up, and at any rate I was reluctant to do so. Instead I just talked gently and patted him, at one time offering him his bottle, which he firmly and tearfully rejected.

"N stayed there a few minutes and then, as if suddenly

giving up on me, turned away and flung himself onto the cuddly elephant, sucking his thumb and burying his face deep into the fur. Then he turned, got up, stood again by the rails and drooped over them, his arms hanging over the edge in an attitude of misery and depression. He again turned and flung himself onto the pink elephant, this time falling into a corner with it. His knees were tucked up under his tummy and he was resting on his feet, although the main weight was on his head and shoulders, which were buried deep into the fur. He sucked his right thumb, at the same time quickly pulling and stroking the fur with the fingers of his right hand. His left hand was buried underneath his body and he looked like a tiny huddled ball in the corner of the crib.

"I was sitting out of his view. Then he suddenly seemed to go to sleep. His eyes shut quickly and he sucked his thumb noisily, using the rest of his fingers to cover his face. His breathing was terribly snuffly from all the crying and obviously not helped by being partially buried in the fur. He stayed like this for a few minutes, his breathing becoming heavier. Then he stirred, half sat up with his eyes open, and then fell down again, asleep.

"A few minutes later he suddenly awoke and sat back on his bottom, banging his head slightly on the end of the crib as he did so. He was clearly only half-conscious and sank back into the elephant almost immediately, still sucking his thumb. His sleep seemed restless and he looked thoroughly uncomfortable, so after a few minutes I moved the elephant to the end of the crib and gently disentangled his arms and legs and lay him stretched out on his side. His thumb had fallen out and he now seemed more deeply asleep, not stirring as I lifted him.

"I tucked a blanket around him and then left."

Next week F again went out—but after the observer had arrived so that the separation could be followed through. At the start of the observation, N was clinging to his mother.

"N was keeping very close to F, and he started clinging to her and crying as her preparations for leaving went on. He held on to her as she squatted on the floor and several times called out 'Mum, Mum,' his face red and tearful. Then, as his mother went off into the kitchen to get her bag, he stopped crying a little and followed her toward the kitchen door. She came out, very quickly said good-bye to me, and hurried out of the door with J (N's older brother) before N was really aware she had gone. N suddenly realized she'd vanished and he crawled rapidly to the door. He stood up by the door, his face working in distress and clinging to it with an expression of horror and shock on his face and his mouth wide open in a noiseless cry. Then about half a minute later the tears came and he burst into loud painful sobs, his body shaking as if quite overcome by the awareness that his mother had gone. Then followed a sequence of emotion much like the first, ending in sleep on the pink elephant."

N's despair, his desperation and catastrophic misery at F's going out, was astonishing and unexpected. There had been nothing like it before. By 14 weeks he could be upset if his mother went into the kitchen. Once F went out into the kitchen, interrupting a happy time following a feeding; the pair had been enjoying each other, and when that suddenly stopped, N started to sob. The separation did not last for long, however, and he was quickly comforted on F's return. An indication that N had been more upset than he appeared was that when he was next put on the floor, he regurgitated his milk. Occasional incidents like this occurred from time to time, but it did seem that N had accumulated rather good inner resources on which he could rely in his mother's absence. Indeed, when he was 10 months old, the family went to Ireland and N was left with a relative while F went to a marriage ceremony and subsequent party. N was "no trouble at all" and was quite happy when his mother returned.

After the two episodes I have described, F decided she could not for the time being go out and leave N. It was apparent, however, that the baby's relation with his mother had become disturbed. He was deeply suspicious of her and became more clinging. Furthermore, it took a long time for the observer to reestablish her relationship with him. He was even more suspicious of her and would have little or nothing to do with her, evidently associating the appearance of the observer with his mother's absence. The pink elephant became an essential concomitant to his sleeping arrangements. It had to be in his crib, together with his mother's pink sweater. The impression given of a fetish rather than a comforter or a transitional object was the opinion formed by the seminar participants. The development had led to a pathological formation.[1]

That conclusion arose from the following reflection: A transitional object is the first "not-me" possession and leads on to play fantasy and dreams (Fordham 1977), while a fetish is a defense system that can lead to sexual perversion. The conclusion that the pink elephant was a fetish expressed better the feeling that N's development had taken on a pathological turn.

Four months later, F went out once more.

"N suddenly became aware she was leaving, looked at her for a moment with an anxious, quivering expression, and then burst into loud sobs. F left and N was distraught, completely rejecting overtures from me or a neighbor, continuing to cry, and then clinging to the brick wall, with his head averted. He cried loudly and resisted me when I tried to pick him up in an attempt to comfort him. Then he stopped crying, went over to his own closed front door, stood right up against it, facing it, his arms at his sides and standing absolutely still and quiet. He stayed like this for several minutes, motionless, and then disappeared up the sides of the flats so that he was out of sight. A few moments later he appeared, bright and smiling, seeming to have completely changed his mood as if his mother's departure had been erased from his mind. It was a disturbingly abrupt

---

1. There is a large literature, to which I have contributed (Fordham 1977), on the differences between a fetish and a transitional object. In that article, I elaborated my understanding of transitional objects and phenomena. I held that the transitional object should be regarded, following Winnicott, as the first "not-me possession" which is ultimately "relegated to limbo" and replaced by transitional phenomena (dreams and fantasies); from these, cultural forms (science, art, and religion) may be derived. The pink elephant did not have these characteristics nor were there any indications of dreams or fantasies deriving from it. It was more like a reaction formation, with the pink elephant representing F.

As to the fetish in psychoanalytic literature, nothing has emerged from Jungian sources as far as I am aware. The classical view is that it derives from the phallic mother (cf. Greenacre 1960), but the data described under this heading have been considerably expanded and the precision of the original definition blurred. I considered the view of the seminar relevant under these circumstances: A transitional object may be regarded as a healthy phenomenon (though that has been questioned), whereas a fetish can lead to sexual perversions.

I rather regretfully add that, contrary to the view that transitional objects are common in infancy, none has been discovered in our rather small number of infant-mother observations.

change: His sudden acceptance of the neighbor and his cheery wave of good-bye seemed just so inappropriate and in such marked contrast to [his older brother's] more healthy sustained and angry protest."

The disaster at separation might thus seem to have been overcome, even though in an undesirable way, but there were serious changes in both mother and child. For some months N continued to be extremely suspicious, especially when the observer arrived. In addition, N, who had always been an affectionate child, became increasingly clinging, and this alternated with violent screaming, yelling, growling, and fierce attacks both on his mother and on the furniture in the house. He even attacked the pink elephant, pulling out the soft stuffing and rubbing it all over his face. Furthermore, he and his elder brother J would combine against their mother, and the whole flat would become pandemonium. F, increasingly exhausted, eventually dispatched J to a day nursery. There followed a period in which a rather over-eroticized "love affair" between F and N took place, of which the following is an example. N was in F's arms.

"As she turned slightly, N banged his head lightly on the edge of the cupboard. He whimpered, rubbed his head into F and said, 'I'm tired,' a phrase his mother used. F laughed with pleasure at his verbalization and repeated in a dramatic voice to him, 'Oh, I'm tired.' N giggled, rather self-consciously, burrowed into F, and then lifted his head, tilted it backwards and turned it from side to side. F laughed and said, 'Show me those eyes' in a gentle, teasing way. N looked up at her out of half-closed eyes in a very seductive way, obviously delighted with himself, and they then both burst out laughing. F then repeated this, saying, 'Show me those eyes,' and N very readily responded with his half-lowered eyelids. Then he gazed into her eyes with an intense seductive expression before again dissolving into giggles, and burying his face into F."

But it did not last. It was all too much, and the distraught mother sent N to a 'foster mother' between 9:00 A.M. and 3:00 P.M. while she enrolled herself in a one-day-a-week course as a nursery attendant, where she was praised for her capacity to work with children.

But, sadly, that would not do. She changed J's day nursery because it was unsatisfactory and complained at length about "Veronica," the foster mother. Here the observation ended, with N being two years old. The observer's final paragraph summarizes N's state at that time:

"N was left with a rather desolate inner world—a world dominated by an excessive dependence on material objects and an over-compensated masculinity, both of which fostered his omnipotent sense of self-sufficiency rather than feeling. His need to defend himself against ruthless archetypal experiences which his mother could not consistently mediate meant a turning in on himself in a way that restricted growth and development. It limited the possibilities of developing thought, fantasy, and imagination, which might have enabled him to deal with new situations creatively rather than just defensively. It meant a lessening of the readiness to have new experiences and to allow for deintegration . . . without which it is not possible to individuate."

The reader will probably agree that to evaluate these heart-rending episodes one needs to know more about N's development and his mother's emotional states of mind. N was a wanted child and, in contrast to his elder brother J, gave his mother an easy time from the start: The pregnancy went well, and the labor was short and easy. N was his mother's Christmas baby, and she enjoyed him. He took easily to the breast. Here is the observer's impression of the first weeks and months of breast feeding:

"N did seem to get a great deal of satisfaction and comfort from physical contact with F, from generous cuddles, kisses, smiles, and caresses which he shared with her. In times of stress and excessive stimulation he was calmed by her voice and touch, and when he was upset, he could be soothed by being very gently stroked. F often responded intuitively to him, sensing his needs, understanding the noises he made, and responding to him in an empathic way: She helped him to adjust to the nipple; anticipated his wind, gently helping him to get rid of the discomfort; reassured him when he was distressed; and facilitated a very warm relationship. N too was accommodating. He rarely cried to be fed and seemed to have a good tolerance of frustration. He recovered fairly easily from upsets and seemed to have some inner stability which facilitated his relation with his mother. However, while there were many peaceful and contented and intimate times between mother and baby with good interaction and easy communication, N's pleasure in the sensuous comfort of feeding seemed to be often unrelated to his mother."

That seemed very well expressed by his tendency to look away from his mother's face and away from her breast. He looked at her dress and especially her pink, fluffy sweater, or over her shoulder as if looking at some object. Right from two weeks old that behavior was evident.

N was a baby who used his eyes a great deal, so his tendency not to look in his mother's face nor look at and inspect her breast seemed significant. He inspected some objects with great care, particularly small objects that he found on the floor, which he either put in his mouth or carefully replaced in the same place from which they had come. Then there was his inspection of F when she was depressed, and sometimes his penetrative looking was accompanied by a possible reflection as if he were experiencing a thought. When it came to bits of soft fluff it was different. He picked at F's sweater, for instance, and that went straight into his mouth. That picking and collecting bits on the floor developed considerably to become a fairly consistent scavenging. The amount of soft materials became quite large and his mother would extract them from his mouth with her finger, with N only making mild protest. Later the scavenging developed to include waste baskets and lavatories. A further development was the acquisition of the pink fluffy elephant, which had featured so significantly in the abandonment episodes.

By and large, however, the observer's description indicates a good fit between mother and baby, which had not been the case with F's elder son, a very aggressive and unhappy boy into whom F had seemed to project all the badness, leaving N as her good Christmas baby. N seemed to know just how to behave so as to constellate all his mother's goodness: He was a sparing baby, not making demands, holding within himself the aggressive impulses which would otherwise be directed at the breast.

The beautiful relationship between mother and baby was not, however, always there. F had periodic depressions in which she felt depleted and developed persecutory fears of cancer. She would say that she "felt like a bit of wall paper" and seemed to feel she was losing her individuality and was quite out of touch with N. The breast feedings became desultory, N became unresponsive to the observer, and N could sometimes be seen "watching his mother with a look of serious concentration on his face." That observation was made when N was 10 weeks old.

Though on the whole mother and baby made a good start, there were defects. There seemed to be a lack of the capacity to contain N and a tendency to rely too much on idealization and sensual enjoyment. F lacked the emotional strength to deal with anything that was not loving. That inference was much more obvious in her relation to J, N's brother who was excessively jealous and violent.

I was not present in the seminar until F's breast feeding had been going on for some months, and when I listened to the proceedings, I could sense that its members were quite apprehensive about the future. F had been doubtful about breast feeding from the outset, quoting her aunts who had brought her up. They were strongly against it because it drained and exhausted mothers. Nevertheless, there was plenty of milk which was enjoyed by N, who to all appearances was a well satisfied baby. F was an intuitive woman whose capacity for insight was sometimes quite startling, but there seemed to be a deprived little girl within her who needed mothering and so was only capable of being a mother in sensory experience and fantasy. The remarkable feature of N was that he seemed to know all that and so did not make demands which could not be met: The seminar concluded that N was a "sparing baby." That capacity contributed to the successful breast feeding.

Weaning took place at around five months, and a change took place in N's behavior. The sparing baby disappeared and a far more aggressive, demanding, omnipotent, and anxious one took his place. He seized food and crammed so much of it into his mouth that F, fearing he would choke, extracted it from time to time with her finger. His scavenging increased and almost anything that he could lay hands on would go into his mouth, including his thumb. But central in that was the fluff he collected from any soft and vulnerable object. It seemed as though he was seeking the softness and sensuousness of the lost breast. But his behavior was also attacking and so was his way of working out his attack on the breast that he had spared. This seemed expressed in the ways he would burrow into his mother's neck or push up between her legs as if he wanted to get inside her. Later he used the pink elephant, attacking it and pulling out its soft stuffing.

During this period N also became increasingly anxious about F's responses, especially her moving about the house. He cried and whimpered if she left the room and sought intimacy by clinging to her skirts or other clothing. At other times he would become coy and give his mother very seductive looks. In addition, he soon started to become jealous of any attention F gave to J. J had always been jealous of N, but N compounded the situation at about 10 months when he became jealous as well.

The teasing episodes between mother and child provide an opportunity to consider their nature in more detail, especially as they lead to insight into the nature of this mother's way of interacting periodically with her baby and older son. I have mentioned that F contained a deprived little girl who herself felt abandoned. Sometimes she induced those feelings of desperation and abandonment in her children, but, having done that, she could also show what a good little girl-mother she really was, essentially to herself but apparently also to her children.

That conclusion may come as something of a surprise, but it follows from the consideration that N's misery and despair are compounded by those of his mother; the containing roles have been reversed.

One of the important emotional interactions between a mother and her baby is that a mother is able to contain her infant's emotional life and, especially in the infant's states of distress, help the child to manage them by metaphorically digesting them herself and feeding them back to her infant in a way that the infant can use. Thus, mental life is facilitated and emotional pain relieved for the baby. In the teasing episodes, N becomes the container, and he cannot sustain that position. The concept of the container and the contained as applied to infancy is essentially the same as Jung's when he applied it to marriage. The one I have used is, however, more dynamic inasmuch as projective and introjective mechanisms are defined. In Jung's description they are implied.

This brief outline of the background to the abandonment episodes and subsequent further despair of F will, I hope, be sufficient. In spite of all that was known about the couple, the episodes were unexpected and the events must have had something to do with N's development. They are easier to understand if we take into account N's violence and his omnipotence. Then it is possible to infer that it was this combination that contributed decisively. If it be assumed that N experienced his mother's absence as the result of his actions—for on more than one occasion he had told her "Go!"—and that he had discovered that his mother could be either a good or bad mother, and if we add that these mothers had now coalesced, then if in his violence he had wished the bad mother dead (to go), he would know that he had destroyed the good mother as well. What an infant can do with that experience is crucial to development: It can lead on to real development, to greater independence, to a greater sense of reality and greater inner resources represented in increased capacity for symbol formation and so for fantasy or thought. That positive outcome of abandonment is, I think, what Jung wanted to depict in the "The Psychology of the Child Archetype" (1969a), but he only depicted the archetypal reflections of experience such as the one that N went through, and so one does not find anything like the "depressive position" on which Melanie Klein (1946, 1952) laid such emphasis. It is sad that such a growing point is not to be found in our series of observations. N seemed to have the possibility of doing it: He could be sad and he could become depressed, though depression is not a characteristic of the depressive position which has failed to develop. Instead he went backwards, using splitting and so becoming persecuted and depressed.

At around six months, N began to use expulsive ways of getting rid of his bad feelings: He would start hissing, blowing and snorting through his nostrils, while looking challengingly and aggressively at his mother or the observer. Another expulsive act was vomiting, which sometimes followed the hissing and blowing and snorting.

While this was going on, it began to look as if N was increasingly afraid of his own violence: Anxious looks appeared on his face and he developed a method of cutting off when J and F were in conflict—treating events as though they did not exist.

All this brought out F's deficiencies as a mother. She met it all with a mixture of tolerance, threats that she could not carry out, and periodical physical blows. In addition, she would resort to a rather cruel way of teasing J, and later N. She did not, I think, intend it to be cruel, but in effect it was. The teasing took on a variety of forms, but the most poignant was as follows: F would say she was going and might hide behind the door; that would made N quite desperate, and he would rush to find her, or if she was present he would look miserable. Then F would relent and say she was not going and might pick him up for a cuddle. It was F's need for reassurance from her children that prompted this teasing.

The home became increasingly dominated by the children's agression: screams, yells, spitting at mother, and fighting amongst themselves, all of which escalated after the abandonment episode. F became more and more exhausted and desperate.

I hope that this has not created too pessimistic a view. We do not know whether N made a more satisfactory adaptation later on. One feature of mother-infant observation is the often astonishing capacity of babies to cope with terrible emotions and an unfavorable maternal environment. Of course, we all wanted to get psychotherapeutic help for mother and baby, but it was not accepted.

One feature of this kind of work is the great difficulty one finds in making predictions, which is in marked contrast to what might be expected from that kind of analysis of childhood that relies on finding causes for mental disorders. So one cannot tell what will happen.

In Mahler's book *The Psychological Birth of the Human Infant* (1975)—a title to which I take exception as I do also to much of her theorizing—she gives very beautiful descriptions of children up to three years of age. One child whose relationship with his mother was almost ideal because of the beautifully empathic capacities of his mother was in a much worse state by three years than another one whose relationship with his mother was rather strained. It is a reminder of the difficulty of prediction.

Consider N with that in mind. While his final state was most distressing, an interesting feature of the observations seems relevant. It sometimes happens that the observer comes to take on a therapeutic function in spite of the best intentions not to do so. In N's case that happened without any intrusion on the observer's part. N just came along and made use of her. He developed quite a close relationship, which was both reliable and soft. So it might be that he will find some person other than his mother with whom that experience with the observer could be continued. Thus he would reinforce the inner resources that seemed so much in evidence during his first months of life.

Such ideas and observations indicate that therapy in infancy is a distinct possibility. Indeed, there has begun to emerge an understanding that remarkable possibilities are opening up. In his book *Dream Life* (1984), Meltzer describes a treatment of a 15-month-old baby who seemed to be developing autistic characteristics. The therapist held weekly sessions communicating in a pre-verbal way, and improvement was impressive.

I said that I did not find Mahler's formulations much help. They are too global. For instance, the symbiotic relationship is either a tautology or a misuse of biological terms. An idea like the mother-infant unity with a single surrounding membrane does not seem to me of much use when observing babies and mothers: It is too general, and furthermore it is misleading. Neither does it provide the language to describe the intense, intimate, and rapidly changing quality of the relationship. Mahler's concepts belong to the time when one thought of primary identity as a state in infancy going on into childhood. These formulations, like many others, seem to have been created out of bewilderment more than understanding.

Neumann's book, *The Child* (1973), suffers from comparable defects. Infant-mother observation and experimental studies on perception have demolished the idea that there is anything like a "primary relationship" in which the infant cannot distinguish subject from object. The idea of a primary archetypal matrix likewise cannot be established. In short, I cannot find much in Neumann's work that has proved useful to me in the line of study which I have pursued. At the same time, Neumann must be given credit for having increased interest in children among analytical psychologists, who have found incidentally some evidence for his ideas in their work with children. This is, however, no place to go into my critical stance, which I have developed elsewhere (Fordham 1981).

Why did I invent, or rather infer, the idea of a primary self in childhood? It was at first a speculation, but over the years it has proved useful in counteracting the tendency to deny an infant a personality of its own. I finally realized that if the idea were to grow, some method for studying the relation between mothers and their babies was needed. But I had no method and was occupied with so many other things that I did not have the time to work one out. Then one was invented and my ideas—especially the sequence integration-deintegration-integration—became embodied in descriptive experience. It is only necessary to observe a good feeding to see what I mean.

A good feeding can be interrupted and much distress evoked, but that also can be part of a deintegrative process if the baby or the mother or both together can negotiate the mental pain. It is usual for a good feeding to end in sleep in which integration takes place and in which the experience can be digested, but not always. N's experience of abandonment was not integrated, and so one can abstract that experience by saying that splitting took place with pathological symptom formation. The sleep grew out of tormented despair, which it, in turn, terminated. Subsequent events confirmed that the effect of abandonment lasted until the end of the observation.

If we dispense with Mahler's kind of thinking, what can we put in its place to develop the idea of deintegration? Many of the required ideas are available in Klein and the group of analysts working in England who were influenced by her. There is the concept of projective and introjective identification, which refers to the way in which a mother can take in her baby's affects and, after digesting them, feed them back transformed so that her baby can use them in mental and emotional growth. That process involves a number of other formulations: the mother's holding and containing capacities and her capacity to keep in touch. All these ideas facilitate observations and have grown out of them. They go near to describing the processes that inevitably arise out of deintegration, an essentially germinating sequence of processes providing experience for growth.

I have not made mention of archetypes, but I regard N's experience as archetypal but without much mental imagery. One is reminded of Jung's metaphor (1969b) of the spectrum, in which archetypal experience took on many forms. At the infrared end, the experiences merged into physical action. It is to this end that we have to look in order to understand what happened.

I have found Bion's scale of experience enlightening (1977). He starts from beta elements, which are psychic and physical rather than mental. Alpha elements, on the other hand, are mental. Then he postulates alpha function, which facilitates the formation of alpha elements. These formulations can be used for giving meaning to what is otherwise meaningless observation. Therefore, what has been called maternal revery facilitates alpha function in her baby, when, for instance, the infant seems to be near forming a bit of mind. Thus when N, at 10 weeks, was seen "watching his mother with a look of serious concentration on his face," that can be thought of as the operation of alpha function; something like a thought may be going to happen or may occur, but we cannot say that it does. Alpha elements arise as the result of alpha function. This idea covers those states of mind in an infant when it seems to have a thought or reflection or even a fantasy, but again that seems to presuppose a state in development that is unlikely. These formulations attempt to penetrate into, to use Jung's metaphor, the infrared end of the spectrum of archetypal action. Finally, mental images, thought, fantasy, and dreams develop and with them words and verbal communication proper.

I have described a progression. But the whole process can go into reverse, and that I have tried to convey. N was a baby who started with good experiences, though at times unrelated to his mother. That was especially well depicted in the use of his eyes. This led to the discovery of fluff and a softness that was somewhat lacking in F. Fluff and softness led him, on the one hand, to interest in objects, and, on the other, to intense sensuous experience, to scavenging, and to open attacks on F. In many of N's actions it seemed likely that fantasies and thoughts had developed, for he was expressing himself in a few words.

How can abandonment be conceived? It requires the loss of a loved and needed person (for N it was F) for whom no substitute can be found (neither Pop nor the observer would do, even though they both behaved with tact and consideration). It starts with misery. Next N tries to use Pop as a replacement, clinging and pulling at his sweater (his mother's sweater was an important part of his relation with her), but Pop does not appear adequate; there is too much persecution, though picking N up makes a change. N's wish to be inside F then appears when he opens the drawer of the chest, but it is no good, she is not there, and he violently attacks the door, presumably because she went out of it. It is here that the observer first uses the word despair, which indeed dominates the picture until N defensively abandons himself to oblivion in sleep.

Though bits of reflection can be witnessed, the main picture of this sequence is one in which beta elements predominate in N's regression. Also, in considering later developments, there is splitting (not deintegration) leading to persecutory despair and mobilization of a radical defense involving the whole of the infant which eliminates external reality or treats it as of no significance. Such a defense I would regard as a defense of the self because it involves more than the ego (cf. Fordham 1974).[2]

I have already suggested the processes which predisposed N to experience an acute abandonment crisis of cataclysmic proportions. I would only like to add that since the step in internalization of the

---

2. I introduced the idea of defenses of the self to help in understanding some features of a delusional transference. Since then it has seemed to me that defenses may be thought of as belonging to two classes: In one, parts of the psyche are rendered unconscious, isolated, etc.; in the other, the whole organism seems to be threatened, abandoned, or in danger of being split up into pieces, and then defenses of the self come into operation. A tentative classification might be: a) defenses of the ego: isolation, reaction formation, undoing, rationalization, conversion, repression, some regressions, dramatization, displacement; b) defenses of the self: projective and introjective identification, some forms of acting out and regression, idealization, somatization, etc. The subject needs more investigation and I offer the above classification as a beginning. In approaching this very difficult subject, one must bear in mind that defenses are both undesirable features of mental life, but they also contribute to growth of the psyche. Here it may be reflected that the circular outline of a mandala is an impenetrable magic circle and so is a defense as well as a containing symbol.

mother image did not take place, the absent real mother leaves her child without her containing and mediating capacities. Under these circumstances, the stark archetypal child breaks through in all the naked ruthlessness so beautifully depicted by Kerenyi (1949).

In conclusion I wish to express the belief that abandonment is a traumatic experience and essentially different from other forms of separation in which sadness, pining, and grief are experienced. In this I am in essential agreement with Satinover (see below, pp. 47–86).

## References

Bion, W. R. 1977. Learning from experience. In *Seven servants*, pp. 1–111. New York: Jason Aronson.

Fordham, M. 1944. *The life of childhood*. London: Routledge and Kegan Paul.

_____. 1957. Some observations on the self and ego in childhood. In *New developments in analytical psychology*, pp. 131–54. London: Routledge and Kegan Paul.

_____. 1969. *Children as individuals*. London: Hodder and Stoughton.

_____. 1974. Defences of the self. *Journal of Analytical Psychology* 19/2:192–98.

_____. 1977. A possible root of active imagination. *Journal of Analytical Psychology* 22/4:317–30.

_____. 1980. The emergence of child analysis. *Journal of Analytical Psychology* 25/4:311–24.

_____. 1981. Neumann and childhood. *Journal of Analytical Psychology* 26/2:99–122.

Greenacre, P. 1960. Further notes on fetishism. In *The Psychoanalytic study of the child*. New York: International Universities Press.

Jung, C. G. 1969a. The psychology of the child archetype. In *Collected works*, vol. 9/1. Princeton: Princeton University Press.

_____. 1969b. On the nature of the psyche. In *Collected works*, vol. 8. Princeton: Princeton University Press.

Kerenyi, K. 1949. The primordial child in primordial times. In *Essays on a science of mythology*. New York: Pantheon 1950.

Klein, M. 1932. *The psycho-analysis of children*. Revised as vol. 2 of *The writings of Melanie Klein*. London: Hogarth.

_____. 1946. Notes on some schizoid mechanisms. In *Envy and gratitude and other works*. Vol. 3 of *The writings of Melanie Klein*. London: Hogarth 1980, pp. 1–24.

_____. 1952. On observing the behaviour of young infants. In *Envy and gratitude and other works*. Vol. 3 of *The writings of Melanie Klein*. London: Hogarth, 1980, pp. 94–121.

Mahler, M. S., Pine F., Bergman, A. 1975. *The psychological birth of the human infant*. London: Hutchinson.

Meltzer, M. 1984. *Dream life*. Clunie Press.

Neumann, E. 1973. *The child*. London: Hodder and Stoughton.

Satinover, J. 1985. At the mercy of another: Abandonment and restitution in psychosis and psychotic character. *Chiron: A Review of Jungian Analysis* 1985: 47–86.

Wickes, F. G. 1966. *The inner world of childhood*. New York: Appleton-Century.

# Abandonment in the Creative Woman

## Marion Woodman

The experience of psychological abandonment in women who are born and reared in a patriarchal culture is their initiation into mature womanhood. It is the experience that confers identity and takes them out of the father. Many women can accept their destiny in a patriarchal relationship, finding within its obvious limitations—socially, intellectually, spiritually—compensations that are important to them. Others accept that destiny and resist the limitations but are forced for financial, political, or social reasons to stay within its framework. Others go through the initiation. These women, for a variety of reasons, only some of which can be discussed within the confines of this paper, are by inner necessity creators in the Keatsian sense of soul-makers. They reject collective consciousness as an imposition from without, and they seek from within to construct an identity which almost inevitably brings them into collision with the very force they are struggling to integrate: the idealized image of the father.

One reason for this is that crucial to their soul-making is their

**Marion Woodman** is a Jungian analyst in private practice in Toronto, having received her training at the C. G. Jung Institute in Zurich. She is the author of *The Owl Was a Baker's Daughter: Obesity, Anorexia Nervosa, and the Repressed Feminine* (1980) and *Addiction to Perfection: The Still Unravished Bride* (1982).

idealized image of the father. The internal father, which in the soul-making process they sought to please, turns on them or appears to turn on them as soon as that father is projected onto a man, or they seek recognition and reward in those creative fields still largely identified with men.

While this situation is now changing, it still has a long way to go. The psychic dynamics of the change are still far from understood. Men and women caught up in those dynamics and even consciously committed to them are still not getting through to each other despite their heroic efforts to do so, efforts that refuse to admit failure even when failure is all they experience. This can be true in the analytical situation. The encounter in the office is often a microcosm of the cultural macrocosm.

"Abandonment" comes from an Old English verb *bannan* meaning "to summon" (O.E.D.). To be among those summoned was to relinquish oneself to service. Abandonment means literally "to be uncalled," symbolically, "to be without a destiny." If that destiny is dictated by the father, however, to be uncalled may be a blessing rather than a curse. Free of the father, the daughter may then abandon herself to the process of her own soul-making.

This rite of passage, containing within it the double meaning of abandonment, is the subject of this paper. Emily Dickinson in her usual elliptical style sums it up in the following poem:

> I'm ceded—I've stopped being Theirs—
> The name They dropped upon my face
> With water, in the country church
> Is finished using, now,
> And They can put it with my Dolls,
> My childhood, and the string of spools,
> I've finished threading—too—
>
> Baptized, before, without the choice,
> But this time, consciously, of Grace—
> Unto supremest name—
> Called to my Full—The Crescent dropped—
> Existence's whole Arc, filled up,
> With one small Diadem.
>
> My second Rank—too small the first—
> Crowned—Crowing—on my Father's breast—
> A half unconscious Queen—

> But this time—Adequate—Erect,
> With Will to choose, or to reject,
> And I choose, just a Crown—          [P. 247]

The "half unconscious Queen," as I define her in this paper, is bonded, for better or worse, to her creative imagination, a bonding that originated in her psychological bonding to her father. Even in childhood she is slightly outside the ban that contains other children. In adolescence, while her sisters are conspiring about bangles, babies, and bans of marriage, she is banished by her own decree. Her creativity is of a different nature: plays, canvases, sonatas, or chemical experiments. On some level she always feels banned from life and yearns for what other people take for granted. Part of her feels abandoned; part of her knows that were she to abandon her own creativity, she would be abandoning her own soul.

Many variables are involved in defining the creative woman. While the lights and shadows in individuals vary in degree, a basic pattern of this particular psychology can be outlined. This is the woman who loves and admires her father, or her image of what her absent father must be. And for good reason. He is a courageous, intelligent, sensitive man, a man of vision committed to his own search. His psychology naturally has taken him into a marriage with a *puella*, usually a father's daughter, whose dream for herself has been cut short by the reality of marriage and family. There is no place in the home for the chaos of unruly children, the "filth" of the chthonic feminine, nor the energies of conscious sexuality. Ostensibly, the father is "the man of the house," but the mother, literally or symbolically, is "paying the rent." Full of resentment and repressed sexuality, she deals with the world as it is and projects her unlived life onto her children. The father, blessed with his wife-mother, is then free to project his young anima onto his little daughter, and together they build a Garden of Eden.

The child is trapped in spiritual incest, even more dangerous than actual incest because she has no reason to be aware that something is amiss. Called to be "Daddy's little princess," she is at once his spiritual mother, his beloved, his *inspiratrice*. She instinctively knows how to act as buffer between him and a judgmental world; she instinctively knows how to connect him to his own inner reality. This is the only world she really understands—this world where she acts as the connecting link between her father's ego and the collective unconscious. Feeding on his vision of Light, Beauty, and Truth, her young psyche can plumb the depths of his anguish or soar to the heights of his dream. If her father is mature enough to value her for herself, then together they share the eternal world of the creative imagination. Its values become her reality. Quick to recognize the illusions of the transitory world, she sets her sights on what is authentic and often finds herself a veritable Cassandra, outcast by her peer group and her parents' friends. Her security lies in her commitment to essence (a commitment, incidentally, which may lead to anorexia, because she either forgets to eat or her throat refuses to open to the food of a world of which she is not a part). She expects all life to be lived on the archetypal edge where life is exciting, fraught with danger, all or nothing, perfect or impossible. She knows little about bread and butter living and does not suffer fools gladly.

If her father was not mature enough to value her for herself, but, consciously or unconsciously, forced her into becoming his star performer, then her trap is a very different one because it involves his rejection of her reality. Unable to recognize her own responses, she simply relinquishes herself to trying to please Daddy.

Daughters of both types of father will be "anima women" but of a very different tempering. Both will dream of themselves in well-lit glass solariums, in perfect blue apartments without kitchens, in plastic bags that threaten to suffocate them. Both will realize there is something between them and the world, something that cuts off their feeling, a veil that men cannot penetrate. Both strive to make life into a work of art, and vaguely realize they have not lived. Whatever that primal relationship was, the father's daughter walks a thin line precariously close to the collective unconscious, unable, like Rilke for example, to separate the personal angels and demons from the transpersonal.

And demons are as immediate to her as angels because she lives so close to her father's shadow. Unless he has been in analysis, the *puer* father is probably quite unaware of his ambivalence toward women. His own bonding to his mother may have created a Prince Charming on a conscious level, but a prince who is nevertheless dependent on women's approval. His shadow hates that dependence and hates the women who make him vulnerable. Unless he has worked hard to bring his own feeling values to consciousness, his shadow may be a cold violent killer, unconsciously destroying the "witch" who would seduce him into her power. Men who live close to the unconscious need to protect themselves from the seduction of the Lamia, as the Romantic artists, dead before 40, make painfully clear. The *puer*'s shadow, however, may murder not only witches, but the femininity of his little daughter as well. On the one hand, he may be mothering, nourishing, cherishing; on the other, he may be creating a *femme fatale* whose psychology with men is kill or be killed. The *femme fatale* lives in an unconscious body: Her femininity is unconscious, her sexuality is unconscious. Thus she may consciously love her father or her father surrogate and be committed to her creativity through that incestuous bonding, and at the same time be lured into violent and dangerous adventures.

Her unconscious sexuality and femininity foundered in her primal relationship to her mother. The *puella* mother who has never taken up residence in her own body and therefore fears her own chthonic nature is not going to experience pregnancy as a quiet meditation with her unborn child, nor is birth a Leboyer experience of bonding. With the psyche/soma split so deep within herself, she cannot accept her baby daughter's body. Her child lives with a profound sense of despair, a despair which becomes conscious if in later years she does creative imagination with her body and releases undulations of grief and wails of terror that resonate with that first rejection. The body that appears in dreams wrapped in wire, encircled by a black snake, or encumbered by a fish-tail from the waist down may be holding a death wish too deep for tears. The security of the mother's body world is not present for her in the original matrix, nor is there reenforcement for her maturing body as she moves toward puberty, attempting to differentiate her own boundaries from those of her mother and the external world. Unable to establish physical demarcations, she literally does not know where she begins or where she ends in relation to *Mater*. During her developmental years when she is attempting to formulate a body image, she is responding to the unconscious rejection of her mother.

The following is a recurring childhood dream that continued to haunt the 50-year-old analysand until it was worked through in active imagination in my office.

Dream: *I am four or five years old. I'm with my mother in a crowded building, probably a department store. My mother is wearing dark clothes, a coat and hat in brown or black, and throughout I see only her back. As we leave the building, I am slowed down by the crowd, and my mother, unknowing, moves ahead and disappears among the people. I try to call to her, but she doesn't hear me, nor does anyone else. I'm very frightened, not only at being lost but at my mother's not noticing we've been separated.*

*I come out of the building onto a long flight of broad steps, rather like those outside the National Gallery in London, but higher. The steps lead down into a large square, empty of any objects, but with similar steps leading to buildings on the other sides. The square, the steps, and the buildings are very clean and white. From my vantage point I look around the square, hoping to see my mother. She is nowhere to be seen. I am alone on the steps. There are other people in the square, but they are unaware of me. I know nothing I do will make them notice me. I am panic-stricken and overwhelmed with a sense of loss, of having been abandoned. It's as though I've ceased to exist for my mother, that she won't bother to come back for me, may even have forgotten about me, that in fact I cannot make anyone aware that I exist.*

*For a moment, and at the same time, I'm an adult observer across the square who sees the small child standing alone at the top of the steps, trying to call out. This is also I, who feels enormous pity for this child, longs to comfort and reassure her, but is unable to reach her. Something—the unconsciousness of the other people or the child's own panic—prevents communication between the child and the adult who cares and understands.*

The dreamer associated this dream with Munch's painting "The Scream," which had evoked a shadow of the same panic in her. While looking at a black and white print of the picture, she was strongly aware "that the background is dark and murky while in my dream the environment is very clear, white and hard-edged, dotted with dark ill-defined but equally hard-edged figures. The screamer is trying to escape from his environment; the child on the steps is trying to connect with hers."

The body's memory, stored in muscle and bone, fuses the desire to connect and the desire to escape so they are simultaneously present in an undifferentiated form. The result—the identity of opposites—is despair, in which there is nothing that can be done and everything to be endured. The "very clean and white" panorama of steps, square, and building empty of any objects, with the dreamer alone, unable to "make anyone aware that I exist," is a characteristic dream of an anorexic. (This woman is not anorexic but her adolescent son is.) She cannot connect with the strangers in her psyche. It is as if *Mater* is concretized outside the body because it cannot be incorporated into it: The baby could not assimilate milk and physical intimacy from a mother who "won't bother to come back . . . may even have forgotten" her. Psychic intimacy and physical intimacy go together naturally, but, where they are split apart at a pre-verbal level, the instinct is isolated. The emotional food that should be incorporated with the physical food is not present;[1] thus the infrared pole of the psychoid archetype, the pole that experiences life instinctively, receives a different message from the ultraviolet pole, where life is experienced psychically. Without the experience of the instincts, the psyche is not embodied; consequently, subsequent emotional intimacy may be undermined by a sense of betrayal. The body is not present. Wholeness, if it is wholeness, resonates physically and psychically. The soul that is, is incarnate. Women who are robbed of that feminine birthright must experience physical acceptance by a woman, whether in dreams or in a lesbian relationship, if they are to find security within themselves.

Bea is also a middle-aged woman with a negative mother complex. Her mother took care of her but could not receive her. The following dream (written exactly as it came to her) was one in a series that brought about a profound religious transformation in her life.

Dream: *There is maybe an offering to be made. I'm in this black body, and there is (or I see) no head, no face, and this black body is to be carried up or sacrificed. Obviously the black body is dead. It's a beautiful naked body and I'm carrying it up to a hill to an altar. I don't know for sure, but there is in my mind for a second the thought that I carry it to a man.*

*I carry this body in my arms like a shawl. I then put the body down. It's so obviously me, my shape, my nakedness. I know it's me. It's a very strange me. The white woman knows that that body is me as well. I am that black woman too. I start to caress her, very softly. I kiss her breast, I put my hand between her legs. She is warm and wet there, and while I touch her there*

---

1. Jung discusses the psychoid nature of the archetype in *The structure and dynamics of the psyche*, in *Collected works*, vol. 8, pp. 213–16 (1960).

*I look up and now I see her face. A smile appears, a beautiful
very soft smile. WOW! I think she's dead but she likes to be loved.
She's so terrific I shake my head. I bend down again either to
pick her up, or to cover her body with my body. I love her so. I
don't know. I just know that black body is mine, whole and
beautiful, and obviously loves to be loved. The body has no
head until I make love to her. WOW!*

In the first section of the dream, the dreamer is about to sacrifice
her own black, headless body. Its blackness suggests her unconsciousness of it, its primitive instincts unconnected to the head.
Momentarily, she thought she was carrying it to a man, as in reality
she had done in her sexual life.

This dream was given after months of dealing with her mother
complex, her "feeling of being left totally alone," her "acceptance
of having no support." She began waking up every morning at 4:00.
Instead of taking sleeping pills, she decided she was struggling with
something in herself, "something to overcome, or to accept." She
often danced, "slow, very slow movements, all this in flannel paja-
mas, and bright, red socks as it was very cold." The love which she
bestowed on her body during those fearsome nights culminates in
an exquisitely modulated embrace. "I feel I carefully have to carry
this black girl, woman," she wrote. "She's delicate unless she's
loved. She's dead unless she's loved. And then she smiles. I feel,
know, she's me, my soul. Loving her is holy for me." The rhythms of
the dream and the exclamations reveal the power of the emotional
experience that brought head and body together. The intensity of
the ego's love touches the soul buried in the dark flesh, and the soul
smiles and is resurrected. Consciously enduring the pain has recon-
nected Bea to her own soul.

The distortion in the body/psyche relationship is compounded
by the symbiotic relationship between father and daughter. There is
confusion at the ultraviolet pole of the archetype, because the love
that she received from her father is the energy that sustains her life.
With this confusion between spirit and matter, she may experience
her body as a prison to be lugged around, while her spirit hovers
two feet above her head at any moment ready to leap "into the white
radiance of eternity" (Shelley, "Adonais"). The body becomes the
prison because the symbiotic matrix, more accurately in this case
termed the patrix, is with the parent of the opposite sex. With her

mother she has learned rejection of her body. With her father she has learned emotional withholding, for although she knows she is his beloved, and knows her mother is no rival, she also senses there is a line she dare not cross. In her adult years, the gender confusion may manifest in her compulsion to be held by a man, not as a lover, but as a mother. Her terror of abandonment then lies not only in the loss of a meaningful relationship but also in the loss of the physical contact that holds her in her body. Locked in her musculature, her feminine feelings are not available to her; thus, if she is threatened with abandonment, she may become catatonic with unexpressed terror and subject to strange physical symptoms. She is losing herself, physically and psychically. Abandonment becomes annihilation because her body with its welter of undifferentiated feeling cannot provide the temenos to protect her ego.

Nor can the collective world offer support. Her preoccupation with the world of the imagination makes her view the mundane, transitory world with scorn and fear. It is a cruel, illusory world in which unreal people clutter their lives with superfluous objects, and clutter is unendurable when the inner world is dismembered.

A woman who is thus identified with the masculine spirit has unconsciously sacrificed her femininity to what she believes is the best in life. In relationship to a man she appears at first to relate superbly because she can so adroitly become what he is projecting onto her. She returns a projection that carries suprahuman dimensions—loving father, loving mother, little less than god and goddess. When father/god fails to live up to the projection, or decides to reject it, he deals the "imperial Thunderbolt" that scalps the "naked Soul" (Dickinson, p. 148). Cut off outwardly from her environment, cut off inwardly from her masculine guide, the woman identifies with the reverse side of the god archetype—the demon lover. Her terrorized ego has no mediator between it and the chaos through which it is falling. The abyss is bottomless. Her solar consciousness asks questions for which there are no answers; her lunar consciousness is not sufficiently mature to accept "meaninglessness." She has done everything to make herself acceptable; she has failed; she is "unlovable," and that verdict resonates right back to the primary abandonment. Life becomes a prison where the password is "renunciation," and the magician becomes the trickster with whom she has colluded in relinquishing herself. Describing loss of soul, Emily Dickinson writes,

And yet—Existence—some way back—
Stopped—struck—my ticking—through.
[P. 212]

Suicide in that situation becomes for her a fulfillment of her destiny. In Sylvia Plath's last "Words,"

Years later I
Encounter them on the road
Words dry and riderless,
The indefatigable hoof-taps.
While
From the bottom of the pool, fixed stars
Govern a life.
[P. 86]

Suicide is a final stroke of vengeance against the savage god who has abandoned her. Paradoxically, it is affirming what he has done to her ego: God has taken her out of life, so killing herself is affirming him. Suicide is a *Liebestod*, embracing the dark side of god, the negative mystical union. It is marriage to the demon lover. The relationship of the woman to the demon is sadomasochistic and her battle with him fascinates because it has within it the elements of violent eroticism. As Shakespeare's Cleopatra says when she puts the asp to her breast,

The stroke of death is as a lover's pinch,
Which hurts, and is desir'd.
[*Antony and Cleopatra*, V. 2. 297-98]

Inherent, however, in such a vision is a sense of total defeat. One battles against a power which is inevitably inexorable. The father animus demands order, justice, meaning, but that meaning is beyond human comprehension. Without the feminine consciousness to allow for a different kind of meaning, life becomes a constant battle against chaos and collapse. The demon lover lures and inflates the ego with *hubris*, but unconsciously the individual knows the outcome must be defeat and final escape from the struggle. It is the last collision of the opposites—the desire to be accepted, the desire to escape. The heart breaks, overwhelmed by rage against the inevitability of loss.

Suicide is the ultimate abandonment, and while few women actually have to deal with a propensity for suicide, many are dealing with abysmal despair, which may manifest in a fatal accident or a terminal illness. They repeatedly go through the anguish of losing the man into whom their saviour projection is hooked; they fail to recognize that the passionate interaction of their relationships is based on narcissistic need; they will not sacrifice the complex and accept "the boredom" of being human. They are forsaking their own soul and their own creativity, the little girl and little boy who repeatedly appear in their dreams. Essentially they are afraid to take responsibility for their own life. If the object of loss is introjected and sealed off, it becomes

> The Horror not to be surveyed—
> But skirted in the Dark—
> With Consciousness suspended—
> And Being under Lock.
> [Dickinson, p. 379]

If loneliness illuminates, the ego sets up a creative relationship with its inner world and releases its own destiny.

Martha, the middle-aged woman whose recurring childhood dream was quoted earlier, is a tall, stately woman with a studied air of confidence. Born into a professional family, she did all that was expected of her at university, married her high school sweetheart, had her family, divorced, held a careful balance between work, children, and men for 20 years. She came into analysis to find out why the pattern of loss kept repeating itself. She fell in love with a highly respected leader in her community, he fell in love with her, and soon marriage seemed inevitable. After one year things began to go wrong; after two years the split came. At that time, Martha very carefully articulated her feelings.

"I don't know where I've been. I am numb. I projected everything I ever wanted in a man onto him. And he left me for another—for an ordinary woman. All I want to be is ordinary. But I don't know how to be ordinary. I am a stranger to others, to myself.

"I think back to my childhood, to that terrible sense of abandonment. I was never at the centre, the living centre of anyone's life. That's all I want—to share my life in its deepest essentials with another. My parents didn't share their deepest core with me. My husband said he loved me, but the most important things of life he did not share. And he went off with a woman who could share the ordinary world with him. I don't know how to do that. I know what the man is projecting onto me. I become what he wants me to be, and at the time it feels natural and real to me. I feel totally alive. And then something goes dead in the relationship, usually in the sexuality. I feel he is manipulating, using power, forcing me to be what he wants me to be. He is making love to his image of me, not to me. I too am projecting. It is not he who is making love to me. Everything swings into unreality. I hate myself for enduring it. I hate him for forcing me. It is intolerable. I go unconscious. Nothing has happened between us. We are both disappointed, resentful, confounded by the seeming intimacy which wasn't intimacy at all.

"I know this lack of intimacy exists between me and my children. They too have developed magnificient personas— lively, efficient, able to cope with anything. Underneath there is grief; it comes out in their poems, their songs. That essential part of themselves they do not share with me. I feel there is a veil around me. When I write, when I am alone, the tragic side of myself surfaces, but I cannot share that with others.

"I know in this situation I could go into my act. I could fly into activity, busy myself with any number of creative things, but that would be choosing the persona again. I won't do that. It's not quite as it was in the past. I'm not incapacitated. I'm not being swung helplessly around. I know something terrible has happened to me, but there is a quiet place at the centre.

"It's the ordinary things that hurt so much, the little human acts we shared together. I stumble along in my numbness. I see the plum blossoms and I'm overcome with slivers of pain. At least the pain is alive. At least I know I am somewhere feeling the reality of what I am going through. Behind that numbness is blind terror. It is the terror of the child within me—the child who knew everything was going wrong, that she was unacceptable, and frantically attempted to try to figure out what to do in order to be loved. It's the terrible aloneness of standing at the top of the stairs crying and no one pays any attention, of knowing that who I am is impossible to those around me. It is standing bereft, hearing mocking laughter in the empty corridor behind me, trying to contort myself into someone who could be loved. I have rejected that child, as everyone else has rejected her. She's still standing there crying, 'What do you want me to be? I don't understand I don't understand. I'll do anything you want, but don't reject me.'

"Well, this time I won't build up my false persona. It can't relate because it can't feel. I know I have to stay with the feeling. I have to experience my vulnerability. I have to allow others to know how vulnerable I am. This is the loss of everything I ever wanted in a man. I am ashamed to be so naive. I respected and loved everything he was. He is gone. I am not young. I may never have such a relationship again. I do not trust that God has something new for me. I do not hope. Hope in me is an illusion. Honest despair is better than a fantasy of hope. This is the confrontation: the abandoning of all I hoped for."

Martha, like other women of her type, is an anomaly to men. Functioning without a strong feminine ego, she nevertheless gives an appearance of being, as she says, "some kind of iron lady who can take anything, and take it alone." And she can go on, "but it's a black rock in the heart." The man who is carrying her positive projections may feel himself quite unnecessary in the relationship, may even feel his masculine ego and his potency threatened. If he withdraws and watches the woman inwardly collapse, he may well wonder what happened. He probably had no idea of the depth of her dependence on him, her need for grounding. As Martha said, "He thought my energy was all going into the analysis and I didn't care about the relationship. What does he think analysis is about?" If in his withdrawal he has swung into an enantiodromia and fallen in love with the opposite type of woman (a shadow sister of the first), a situation may arise such as the one in Barbara Streisand's *Yentil*, where the masculine-oriented Yentil projects her femininity onto her beautiful rival and sings, "No wonder he loves her," thus passively surrendering what is crucial to her existence. In fact, it is quite possible that the projection of her own femininity onto a shadow sister may be the trick of the magician animus. When he knows his woman is falling in love, he will do everything he can to destroy the possibility of authentic relationship. Once her shadow energy is thus projected, her lover's anima may also split: He loves her for her strength, her shadow for her sexual vulnerability. Instead of contacting her own feminine rage and jealousy, she may retreat into her abandoned child, harangued by her negative animus. "This is the way it always ends, will always end. When the chips are down, never trust a man. You can stand alone. You always have. You're a better man than he is. You're not sweet and feminine like her. If only you hadn't stood your ground in discussions. If only you'd pretended the issues didn't matter. If only you hadn't tried to make him more conscious. If only you had been more sensitive to his sexuality. If only . . . if only . . . if only. . . . Never mind. Take it like a man."

Instead of withdrawing her projections and looking the man straight in the eye, honoring his manhood and her own womanhood, and saying, "What the hell is going on here?" she stands helplessly crippled by her own self-recriminations. She does not fly into a childish tantrum. She does not whimper and cry. Her masochistic feminine is asking rational questions and understanding rational answers. She knows she's not dead because she's still standing up. She plays the role of the perfect gentleman.[2]

## Analyzing the Creative Woman

While many creative women choose to work out their destiny through their own art, others enter analysis when they see a destructive pattern undermining their relationships to men. Sometimes they are shocked by their own *femme fatale*; sometimes they are grieved when their sexual relationship with their husband whom they love has failed. Often they are driven into analysis by mysterious body problems which medical science has termed psychosomatic, but can do nothing to relieve. Sometimes they are despairing in their separation from life; sometimes they are stricken because their creativity is blocked; sometimes they are terrified of madness.

Working with such a woman is like working with anyone else except that the ambushes are more immediate, precipitous, and treacherous because the unconscious is her home and native land. The analyst must take full cognizance of the power of her imagination, her capacity to abandon herself to the archetypal world, and her lack of relationship to her own body. Male or female analyst will become her *inspiratrice*, her connecting link to the unconscious. If her father was her companion rather than her guide on the inner journey, then the analyst is treated as a partner, a *frater* or *soror*, daring the dangers and sharing the illuminations. Together they set up a world of imagination, rich with imagery and insights. She makes an exciting analysand because she is not afraid to enter the

---

2. Private conversation with Dr. Anne Maguire, 1984.

underworld, and she brings back to the analyst riches, personal and transpersonal. She understands Silence, and if the analyst can endure the intensity of her world, every session becomes a happening.

If she is an Ariadne, betrothed to the god before her birth but side-tracked into her love for the sun-hero Theseus, then in her abandonment she may give herself up to death. She may surrender to deep depression, and, at the nadir of that experience, recognize the light in the darkness. She may in fact find her true destiny: surrender to the God. Not many modern women want to face the nun in themselves, but not a few in analysis are forced to put the archetypal projections where they belong, separate personal relationship from archetypal, and work out their own salvation in harmony with the God/Goddess without the support of a church or the containment of the nunnery walls.

Another possible direction also involves the death of an illusion. The abandoned woman becomes conscious of her own abandonment to her own illusion. She recognizes that her problem lies in falling in love with her own projection, attempting to create herself in an image which is being projected onto her, thus abandoning her own being. As the relationship develops, she herself rejects that image and cannot continue the pretense. As she reveals more and more of herself, the man experiences her as the betrayer because she has withheld so much of her true nature in order to play "Daddy's little girl." Unconsciously, her rage toward the man and toward herself as self-betrayer unites with his rage, thereby creating the bomb which must inevitably be exploded. The two shadow figures will have their revenge. If healing is to take place, she must not act like a gentleman; she must not try to understand why he is abandoning her. She is angry and her rage is killer-rage and killer-jealousy that needs an acceptable channel. The pent-up fury of a lifetime has to be released from the body to make room for the healing love. That personal rage has to be experienced before the transpersonal understanding and compassion can flow in. Somewhere in the anguish and anger, the woman will realize that she has not been abandoned by the man she loves. The man she loves does not exist in human form. Never did. She has been projecting an illusion. Her mirror has shattered, and she can either die or accept reality. And the reality is that it is not that actual man she grieves for. She grieves for her perfect lover. And for the beautiful woman she was when she was in love. Taken to her naked truth, she grieves for her own child, the child she herself abandoned when she first set out to please Daddy. That child in all its childish and childlike faith, hope, and love is the one who cries out in its aloneness. In spite of its vulnerability, it has to trust life if the woman is ever to bring her essence to maturity.

Her original abandonment by her mother and her creative relationship with her father may make her feel that women are a waste of time. She may know, however, that she does not "want to go through the hassle (or inconvenience) of falling in love with a male analyst" and, therefore, chooses a woman. In the transference the analyst then carries the projection of the loving mother the analysand never had. Together they nurture and discipline the abandoned child, giving it a safe place to play and cherishing it into maturity. It is that child who has suffered outside the limits of society, yet is still holding to its own innate wisdom, refusing to die. Its vulnerability and strength, born of its aloneness, give it the detachment necessary to the artist and the clown. In my experience, that detachment, simultaneously personal and transpersonal, is the only energy strong enough to depotentiate the trickster father.

Let me illustrate that point with a brief story. One Christmas Eve I happened to be in the Chalk Farm underground station in London, England. The trains were nowhere to be seen. The few prodigals who stood shivering in that dank cave were dreaming of the fireside they were attempting to reach or the one they didn't have. Suddenly a drunken, high-pitched roar echoed through the vast cavern. A slovenly, massive woman lurched through the entrance with two little girls, one perhaps six, the other four. They had no coats; their little arms clutched at this heaving mass roaring her obscenities into the emptiness. Her Cockney humor was outrageous, so frank, so visceral, so true. Shocked laughter of the bystanders bounced off the walls. In one crystal clear cry, the four-year-old stood to the full height of her tiny frame and shouted, "Don't you laugh at my mum." Silence. And not a dry eye on the platform. That little girl's innate wisdom ripped the veils off every adult, including her drunken mother. She was the only one, at once detached and connected enough, to see the Reality. She was the unexpected guest that Christmas Eve.

Now to return to the creative woman. Because her body has so often been the scapegoat, loving attention needs to be paid to its attempts to make itself heard. There may be severe digestive problems, migraine headaches, skin rashes, and allergies. These are a part of any analysis, but the artistic temperament, flying with its intuition, may overlook an ulcer and be possessed by a pimple. Old patterns of avoidance and repression, often involving eating disorders, may reemerge. With increased body awareness, the feeling values that are being differentiated verbally are being reenforced by the emotions released from the muscles—a reenforcement that comes as a shock to the woman who is a stranger to her own body. If she falls in love with the analyst, that must be dealt with openly, because the mourning in relationship to the mother repeats itself and now that grief can be handled creatively. If the analyst chooses to touch or embrace the analysand, she must be very aware of the difference between personal and transpersonal touching. That awareness can come only from her own sense of detachment. As the analysand learns to listen to her own body, her sexuality gradually becomes connected to real feeling and the lesbian dreams are either replaced by heterosexual dreams, or the analysand chooses a lesbian relationship. It is a period of building a strong ego, well grounded in the feminine body and the emotions springing from that body. The artist particularly needs a strong foothold in order to be able to surrender to her creative imagination with the full assurance that she will be able to return to her own ego and relate to the world.

As the analysand gains confidence, the analyst may find herself increasingly in the role of *inspiratrice*. The analysand may ask for critical appraisals of her creations, looking for encouragement to dare to put her work before the public. There is a double danger here: First, the analyst could quickly turn into negative mother; second, she could make the artist totally dependent on her, both creatively and critically. If critiques are left to the critics, the analysis remains uncontaminated.

In my experience, there is one very dangerous passover to be made with creative women. If they are in a midlife crisis, have recognized that they have not yet taken responsibility for their talent, have lived a basically persona or animus-oriented life, they may suddenly reclaim their abandoned child and attempt a 180-degree turn with all the determination of the outcast about to come into her kingdom. Either the archetypal influx is too much for the immature body, or the ego is not sufficiently related to the body energy, or the psychic shift is too sudden for the body to move in harmony with it. Whatever the cause, there may be serious physical symptoms. It is as if the initiation rites that were not assimilated at puberty have now to be integrated before the rites of menopause can be endured. During this period, the forsaken body has to be claimed, cherished, inhabited before it surrenders to becoming a vessel for creativity. In this situation it is difficult to distinguish the adolescent from the menopausal woman, but careful differentiation of the two phases of lunar consciousness help her to own her own life instead of bitterly yearning for what in fact is hers for the claiming. This can be a very threatening passover. Unless solid body work has embodied her emotions, the analysand may once again feel herself doomed to abandonment.

This type of woman working with a male analyst may constellate a very different situation. In him she may see the positive father whom her psychology naturally makes into her own positive animus. The outcome can be destructive, largely because of the peculiar strength of the male ego in the Western patriarchal world. While the male analyst encourages the healing activity arising out of the analysand's constellation, his countertransference may go well beyond encouragement to become a father's pride in his daughter's achievement. Since historically the daughter's achievement has always counted for less and been measured by quite different standards, the father-analyst's pride in his daughter-analysand's creative work now, in the new feminist ethos, takes on an added dimension. There is the sense of breaking new ground, establishing a new alignment between the sexes, building a new cultural matrix. What too often is not seen is that none of these things is happening. On the contrary, what has been constellated is the old patriarchal dominance in which the father's fathering of his daughter with all the incestuous currents that energize it give the illusion of healing, creativity, and change. What in reality may be constellated is the father-complex, which is probably what brought the woman into analysis in the first place. The moment the countertransference is recognized and withdrawn (as eventually it must be), the analysand will not only be back where she started, but, what is worse, she will know herself to be seduced or deceived in the most treacherous possible manner.

What the male analyst may fail to recognize in the psychology of the creative woman is the profound split between her imagination and her body. For her, the imagination is the real world and the father-man who can penetrate and impregnate that world brings "light to the sun and music to the wind." He is her beloved. Here is where her intimate intercourse is. Here is where incest is legal. Since her physical sexuality is basically unconscious, she may have relationships outside the analysis which she may not bother to mention. Ordinary men are outside her sphere, barely worthy of her *femme fatale*. Her energy is focused on the man she loves in her imagination; the alchemical vessel with the adept and his *soror mystica* is tailor-made for her. And tailor-made for her destruction if the male analyst becomes frightened, is seduced, or misappropriates his power. If the vessel explodes, she has no body to return to, no world to return to. Putting her animus to work is no answer; he has driven her all her life to please Daddy, university professors, husband, boss, any male authority. His laughter can be diabolic when he has vanquished another rival. She needs to be finding her own life in her own body, differentiating her own femininity (which is going to involve her rage against men), and integrating her own masculinity and femininity.

Unless the analysis has opened up space for the trickster father, i.e., made room for the trauma at the center of her psyche, she is eventually going to be abandoned again, and nothing, not even incest, so arouses the full range of patriarchal feeling as the abandoned daughter. Historically, in ancient cultures, daughters were often abandoned because only male offspring were of real value. When the analysand experiences her abandonment, the whole patriarchal myth at its most primitive origins has been constellated. The urgency with which the unconscious takes hold to effect the sacrifice (Tess at Stonehenge, for example) is apparent in the abandoned and sacrificial role of the woman in Western literature. To find oneself abandoned to, or at the mercy of, this myth can, and usually does, evoke a profound passivity on the part of both persons involved, as if what is happening is both necessary and inevitable. Fate, Destiny, Karma—everything comes into play to support what has happened and is happening.

What needs to take place is a profound, revolutionary realignment of the relationship—a realignment that is as huge a challenge to the male ego as it is to the father complex that feeds that ego. The analyst who has been the best little boy in the world and has tried to be the most loving father in the world may have a very caring professional persona, but when it comes to real feeling, he may find himself at a total loss. A woman who is fighting for her own life is going to demand genuine feelings, and she has a right to an honest response. The truth may set both analyst and analysand free. The truth may be given; something new, unknown to either, may emerge. Abandonment in the negative sense of betrayal, loss, exposure, death may become abandonment in the positive sense of open, spontaneous, free. To go with that is to break out of the magician father constellation into the unknown, where true creativity resides. Then and only then is the delusion of the old pattern seen, because the illusion it contained is now seen as a reality struggling to break out of the trap that imprisoned it.

The dangers in transference/countertransference between the female analyst and the creative man also deserve close attention. The parameters of this paper do not allow a full discussion of those dynamics. Let me point out, however, that the female analyst may constellate the positive mother in the male analysand. If the unconscious is his native land, together they may mine that configuration for all the energy it contains. Together they may tap into a geyser of creative life that erupts with poetry, music, drama, pottery. She becomes the muse of her spiritual son, as Venus-Urania was the muse of Adonis. That such a relationship is fatal, that Adonis then assumes a strength that is not his which leaves him unprepared to confront the other more incestuous, more instinctive lover of Venus—Ares the boar—is not seen in the first flush of creative renewal. Releasing Ares requires of a female analyst a fine differentiation of her own virgin, that is, a feminine consciousness no longer identified with the mother, a consciousness that is receptive to her own creative masculine, freed from the tyranny of the father.

If the analyst, male or female, recognizes from the beginning the psychic dynamics inevitable in the relationship and can handle the countertransference, the process need not be traumatic. Somehow the power of the dark magician and the omnivorous witch must be depotentiated. While these negative complexes can act positively in that they force the analysand to do the inner work in order to escape their clutches, in this particular psychology, they can destroy before the individual is strong enough to withstand their energy. A flash storm, a tornado, a seering fire can rip the center out of the psychic house. Jung has pointed out that an unconscious woman and the anima of a man are identical; similarly the unconscious man and the animus of the woman are identical. In any intimate relationship, the love/hate dynamics among the four are going to constellate. If the analysand falls into persona identification, the persona and the defensive ego will operate at all costs to hide the inner world, and that world includes the instincts. If passionate eroticism is not consciously discussed, the body is once again abandoned, and the shadow will take revenge in physical symptoms. At the point of highest tension between analyst and analysand, one or the other may fall into unconsciousness and accuse the other of wanting power. Each may accuse the other of wanting "more and more and more" and both be saying, "That's not true." The conflict arises when the shadow projections are constellated: The negative mother's "more" wants quantity, whereas the negative father demands quality. The feminine may feel she is being psychically raped, and the masculine may feel he is being sucked dry by the terrified child. Enormous hostility built up in the unconscious toward the opposite sex may erupt. Unless the analyst can instantly move to a strong ego position, a position well fortified by authentic feeling, there is no mediator between the conscious and unconscious. This is no moment for wimp masculinity, nor masochistic femininity, nor tyrannical father, nor positive mother, nor any musical chairs combination of the four. Both must speak and both must be heard. The old map is useless in new country.

The analysand who has allowed her femininity to evolve has passed the frontier of the anima woman operating out of a male psychology. She finds herself saying things she never said before, verbalizing questions she never asked before. She tries to speak from her feminine reality at the same time aware of the masculine standpoint. She is caught between two conflicting points of view: the rational, goal oriented, and just versus the irrational, cyclic, relating. A woman who has devoted her life to examinations and scholarships knows how to organize her mind in obedience to the laws of unity, coherence, and emphasis. What she has lost in training herself into that rhetoric is faith in the values that come from the heart. When she attempts to speak from that place, she contacts her abandoned soul. Fearful of appearing "childish and stupid," she feels her face going red, she clutches at her neck to try to get the words out, she breathlessly plummets on hoping she won't be stopped, hoping she won't collapse in her own confusion and lose her vocabulary. She is trying to articulate her feminine being, trying to transcend the either/or prison which locks her into contradiction. That old model is now untenable. She is trying to move toward paradox, where two mutually exclusive aspects of reality may be held at the same time. The rhythms there are circuitous, slow, born of the feeling that comes through the heart. Many people know that place exists; few have the confidence to talk or walk from that center.

Martha did confront her own abandonment of all she had ever hoped for in relating to men. Commenting on her last relationship, she said:

"Maybe I am too strong. He said he experienced me as critical; I experienced him as judgmental. I know my little girl is too needy, too demanding. She is so uncentred she attempts to find centre in a relationship—man as god and mother. I was trying to let her grow up. I cannot help feeling that I did the right thing. I told him honestly what I felt. I tried to understand how he felt. We could not communicate. I was true to my feeling values, but he wasn't willing to rise to the challenge. He recognized his persona problem, but he didn't want to work on it. He wanted to go back to his uncritical mother. He did. He married her. So long as we had our paradise, it was fine. When it came to the real problems of relationship, he wasn't there. Yes, it is the old pattern, but I'm conscious this time. Consciousness makes it worse, also makes it better. Maybe it is Fate. Maybe we weren't meant to be together."

After a session of reflecting in this manner, she had the following dream:

Dream: *I'm sitting up in my very first bed. I'm facing the head as a child might in play. Leaning against the headboard is Laurence Olivier, the object of my most varied and detailed adolescent fantasies. In my dream, he is old, but still enormously attractive, with an abundance of snow-white hair. We are in a relationship, have been for some months at least—a settled sort of thing. The thought comes to me that it's rather delightful to have my adolescent fantasy come true almost as I fantasized it. At this point we are both assailed by an overwhelming sexual desire, which we are about to give in to when I awaken.*

"I awoke with a boot in my stomach," Martha said. "I felt crushed, overwhelmed. Then relief. At least I know what I've been living with all my life. I recognize the fantasy world." The dream suggests that the fantasy world has been with her "for some months at least," a poignant understatement in light of the setting in "her very first bed." Laurence Olivier, the elegant father-figure, is very old, an image that clearly suggests that this fantasy attitude is outworn.

This dream clarifies in no uncertain terms the cross that Martha has been on all her life, and at the same time delivers "the boot in the stomach," the transcendent that can release her. Here is the same conflict that was inherent in her recurring childhood dream: the desire to escape, the desire to connect. Escaping into the complex (abandoning herself to Sir Laurence) protects her from the pain of connecting to life. It also separates her from her own authentic being in her own body. It is the actual experience of the kick in the stomach that makes her wake up to where she has been all her life—in a compromise with an illusion. That fantasy world is a pact with the devil. The kick is the wound from the Self through which the god can enter. The dream has thrown the ego out of the crib and into the fire. Having abandoned the fantasy, the dreamer is now the abandoned one, free to abandon herself to her own life.

Martha, like so many of her contemporaries, is now attempting to make the leap into freedom. She is attempting to be who she is, determined to put her energy into her creative work. The contradiction at the core of her life becomes more clear to her.

"I am still split on some level. I am still unreconciled, angry. Intellectually I feel I set up an impossible situation for him. I think I was unconsciously very negative. I think he read the real message which was very critical. I think I was demanding perfection. My anger is directed not at him but at all men. It's an intellectual construct: deflect my anger off myself by making him wrong. It's myself I'm angry at. I betray my own soul, my own little girl. It's horrendous really. I realize there is no mature femininity there at all. It's still a problem of commitment. I'm still trying to escape when I'm trying so hard to commit. All the time my arms are out begging to connect, something else is pulling back not wanting to commit. Something in me is not responsible. I'm waiting for someone to say, 'You're great. What you're doing is worthwhile.' I look for reenforcement from outside. Rather than waiting for my own inner authority to come up, I shift into pleasing. I'm terrified to connect because I'm sure I'll be found inadequate. I keep trying to justify my existence instead of just being.

"You know what it is? It's a problem of loving. I don't love myself enough. I understand love in my head, but when it comes to opening my heart, I don't know what that means. When I feel myself tight, I relax, I breathe into my heart. Then I can take the chance. I listen with my heart. I can feel what I'm feeling. I want, I want so very much, for that little girl to grow into mature womanhood."

Feminine consciousness, not to be confused with mothering, is evolving in many men and women. While a few great individuals in the past have articulated its territory, it is now coming to consciousness as a cultural phenomenon. It is our responsibility not only to hear it but also to act on it and to accept the consequences of our lives being turned inside out. If we choose to abandon it, it turns its dark face—angry, revengeful, depressed, suicidal. If we abandon ourselves to it, we will seek and we will find.

## References

Dickinson, E. 1960. *The complete poems of Emily Dickinson*, T. H. Johnson, ed. Boston and Toronto: Little Brown.
Plath, S. 1965. *Ariel*. London: Faber and Faber.

# At the Mercy of Another: Abandonment and Restitution in Psychosis and Psychotic Character

## Jeffrey Satinover

*Irrationally held truths may be more
dangerous than reasoned errors.*
T. H. Huxley, *The Coming
of Age of "Origin of Species"*

### Introductory Remarks

The purpose of this paper is to delineate certain essential features of a clinical theory of psychosis and related conditions, integrating the pertinent insights of Jungian thought, but modifying these in the light of clinical experience.

I am calling conditions related to psychosis "psychotic character." These are conditions of personality in which a mental organi-

**Jeffrey Satinover,** M.D., is a Fellow of the Child Study Center at the Yale University School of Medicine and has a private practice in Connecticut. He is a graduate of M.I.T., Harvard, the University of Texas, and the C. G. Jung Institute in Zurich. His most recent article, "Jung's Lost Contribution to the Dilemmas of Narcissism," is forthcoming in *Journal of the American Psychoanalytic Association.*

I would like to thank my wife, Julie, for her extensive editing of this paper, for her many helpful clarifications, and for the fact that at times she understood what I was trying to say better than I did.

zation prevails that shares certain features of overt psychosis, but not all, and usually in lesser degree. I have adapted the term from Frosch (1983), who uses it to describe a kind of patient likely today to be diagnosed as borderline.

Some important nosological questions lie behind Frosch's term and my own use of it. As was also true of the earlier Kraepelinian system, current psychiatric nosology is essentially descriptive. It draws sharp distinctions between disease (that is, symptom-complex) categories. From a psychodynamic point of view, these distinctions often seem arbitrary. Thus, to label one group of patients "psychotic" and another "borderline" exaggerates their differences (the presence or absence of gross reality-testing) and minimizes an essential similarity (poor self/object differentiation and instability of the self). The term "psychotic character" is meant to emphasize the chronic, structural nature of self-instability and of poor self/object differentiation. Within this characterologic domain, overt loss of reality-testing may or may not occur.

Consistent with this distinction is the possibility that the specifically heritable component of psychosis is the proclivity to lose gross reality-testing. That this proclivity might be related to a specific abnormality in the biochemistry of brain function is indirectly supported by certain common observations. Thus, on the one hand, street drugs (LSD, mescaline, amphetamines, cocaine, PCP, etc.) can induce quasi-psychotic states whose most prominent features are perceptual distortion and gross loss of reality-testing without altering character. On the other hand, antipsychotic medications can reverse (phenothiazines, butyrophenones) or prevent (lithium, carbamezepine) the gross loss of reality-testing without improving character or level of defense.

Frosch's term "psychotic character" suggests a kind of low level of borderline functioning prone to overt psychotic fragmentation. However, Frosch makes it clear that many patients he would diagnose as "psychotic characters" are quite highly functioning. I agree with this broad usage. I think that such conditions are common, and a gifted sufferer may be driven to quite extraordinary achievement (Hermann Hesse might be an example; see especially his *Steppenwolf*, which he acknowledges as largely autobiographical). Thus, narcissistic personality disorder may be considered the characterologic background to (or milder version of) bipolar disorder, and the successful narcissist is today thought of as pandemic. Viewed dynamically, the irritable mania of bipolar disorder or the elative grandiosity of the narcissist both represent a manic defense against depression (self-fragmentation). The achievements wrought in such a state of defense may nonetheless be considerable. In my use of the term psychotic character, the narcissistic personality would be one form of psychotic character just as mania is one form of psychosis.

In an individual without the genetic loading that predisposes to the loss of reality-testing, certain developmental factors (centering on the early experience of "abandonment") will lead "only" to a psychotic character. In an individual with such a predisposing genetic loading, the same factors that lead to psychotic character are likely also to lead, when reexperienced in the present, to an overt break with reality.

In a way, then, psychosis may be thought of as a model for the entire spectrum of psychotic character disorders. In overt psychosis, because of the loss of reality, we see as if through a microscope greatly enlarged versions of the kind of pathology which, in milder form, characterizes the entire spectrum.

For example, the most characteristic feature of psychotic character is what Erikson (1968, p. 212) calls "identity diffusion." It is also characteristic of adolescents, normal or prolonged. Like Woody Allen's Zelig, such individuals have only a poor sense of their identity and tend to take on the roles and attitudes of the people around them. But although a person with a psychotic character, or a teenager, or to some degree anyone, may be uncertain as to "who he is" in this existential sense, he has no trouble recognizing that he is not literally the same person as the one he is currently identified with. Self/object differentiation may be weak and will lead to unstable life choices, but reality-testing is intact.

But if identity diffusion is compounded with loss of reality, the result is overt psychotic identification (fusion). In such a case, the sufferer may not be capable, at times, of distinguishing himself from others, in particular from his family members or his therapist.

When we consider how common are such problems as identity diffusion—not going so far as to overt psychotic identification—we might almost agree with Jung when he wrote of his discovery at the Burghölzli Clinic "that a general psychology of the personality lies concealed within psychosis" (1961, p. 127).

Although I will be using psychosis as the model, I am addressing the entire spectrum of psychotic character problems, that is, all those human difficulties which have at their heart some degree of instability in the self and some weakness in self/object differentiation.

I remarked above that we might *almost* agree with Jung's notion that a general psychology lies concealed within the psychoses. I say "almost" because, although a wide spectrum of personalities shares with psychosis the difficulties that arise from inadequate differentiation of the self, this is not true of all personalities. In brief, I believe there are two main types of personality problems. These may be roughly characterized as "psychotic," in the broad sense outlined above, and "neurotic." The former are characterized by problems of self-differentiation, the latter by unconscious conflict within an adequately structuralized (stable) self. The primary goal in the treatment of the former is differentiation and stabilization of the self (Satinover 1980); in the latter, it is the undoing of repression. "Unconsciousness" in the former refers to mutual autonomy of sectors of the personality; in the latter, it refers to the forgetting of unacceptable impulses. Thus, Winnicott (1964) comments: "It is not possible to conceive of a repressed unconscious with a split mind; instead what is found is dissociation."

Jung focused on problems of self-differentiation and expanded the conceptions that followed into a general psychology of individuation. Freud, focusing on intrapsychic conflict (with a stable self as a given) similarly expanded *his* concepts into a general psychology of repression. Both men subsumed large-scale cultural phenomena under their respective theories, including art, religion, and social structure.

I agree with Winnicott who, in reviewing Jung's autobiography, commented:

> The search for the self and a way of feeling real, and of living from the true rather than the false self, is a task that belongs not only to schizophrenics, it belongs to a large portion of the human race. Nonetheless, it must also be recognized that for many, this problem is not the main one. (1964, p. 455)

We know that abandonment is the most powerful precipitant of psychosis, and also that Jung's theory of the psyche is most powerful when applied to psychosis and related conditions. In one of his earliest studies (1909), abandonment not surprisingly figures prominently. Later, however, it drops from sight as a crucial issue, and the quest for meaning takes its place. It is in relation to this lacuna that Jung's theories require modification.

Jung and, to a greater extent, Jungians attribute to the "self" a greater overarching capacity for internal homeostatic compensation than is clinically observable. The "self" is both treated as infallible and as having the synthetic and integrative capacities that, I believe, are features of the well-functioning ego. This view of the "self" is as if it were the picture held by a poorly functioning ego looking yearningly at what it might be, externalizing and idealizing it much as a young child idealizes and yearns to be like his or her father. This attribution of infallibility to the self is a defense against the narcissistic wound inflicted both by object loss and by relinquishment of infantile fantasies of omnipotence. This kind of defense is typical of psychosis and psychotic character, hence the frequency of both grandiose and paranoid delusions in the psychoses. One experiences this infallibility as self-sufficiency, the perfect antidote to profound need for and fear of abandonment by the object.

The "self" is sometimes thought of as the archetypal basis of the ego-complex. This formulation points up the special connection between the ego and the "self," but, as the word "archetypal" has come to imply, this also suggests a superordinate, innate caretaking (one might say, parental) function that stands behind, guides, and supports the ego. As I have suggested above, I am skeptical of this formulation. But what of the "self" that is directly experienceable? As I have outlined elsewhere (Satinover 1980), the defining feature of the experienced self is continuity of identity. (Hence discontinuity of identity is the defining feature of disorders of the self.) This continuity, subjectively experienced, corresponds to what Federn (1952) called "ego-feeling," and is the sense of a firm "boundary" about one's ego.

Consistent with this view, the *idea* of an overarching, superordinate, and omnipotent "self" is itself a manifestation of what Kohut (1971) calls the "grandiose self," i.e., an externalized exaggeration of ego-feeling that compensates for an introspectively sensed weakness of the ego. Thus paranoia and grandiosity, the emotional states most typical of psychosis, are the most prominent responses to threatened ego feeling.

Where does the self come from, then, if it is not innate? In brief, the experience of the self is a function of the stable ego (expending narcissistic energy in a normal form of introversion, as a kind of background process of self-awareness). Like other products of the ego, it is a variety of creative achievement. To the extent that the introverted energy the ego expends has been neutralized (Hartmann 1952) and is thus conflict free, it represents the highest possible level of defense against drive conflict. In short, the self is every person's unique solution to the inherent problem of being human. In my view, the self is not given, it is forged. I will later take up in somewhat greater detail the question of what may be innate and what may not be. Needless to say, many dispositions of the personality that will later be integrated into the self are innate, as are the maturational processes (for instance, of the nervous system) that support this integration.

I approach the topic of abandonment from three different but closely related directions. Each direction has its own rationale and each leads to a different part of the same conclusion.

The first part of this paper explicates a clinical theory of psychosis and psychotic character that, in contrast to the established Jungian view, restores to its central place in a Jungian model of their etiology the role of object loss (abandonment). The reader familiar with object-relations theory (not extensively referenced here) may hear in this argument an echo of the British Object Relations School. Such a connection could be articulated, but this would detract from the (historically and theoretically) more compelling reconnection to Freud's own theory and to classical psychoanalysis. By emphasizing the role of object loss in psychosis, I hope to draw attention to the role of the classical instincts—love and aggression—which are object-oriented, in distinction to the so-called "instinct for meaning" (Jung 1936, par. 241; Langer 1953), which is self-oriented. Object-relations theory may itself be seen as a recasting of instinct theory in a form that lends itself to the concept of an "inner world," halfway to the world of archetypes (and eventually to a *mundus imaginalis* stripped of even a compensatory relationship to the real world). By pursuing an increasingly introverted style of conceptualization, which eventually becomes solipsistic, instinctive aims become object-representations, then undifferentiated self-object representations, then introjects, and finally parts of the self. Glover (1961) may thus damn object-relations theory as, precisely, "Jungian." In a seeming paradox, the object-relations approach may actually draw attention away from the relationship to objects.

The second part of this paper is devoted to an examination of Jung's own near-psychotic break, his "Confrontation with the Unconscious" (1961). This examination is useful for a number of interrelated reasons. Jung felt that his theories should be considered a contribution to science, but to an extent unusual for science, Jung translated personal inner experience directly into theory. Thus, for instance, the prototype of Jung's concept of the anima was Jung's own compelling fantasy image; or, more generally speaking, the prototype of the individuation process was Jung's own psychic process both as he experienced it and then theorized about that experience by using the images that came to mind as concepts. We should not be surprised if necessary revisions in his theory should prove to be closely related to the ways in which Jung (intellectually) managed his own (emotional) experiences. Further, Jung makes it clear in his autobiography (1961) that the act of forging a scientific theory played an important part in stabilizing his personality following the "confrontation with the unconscious." But if that is true, and I believe it is, then those theories may justly also be studied as symptoms that helped Jung homeostatically to regulate his disorder. This is only another way of stating Jung's view of the prospective— that is, self-healing—function of symptoms.

Such an ad hominem approach would usually be strictly rhetorical, and in any case it cannot support or refute the truthfulness of a hypothesis. But because of the unusual extent to which Jung's theoretical ideas and inner processes are interrelated, this ad hominem approach is merely the obverse of the uncritical appropriation of Jung's ideas in the hope of emulating his inner process. The *imitatio Jungi* is widespread enough within the Jungian movement to call for such a critical reexamination of basic principles and of the way they were reached.

In his "confrontation," Jung was indeed reenacting a prototypical process having to do with self-differentiation. But Jung's inner process was also typical of psychosis or psychotic character in avoiding a direct confrontation with object loss, and his theories after the break from Freud came to reflect this avoidance. In those areas where they need revising in the direction of greater attention to the object, Jung's ideas truly were symptomatic of the processes they described, which are the subject of this paper.

The third part of this paper provides an example of a revision in the theory of the archetype, consistent with the principles established in the first two parts. This proposed revision finds external support in recent findings about development that have emerged from the study of infants. It is but one instance of a kind of revision that will be necessary if Jung's contribution, instead of being a myth for our time, is to achieve its full clinical potential.

## Psychosis

No form of psychopathology is so difficult to comprehend and treat, nor so devasting to its sufferers, as psychosis. Its protean manifestations, both biological and psychological, have tantalized researchers since the turn of the century. While Jung was still a resident under Bleuler at the Burghölzli Clinic, he was one of the earliest investigators to propose that psychosis was caused by the interraction of biochemical and psychosocial factors (Jung 1909, 1919, 1939, 1957, 1958). Arguing against the strictly descriptive psychiatry of Kraepelin (1919) that prevailed, Jung attempted to demonstrate the psychological meaning of the psychotic patient's florid productions (1909, 1916). Three important interrelated facts emerge from this work.

1. Jung's Model is an *Einheitspsychologie*. Bleuler was the great psychiatric innovator of Jung's formative years. Bleuler's contribution (1950) was to counterpose a psychodynamic nosology to Kraepelin's descriptive one. In so doing, he created an *Einheitspsychologie* that influenced Jung.

As a result of the view that everyone shares the same psychology (*Einheitspsychologie* = one common psychology), Jung came to define psychosis as a particularly extreme form of otherwise common, even normative, psychological problems. This view of psychosis is paradigmatic for his general theory of psychopathology, as well as for the individuation process (Levene 1982).

Bleuler's nosology was shaped by Freud's emerging psychoanalysis. The steady stream of psychoanalytic investigators who have followed also tend to see psychosis as related to other normative psychic processes. Most of their theories thus show a greater affinity to Jung's thought than do the psychological theories of those psychoanalysts who concentrated on the neuroses. A good example of this affinity, arising out of a consideration of primitive mental states, is the close affiliation of the Jungian and Kleinian schools in London. Exceptions would be Arlow and Brenner (1969), who are of the classical psychoanalysts the most successful in incorporating psychosis under a strict version of the structural hypothesis. Heinz Kohut is the modern analyst most readily compared with Jung (Satinover 1983), and his theories about narcissistic personalities are more accurately applied to psychotic and psychotic character patients than to more highly integrated ones.

In short, with a concept of individuation rooted in his studies of psychosis, Jung delineated a critical dimension of personality development: self-differentiation. It is in this dimension, too, that a spectrum of related psychopathologic states resides. In a non-pejorative sense, these are all more-or-less psychotic in that they all involve a degree of pathology of self-differentiation. The spectrum runs from schizophrenia at one end, through mania and psychotic depression and the transient micropsychotic episodes of borderline individuals to, at the other end, the narcissistic problems of the *puer aeternus.*

2. Jung's Model is Organismic. As the subtitle of this paper ("Abandonment and Restitution") suggests, the great overarching metaphor of psychotic process is death and resurrection (or, equally, world-destruction and world–re-creation). The metaphor may broadly be understood as a representation of homeostasis or self-regulating (healing) psychic processes. Jung's model of psychic death and rebirth is organismic in that it conveys a view of psychic process that is homeostatic.

In medicine, disease states fall into two broad categories: those caused directly by the pathogenic factor and those caused by the body's attempt to respond to the pathogenic factor. Thus, tissues of an immunocompromised host infected and killed by bacteria are in a diseased state caused by the bacteria. But the inflammation and exudate at the same site in a normal host, as well as the elevated white blood cell count in the bloodstream, are normal homeostatic responses of the body to the bacteria. Although they are symptoms of pathology, inflammation, pus, and a high white count indicate purposeful mechanisms for eliminating the infection and returning the body to health. The immunocompromised host, on the other hand, will die rapidly—without swelling, pus, or a high white count—of what in another individual would be trivial (as happens, for example, to AIDS victims).

Another example of a normal homeostatic response that is nonetheless a pathologic state is the dilated heart of congestive heart failure.[1] The heart enlarges in order to compensate for its

---

1. This is not to be confused with the hypertrophic heart of chronic hypertension. In that case, the hypertrophy is due to a growth of extra tissue needed to create greater outflow pressures to overcome the greater resistance of the vasculature that is the cause of hypertension. Homeostatic processes are ubiquitous.

intrinsic weakness. This tissue weakness (which may have many causes) is the true disease, and the subsequent dilation is a homeostatic response that preserves life (because stretched heart muscle fibers contract more strongly, up to a point [Starling's Law]), but at a cost.

Jung's view of psychosis (and later of neurosis, too) is similar. He saw the florid productions of psychosis (fantasies of death and rebirth) as the symptoms (representations) of a homeostatic process for restoring the integrity of a diseased personality. The psychotic symptoms are not the illness. Rather, they are the psyche's attempt to restore health. It is the normality and ubiquity of these processes—even in states that are not clinically psychotic—that is emphasized in the general Jungian view. But what is also emphasized is that the new state of homeostasis is either normal or in some sense better than normal.

3. The Unifying Principle is Self-Differentiation (Individuation). Jung proposed that there is an innate maturational drive toward the establishment of a stable sense of self that encompasses as much as possible of the whole person. As the name for this drive implies, individuation refers to those aspects of personality that are relatively immutable and independent of external circumstances (i.e., objects). As Jung's own personal account (1961) explicitly states, this component of personality separates the individual from his place in a specific sphere of personal relationships but also relates him to humanity as a whole. It is important to note that this latter is an abstraction.

To summarize these three points: self-differentiation is a critical dimension of normal development; psychosis is the most severe, and in some ways the most typical, instance, of the disorders of self-differentiation; the symptoms of psychosis are the representations of a homeostatic attempt on the part of the psyche to reestablish an autonomous, differentiated self.

Consistent with this point of view are various other tenets of Jungian theory. For instance, the self is defined as common to all individuals but also as located "in" the individual. In other words, it does not require other people in order to exist. Also there is the idea that archetypes are inherited aspects of the individual psyche. (In Jung's analogy, they are the organs of the mind, located in the individual, thus inherited with the brain, though similar in all people.)

The most integrated exposition of these ideas as they apply to psychosis is John Perry's (1976). He interprets the symbolism of psychosis as the autonomous self-representation of a spontaneous healing process that occurs within the individual. Indeed, so thoroughly is this healing process "within" that although "the therapist must be receptive and attentive to the psychic process . . . the psyche does the work of healing" (Perry, p. 22). Perry then explains his overall point of view, contrasting it to the psychoanalytic model:

> If one starts from the premise that the human being is fundamentally a biological animal . . . the ego's primary concerns are, then, object-relations handled with . . . a well-developed capacity for reality-testing. . . .
>
> If, however, one's premise is that we have become primarily psychological beings, whose basic drive is . . . awareness . . . of the meaning of our life, then . . . [psychic] processes strive to single out my individuality from all the various influences, pressures and identifications that have impinged on me since birth. . . . The myness of my world view . . . is the substantive expression of my nature. The quest for meaning . . . is the same as the effort to become the person that I am. (Ibid., p. 23)

Perry's dichotomy between a psychoanalytic view and a Jungian one is false. Self-differentiation, and the accompanying sense of meaning, occurs in the context of maturing object-relations and, conversely, functional psychosis occurs in the setting of a perceived abandonment by significant objects. For this reason, the Jungian and psychoanalytic conceptions of restitution in psychosis are each in part correct. The symptoms of the restitutive phase both represent an attempt at internal reordering, and then substitute for the lost object (Burnham 1955).

Perry's formulation is consistent with traditional Jungian theory and with Jung's model of personality as he formulated it during his break from Freud. The schizoid cast to it is ironic and illuminating. A theory that views restitution in psychosis as a purely internal phenomenon and has as its aim an abstraction—such as "meaning"—shares with psychosis itself a defense against the pain of object loss.

Conversely, that which we experience in our closest and most special relationships is meaningful enough. The missing element, which needs to be added to the three implicit in Jung's view, is the object.

What I am suggesting is akin to Martin Buber's accusation that Jung was a gnostic, although the concepts I am using are not theological: Buber complained that Jung eschewed the importance of relationships and instead sought spirituality through gnosis. In his reply to Buber, Jung acknowledges this: "the objective psyche . . . forms the counterposition to the subjective ego. It can therefore be designated as a Thou" (1952, p. 665).

Jung is here restating, in Buber's terms, a well-known theoretical maxim of his. However, this theory has its roots in his own personality. (A much chuckled-at story of Jung told in Zurich is how his wife thought he was more interested in the collective unconscious than in people.) A truer conception of the problem of self-differentiation would need to take into account the bias present in Jung's own formulation of the problem, even though Jung was the first psychoanalyst to characterize it.

## The Development of Jung's Theoretical Position

As stated, Jung's view of the compensatory function or the psyche was rooted in his study of psychosis. Only later did he explicitly broaden his theory to the entire domain of psychopathology, including the developmental vicissitudes of maturity. Thus, in 1954 he wrote to John Perry:

> the regression that occurs in the rebirth or integration process [restitution] is in itself a normal phenomenon inasmuch as you observe it also with people that don't suffer from any kind of psychopathic ailment. When it is a matter of a schizoid condition, you observe very much the same. (Jung 1975, p. 148)

Jung's original idea was that the regression in schizophrenia was purposive, aimed at reintegration of the personality, and that it expressed itself in death and rebirth fantasies. This was the central hypothesis of the two *Jahrbuch* articles (Jung 1911, 1912) that contributed to his personal break from Freud. Jung wrote these articles in direct rebuttal to Freud (1911), who in turn countered with his seminal, but still controversial, "On Narcissism: An Introduction" (1914).

### The Problem of Libido in Dementia Praecox

In numerous letters to Jung, and finally in a 1911 article (quoted below), Freud noted that individuals who suffer from paranoia or dementia praecox seem to be absorbed excessively in themselves to the same degree in which they lack interest in others. (Freud accepted and used Jung's term "introversion" to characterize this.)

This imbalance, he further noted, corresponds to the loss of their reality function. He proposed, therefore, that in dementia praecox, the loss of reality is due to a withdrawal of libido from objects and its secondary reattachment to the ego.

Thus, in certain circumstances, the ego could be cathected not only with its own proper energy, but with additional sexual energy as well. Freud called this state "secondary narcissism." He laid out this conception in his analysis of the case of Schreber, a previously published autobiographical account of psychosis brought to Freud's attention by Jung. Freud's own formulation therein is as follows:

> We can no more dismiss the possibility that disturbances of the libido may react upon the ego-cathexes than we can overlook the converse. . . . It therefore appears to me far more probable that the paranoiac's altered relation to the world is to be explained entirely, or in the main, by the loss of this libidinal interest. . . . It would resemble dementia praecox insofar as the repression proper would have the same principal feature—detachment of the libido together with its regression onto the ego. (1911, p. 75)

At the time he was reading this passage, Jung was at work on his own analysis of "The Miller Fantasies," a case of prodromal schizophrenia published by Theodor Flournoy (Miller 1906). This analysis was to become Jung's "Wandlungen und Symbole der Libido," a two-part article he published in the 1911 and 1912 *Jahrbuch für psychoanalytische und psychopathologische Forschungen*. Jung felt so strongly that the article would be considered by Freud a betrayal of psychoanalytic principles that he delayed its completion for months, agonizing over the dreaded and wished-for break from his mentor. Even his wife, Emma, got caught up in the drama and attempted to intercede with Freud on her husband's behalf, pleading with him not to take the theoretical differences personally. In a letter predating the August 1912 publication of the more heretical Part II, Jung wrote to Freud (Dec. 11, 1911):

> As for the libido problem, I must confess that your remark in the Schreber analysis . . . [the passage quoted above] has set up booming reverberations. This remark, or rather the doubt expressed therein, has resuscitated all the difficulties that have beset me throughout the years in my attempt to apply the libido theory to [dementia praecox]. The loss of the reality function in [dementia praecox] cannot be reduced to repression of libido (defined as sexual hunger). Not by me at any rate. . . . I have now . . . arrived at a solution . . . . (McGuire 1974, p. 471)

In the resulting *Jahrbuch* article, which indeed contributed to the break with Freud, Jung wrote:

> If [one] believes that through the withdrawal of the libido from the outer world the paranoid system of the schizophrenic symptomatology results, then this assumption is not justified . . . because a mere libido introversion and regression leads, speedily, as Freud has clearly shown, into the . . . transference neuroses, and not into dementia praecox. Therefore the transferring of the libido theory to dementia praecox is impossible, because this illness produces a loss of reality which cannot be explained by the deficiency of the libido defined in the narrow sense. (1916, p. 143)

Put briefly, Jung claimed that the loss of reality was unrelated to the experience of object-loss.

### Jung's Monistic, Genetic Libido

Jung then proceeded in a number of directions seminal for his later psychological theory. But certain of his hypotheses were contradictory and were later modified or dropped. (Unfortunately, they do not appear in unrevised form in the *Collected Works*, so that a reader of these loses an important perspective. The 1916 English translation of "Wandlungen . . .," entitled *Psychology of the Unconscious*, is long out of print and contains some astonishing material.)

First, in his *Jahrbuch* article Jung proposed a specific alteration in the psychoanalytic theory of the libido, a proposal not to be found in later editions of the same work nor elsewhere. This is the notion of a "genetic" component to the libido (genetic in a biological sense). In the letter to Freud quoted previously, Jung continued: "The essential point is that I try to replace the descriptive concept of libido with a genetic one. Such a concept covers not only the recent-sexual libido but all those forms of it which have long since split off into organized activities" (McGuire 1974, p. 471).

In the article itself, Jung described a primordial energy of primitive organisms that could be considered essentially sexual, i.e., the core drive of this organism was to reproduce. In the course of evolution, however, other functions developed that were needed to maintain the organism so that it might reproduce successfully. (The modern analogy to this theory—only partly tongue in cheek—is to view life as a mere support system for the maintenance and replication of nucleic acid.)

Thus, the original sexual energy had become modified, with only a portion of it now remaining at the service of sexuality per se. The remainder had long since become fixed in maintenance functions which, having evolved, were now inherited. In Jung's words:

From that sexual primal libido which produced millions of eggs and seeds from one small creature, derivatives have been developed associated with a great limitation of fecundity; derivatives in which the functions are maintained by a special differentiated libido. This differentiated libido is henceforth desexualized because it is dissociated from its original function . . . nor is there any possibility of restoring it. . . . This now presupposed a very different and very complicated relation to reality, a true function of reality. . . . Thus the altered mode of procreation carries with it . . . a correspondingly heightened adaptation to reality. (Jung 1916, p. 149)

Second, Jung hypothesized a monistic, overall "psychic energy (which he continued to call "libido," a point of contention with Freud). There is a crucial flaw in this idea. Jung equated his monistic "libido" with the "primal libido" described above.

He wrote of his new idea that "it regards the multiplicity of instincts as issuing from a relative unity, the primal libido" (Jung 1916, p. 149). Yet, as quoted above, he also said "nor is there any possibility of restoring it." But if there is no possibility of restoring the multiplicity of instincts to their original unity, the primal libido, then there is no *real* difference between Jung's supposedly original concept and Freud's. For all practical purposes, Jung failed to establish a monistic concept of libido. One would be born anyway with multiple, non-interconvertible instincts, their monistic origins notwithstanding. In his later writing, Jung consequently dropped altogether his "genetic" conception and reiterated instead his proposal of a unitary psychic energy. He thereby preserved the disagreement with Freud on the nature of libido and laid the groundwork for his later non-conflict—based model of the psyche.

Third, although he continued to assert the monism of psychic energy, Jung's later conception of the psyche is fundamentally dualistic (though non-conflictual). But whereas Freud's dualism was, at least originally, an analytic one of ego versus libido, Jung's is a more synthetic one of good and bad aspects of the self. The "archetypes," which are the equivalent to primitive self/object representations, or introjects, divide along these lines.

### Ego-Regression in Dementia Praecox

The value of Jung's biological speculation is in its implicit assertion of an evolved, independent (conflict-free) *energy of the ego* that supports the reality function. He located the primary source of schizophrenic psychopathology in disturbances of this energy, rather than in disturbances of the libido. (Later, Jung would refer to the self in this connection. Hence, the self became what, for the psychoanalysts, remained the ego.)

A version of Jung's thesis persisted in psychoanalysis after Jung's departure. Although Abraham continued to develop the idea that the withdrawal of libido from objects explained the symptoms of schizophrenia (in particular, megalomania—[Abraham 1908]), this idea was increasingly challenged by theories that emphasized disturbances in the ego per se. Ferenczi's classic 1913 article "Stages in the Development of the Sense of Reality," asserted the primacy of sexuality in the genesis of the reality function, but it focused greater attention on the ego-instincts. And, as do later theorists of narcissism such as Gruenberger (1979), Ferenczi ultimately located the origin of infantile omnipotence not in self-love, but in a dim recollection of intrauterine self-sufficiency.

As Van der Waals put it in 1965:

> Freud was critical of Jung, who could not accept Freud's hypothesis that the detachment of libido from the object and its withdrawal onto the self could cause the loss of reality in psychosis. Nowadays, we can appreciate the doubts of Jung, and I believe that ego-regression is the central problem. (P. 303)

The same conflict about the nature of psychosis has persisted within psychoanalysis itself. Most modern psychoanalysts speak not of ego-regression, as does Van der Waals, but rather of an inherent defect of the ego (or, in some theories, of the self). But those who speak of such defects oppose the adherents of the more traditional view that in psychosis there is a regression of libido (i.e., of investment in objects) as a defense against conflict. This is simply another way of stating Freud's original observations in his 1911 Schreber article. The defect-defense controversy is thus, in somewhat different guise, the same controversy that sprang up between Freud and Jung and played such a central role in the theoretical component of Jung's apostasy. In the defense view, psychosis is one way of handling overwhelming loss in relationships; in the defect view, psychosis results from a flaw or inadequacy in the ego or self. In the defense view, the compensatory restitution of a psychotic (i.e., grandiose) self-image is a compromise or substitute formation, meant defensively to assuage the unacknowledgeable pain of external loss; in the defect view, the compensatory restitution is an attempt at internal homeostasis (rebirth).

## A Restatement of the Nature of Psychosis

There is a third way of putting it that adjudicates the Jungian and psychoanalytic positions. If correct, it would require some important alterations in our theory of the psyche. This third way is as follows:

There is no such thing as a self independent of its objects. Although an innate, heritable defect may predispose to it, the shattering of the self which occurs in the acute phase of clinical psychosis, or as a chronic weakness in psychotic character, is caused by perceived abandonment by important objects. Psychotic restitution of the self-image is a form of homeostasis. It is the psyche's means of protecting itself from total destruction, but at a cost. The cost is a diffusion of identity and at times decreased capacity to grasp reality. At the same time, the constellated archetypes (primitive self/object representations) substitute for the lost object.

This formulation is a less hopeful one than pure homeostasis, but does greater justice to the clinical facts at both ends of the self-pathological spectrum. At one end of that spectrum, psychosis is extraordinarily destructive. Psychotic regression is usually only partly reversible and almost always ends in a decrease of functioning in both work and relationships.

At the other end of the spectrum the much less severe pathology of the *puer aeternus* is nonetheless quite intractable and modified only with great difficulty. As a classical psychoanalyst would put it, the most difficult analysand is the successful narcissist.

To draw on the heart failure analogy once more, enlargement of the heart in congestive heart failure is the body's attempt to heal itself. It does not correct the original deficit, but compensates for it. Similarly, because psychosis leaves so wide a swath of destruction in its path, the alterations in personality that follow an acute psychotic episode are self-healing only in this limited sense of being the best possible resolution. In both enlargement of the heart following heart failure and in enlargement of the self following failure of the ego and object loss, the compensated state is the best possible one, but is nonetheless pathological. In neither instance can one reasonably hope for full restoration of normal function.

In psychotic characters, the pathological nature of the compensatory restitution is more difficult to see. Furthermore, the compensated state may utilize creative expression in an extremely interesting and valuable fashion, so that the substitution of inner for outer objects may be seen more as a matter of choice (or of innate disposition) than dynamically. Finally, the narcissistic investment in considering oneself not ill is so great that even obvious instances of pathology are subtly normalized.

The conventional Jungian view of compensation in the psyche is that it represents an ideal homeostasis, one that aims to return the personality to a truer baseline than preceded the decompensation. As quoted above, Jung referred to this restitution as "the rebirth or integration process [which] is itself a normal phenomenon inasmuch as you observe it also with people that don't suffer from any kind of psychopathic ailment" (Jung 1975, p. 148).

I disagree. The death and rebirth phenomenon, with its characteristic introversion of libido and heightened compensatory cathexis of archetypal figures is indicative of those conditions whose extreme version is clinical psychosis.[2] While such conditions, especially in their milder forms, are quite widespread (and in *that* sense, normal), "nevertheless it must also be recognized that for many, this problem is not the main one" (Winnicott 1964, p. 450). As Winnicott remarks:

> Jung, in describing himself, gives us a picture of childhood schizophrenia, and at the same time his personality displays strength of a kind which enabled him to heal himself. At cost he recovered, and part of the cost to him is what he paid out to us, if we can listen and hear, in terms of his exceptional insight. Insight into what? Insight into the feeling of those who are mentally split.
> . . . I have stated elsewhere that it is in the area of psychosis rather than that of psychoneurosis that we must expect to find cure by self-healing. Jung provides an example of this, but of course self-healing is not the same as resolution by analysis. (Ibid., p. 451)

Winnicott's observation has many corollaries, despite the unlikelihood of his specific diagnosis. (While Jung's pathology was probably within the psychotic spectrum, broadly conceived, it does not appear to have been nearly so severe as what today we would call childhood schizophrenia.) First, self-healing differs from analytic resolution in that it is too optimistic to think that autonomous compensatory processes lead to higher levels of *overall* integration than existed prior to a decompensation. To use William James's

---

2. As I have suggested elsewhere (Satinover 1984), the widespread belief in a dying and resurrecting god may be thought of as the collective solution to this problem, available to those who required it in cultures where metaphysical belief was still possible.

(1901) metaphor, the once-born are the healthiest and luckiest. Some of those who require death and rebirth may achieve extraordinary insight as a result, but the mortgage is high and continues to be paid. It is true that a higher degree of functioning in certain areas will result, perhaps even a hypertrophy of function—that, after all, is why compensatory processes exist. But a careful examination will reveal the cost. To use the extreme case, one commonly observes in chronic schizophrenics that a highly integrated paranoid delusional system will enable the person to function at a higher apparent level than prior to the acute phase of the illness. Indeed, in psychotherapy with such people, one must reach the person during the subacute phase (Pao 1979), prior to the crystallization of the delusions. Otherwise, the new homeostasis stabilized by the delusion will be very difficult to alter. It may require another decompensation to do so, the outcome of which may prove to be worse.

Once a delusional system has become established, the areas of increased functioning outside its domain are discrete. For example, an engaging 52-year-old man was convinced that people put itching powder in his food. Except for this conviction (which entailed a complicated scheme to rationalize how people managed to do this), he appeared quite normal and handled his life as a rugged outdoorsman quite well. However, it became apparent that the delusional idea was directly related to his fears of intimacy. No sooner would he grow close to someone than he would "get the itch" and distance himself. He would find himself disturbingly attracted, usually to other men, but he would only admit how they "got the itch" for him. Because his need was intolerably coupled to fear, this became a paranoid idea: They were attacking him and putting itching powder in his food. His highly functional, nomadic outdoorsman's existence was part of his homeostatic adaptation. He was rarely at close quarters with other people for very long, and he moved in his camper from place to place, effectively precluding any threatening ties. Nonetheless, his internal world was populated with figures of extraordinary importance. He was the sole object of their attention. In this fashion he remained contentedly isolated and celibate for over 20 years—since the day his wife left him—though to all outward appearances he was normal.

The pathological nature and compensatory function of such ideas as this delusion are easy to identify because the idea contrasts so starkly with simple reality. Indeed, the capacity for reality-testing is the conventional means of drawing a line between psychotic and non-psychotic states. It is much more difficult to identify the more mildly pathological nature and compensatory function of abstract ideas held by more creative and intelligent personalities. This is especially so when the ideas are, at least in part, useful abstractions of reality. In such cases, it is tempting to throw up one's hands and mumble something about the connection between genius and madness.

A more constructive approach exists. The self-curative process in psychosis leaves a residue, as it were, in the personality. As in the case above, following reconstitution (rebirth) of a decompensated personality (death), the primary area where such residua will be found is in *ideas.* The thought disorder in psychosis, while typical, is thus not primary, but a consequence of the homeostasis. The pathological component of these ideas is in the way they function to create distance from people (because of a primordial fear of abandonment). I believe that this is also the case, amplified by genius of unusual depth and complexity, with Jung and his theories about the psyche.

This brings us to the second corollary to Winnicott's comment. Because self-cure is not the same as analysis and does leave a residue, Jung's theories about the primitive core of the psyche are a mixture of profound insight and defensive compensation which need to be disentangled.

The defensive component is contained within its optimism, the failure to acknowledge pathological consequences of the rebirth process. This failure is itself the residue of Jung's own "death and rebirth." Specifically, Jung's hypothesis of the archetype is an incisive conceptualization of primitive inner experience. But his assertion and belief that the archetypes are innate and irreducible, and thus also true "Thou's," serves as a defense against profound fear of object loss.

## Jung's Confrontations: With the Unconscious and with Freud

As has often been noted, Jung's autobiography is remarkable for its absence of attention to the outer world and to other people. The one person, the one relationship, that merits a chapter is Sigmund Freud. It seems to me a crucial part of Jung's psychology and the peculiarity of his genius that his life after Freud was essentially a great containing and re-elaboration of the near-psychotic experiences that occurred upon the rupture of this relationship. It is also typical of his psychological approach, in both its brilliance and its blind spots, that he says the following, without mention of that person whose loss is the central event in Jung's personal life and professional development:

> In the end, the only events in my life worth telling are those when the imperishable world erupted into this transitory one. That is why I speak chiefly of inner experiences, amongst which I include my dreams and visions.
>
> All other memories of travels, people and my surroundings have paled beside these interior happenings. . . . Recollection of the out-ward events of my life has largely faded or disappeared. But my encounters with the "other" reality, my bouts with the unconscious, are indelibly engraved upon my memory . . . . [E]verything else has lost importance by comparison. . . . Outward circumstances are no substi-tute for inner experience. Therefore my life is singularly poor in outward happenings. (1961, p. 4)

Most of Jung's autobiography deals with these inner experi-ences.

As noted previously, one of the most striking and typical aspects of the fantasies, dreams, and hallucinations of individuals suffering from acute psychotic states (and true also of Jung's "Confrontation with the Unconscious"[1961]) are images of world destruction. This was a prominent feature of Schreber's fantasies, for example. The meaning of the world-destruction motif has been a point of conten-tion in the literature ever since. The more clinical of the Jungian understandings has been to take such fantasies as direct, metaphoric representations of the state of the personality (Perry 1974); the less clinical understanding is that they are literal prophesies referring to the real world or to the state of the collective unconscious. There is general agreement, however (excluding, perhaps, the adherents of the latter point of view), that the presence of such fantasies is typical, though not pathognomonic, of psychosis. In general terms, world destruction and re-creation parallel the motif of death and spiritual rebirth (also of cultural revivification [Perry 1976]) that is equally prominent in psychotic fantasy as in myth and religion. The following psychoanalytic points of view concerning world destruc-tion have been elaborated:

1. World destruction represents the subjectively experienced loss of, abandonment by, or fantasied destruction of the patient's object-world. It is thus a picture of the organismic panic (Frosch 1983) that results from abandonment by a primary object. Such subjectively experienced abandonments are frequently the specific

precipitants to a patient's presentation in a psychiatric emergency room.

2. World destruction represents the wished-for effect of the patient's excess unmodified aggression on his object world. In this view, an unmanageable excess of aggression—due to some combination of innate and environmental conditions—is central to the etiology of psychosis. The violence of many paranoid patients, and the violent content of much schizophrenic fantasy, is consistent with this view.

3. World destruction is a direct, symbolic representation of the patient's shattering self. This is a more recent view that has arisen because of the renewed interest in narcissism and in particular the contributions of Kohut.

4. To the above, we can add the more specifically Jungian views. On one hand, world-destruction fantasies represent a purposeful overthrowing of an inadequate consciousness by a dissatisfied superordinate self. This destruction aims at renewal. On the other hand, world-destruction fantasies represent the overthrowing of a dominant collective mode of consciousness, because of an alteration in the collective unconscious. According to this latter view, susceptible individuals are the "carriers" of this alteration and suffer the sea-change on our behalf. This view cannot take into account the frequency with which such fantasies occur in response to personal crisis in susceptible individuals, nor the fact that they tend not to occur when even susceptible individuals are in stable relationships, therapeutic or otherwise. Similarly, even severe crisis will not provoke such fantasies or the corresponding panic and destabilization of the self in individuals who are not susceptible. A recent investigation, presented at the Annual Conference of Jungian Analysts in New York, showed few such dreams in the general public. Further, there was a predictable lack of correlation between dreams of nuclear holocaust and conscious fears of world destruction. (Conversely, that few people are now dreaming of nuclear war should be of no comfort to anyone.)

Jung developed the essentials of his theory while he was experiencing just such fantasies and the primitive emotional states that typically accompany them. Strikingly, he attributed to his own world-destruction fantasies (hallucinations, dreams) the most impersonal meaning at the very moment when his personal relationship with Freud was collapsing.

When a patient suffers an acute or subacute psychotic decompensation, disruptions in his close relationships to others are almost invariably the precipitants. Frequently, we can obtain enough information about a patient's present life to understand what these disruptions are, and about that person's past life to understand why they are experienced as so severe. In such instances one sees clearly how images that relate to these past and present relationships reappear—defensively cloaked—in dreams and hallucinations. In general, when these images refer to the self in that relationship, they assume a grandiose (haughty, self-sufficient) nature; when they refer to the lost object, they assume a persecutory cast.

In his autobiography, Jung carefully details his inner experiences during his crisis. However, he does not relate them to events happening in his personal relational life, except in a general way. He does place his chapter on "Confrontation with the Unconscious" after his chapter on Sigmund Freud, but one is left with the impression that this was simply a matter of chronology. Further, in his introduction he minimizes the significance of these relationships to the inner experiences he concentrates on. He interprets his confrontation in terms almost exclusively impersonal, and his theory buttresses this approach.

Jung thus leaves the reader with the impression that his confrontation with the unconscious was but a reflection of events in the objective psyche and specifically a reflection of the same general factors that gave rise to World War I.

However, a great deal *was* going on in his personal life while Jung was confronting the unconscious. The events outlined in the chapter "Confrontation with the Unconscious" can be rearranged chronologically, and the events in the chapter "Sigmund Freud" intercalated with them. Thus, as it was written, "Confrontation with the Unconscious" follows "Sigmund Freud" and begins: "After the parting of the ways with Freud, a period of inner uncertainty began for me. It would be no exaggeration to call it a state of disorientation" (Jung 1961, p. 170). But actually, the period of disorientation began during the tension with Freud, not after.

If one adds to this intercalation of events the corresponding letters between the two men, something striking emerges: Each of the critical inner events that Jung documents (some of which have come down to us with an aura of prophesy) corresponds to critical events in the drama unfolding between him and Freud. Further-

more, these inner events strongly echo the inner events that occurred in Jung's childhood, during the period of his parents' separation and his mother's hospitalization.

In this chronology, certain features typical of psychotic fantasy
stand out:

1. Parental (specifically father) murder, first denied, then implicitly acknowledged;

2. Death, and the dead not remaining dead but coming to life
or living on;

3. The reactivation of childhood conflicts related to abandonment;

4. Emotional flooding, accompanied by dreams and hallucinations of a morbid nature;

5. World-destruction fantasies;

6. The fear of the destruction of the self (fear of psychosis) in
the setting of weakened self/object differentiation;

7. The elaboration of a set of ideas that both explains the above
and distances the individual from the personal aspects of it while
also reintegrating the self;

8. The emotional experiences that are part of the psychosis and
their systematic reintegration, which persist as the focal point of the
rest of the individual's life.

There is not enough space here to detail this chronology and
illuminate all the interweaving threads. However, I would like
briefly to touch on a few of the highlights.

In his chapter "Sigmund Freud," Jung recounts a number of
instances where he believes that Freud was implicitly or explicitly
attributing to him (Jung) murderous, unconscious wishes toward
Freud. Jung not only denies the presence of any such wishes, but
reinterprets the same material as suggestions of the collective unconscious. What was happening at that time? Early in 1909, Jung was
entangled with Sabina Speilrein (McGuire 1974) in a curious triangle involving Freud. Although it appears that he did not actually
have sexual intercourse with his then-patient, Jung presents himself
to Freud in this matter as a guilty supplicant to his paternal confes-
sor. In one of these letters he also comments to Freud: "Nothing
Fliess-like is going to happen" (McGuire 1974: p. 212). Thus, the
fantasy of an oedipal betrayal is already present.

In late March of that year, Jung visited Freud in Vienna. At that
meeting, the well-known parapsychological discussion occurred
(Jung 1961, pp. 155ff). In the first letter to follow, Jung commented:

> It seemed to me that my spookery struck you as altogether too stupid and perhaps unpleasant because of the Fliess analogy. (Insanity!). . . . I had the feeling that under it all there must be some quite special complex, a universal one having to do with the prospective tendencies in man. If there is a "psychanalysis" there must also be a "psychosynthesis" which creates future events according to the same laws. (I see I am writing rather as if I had a flight of ideas.) . . .
>
> That last evening with you has, most happily, freed me inwardly from the oppressive sense of your paternal authority. (McGuire 1974, pp. 216–17)

Freud replied:

> It is strange that on the very same evening when I formally adopted you as eldest son and anointed you . . . as my successor and crown prince, you should have divested me of my paternal dignity, which divesting seems to have given you as much pleasure as I, on the contrary, derived from the investiture of your person. (McGuire 1974, p. 218)

And, also in the same reply, that which Jung would later characterize as "synchronicity," Freud went on to call "the undeniable 'compliance of chance,' which plays the same part in the formation of delusions as somatic compliance in that of hysterical symptoms, and linguistic compliance in the generation of puns" (McGuire 1974, p. 220).

Thus, even in this brief (but crucial) interchange, the essentials of the future break are laid down: Behind Jung's ambivalence toward Freud lies a father-complex (i.e., in part a wish to murder the hated rival, in part to identify with him—the Fliess analogy). Jung's response to this complex is to generate a manic defense (the flight of ideas that he senses) and to turn the personal conflict into magical abstractions that, as Freud perceives, are akin to delusions. Within this complex, crucial elements of Jung's future theory are germinating. For example: 1) the prophetic, parapsychological dimension of the psyche; 2) the psyche's prospective tendencies; 3) the idea of psychological "synthesis" in opposition to "analysis" or reduction. This germination, in the form of a flight of ideas, occurs just as Jung feels himself freed from the oppressive sense of Freud's paternal authority. In the primitive language of the unconscious, Jung wishes to "kill" Freud with his parapsychological demonstration.

Later in 1909, the two men met again in Bremen. Jung commented that it was a decisive year for their relationship. At Bremen occurred the well-known discussion of the peat-bog corpses and one of Freud's fainting episodes. Jung ridiculed Freud's belief that father-murder was then in the air between them. Later that same year, Jung dreamed of skulls and *anticipated* that Freud would interpret them as death wishes against Freud. This assumption appears to have been the first thought Jung had in connection to this dream. He therefore lied and presented to Freud some "invented" associations. For himself, he considered the dream an intimation of the collective unconscious. But the dream led him to Friedrich Creuzer's work on mythology. Ironically, he used Creuzer's book to interpret the Miller fantasies in the later *Jahrbuch* articles, which indeed attempted to throw over the cornerstone of Freud's theory and capped his break from Freud. As with Oedipus, Jung's attempt to avoid the predicted father-murder led directly to it.

While Jung was working on this *Jahrbuch* article, he had a dream about an Austrian customs official who, though dead, would not die. Jung recognized that this dream presaged the break from Freud and commented: "*I could not refuse to see* the analogy with Freud" (1961, p. 163; italics mine). He speculated, "Could that be the death-wish which Freud had insinuated I felt towards him?" (ibid., p. 164). He rejected this possibility in favor of compensation, i.e., the view that he had valued Freud too highly and must take him down a peg. Again, as in the case of the lie, he did not see that this very thought was itself a derivative of the aggression he was denying.

The dream hearkens back to a letter of November 1907 when Jung wrote to Freud of his first visit to Vienna earlier that year: "I dreamt that I saw you walking beside me as a *very, very frail old man*" (McGuire 1974, p. 96). In this letter, which followed a confession of his "religious crush" on Freud, Jung commented that the confession had enabled him to realize the meaning of the dream, which until the confession had remained obscure: "The dream sets my mind at ease about your dangerousness" (ibid.). Jung inserted three crosses after writing "Gefahrlichkeit! "[dangerousness!]". That is, the dream "compensates" for Jung's fear of the object of his "crush." (See Burhnam et al. [1969] on the "need-fear dilemma" in schizophrenia.) Among peasants of middle Europe, three crosses were chalked on the inside of a door to ward off danger and echo the death of Christ and the two thieves. Thus, the context of the customs official dream points to love, death, danger, and defense, and therefore to a subjective need for compensatory undervaluation. The three crosses will appear again at a critical juncture.

In the summer of 1912, the first overt anger appeared in the correspondence between the two men, and it escalated rapidly. In September Emma Jung sent Freud a copy of the critical second part of the *Jahrbuch* article. In November Jung castigated Freud for supposedly snubbing him on a visit to Kreuzlingen, calling it a "lasting wound" and asking for a "personal confrontation." On November 14, Freud changed the salutation on his letters from "Dear Friend" to "Dear Dr. Jung" (McGuire 1974, pp. 517–20).

Following Freud's abandonment of the personal form of address, there followed an extraordinary salvo of angry and sarcastic letters. In his account of this period in his autobiography, however, Jung describes a dream and comments only that it indicated "an unusual activation of the unconscious" (1961, p. 172). He says nothing of what was happening with Freud.[3]

On November 24, 1912, Jung and Freud met in Munich at a psychoanalytic conference and effected a reconciliation regarding the "Kreuzlingen gesture." The content of the discussion at the Congress is as interesting for what Jung neglects to report as for what he does report.

Jung writes that "someone had turned the conversation to Amenophis IV." This person claimed

> that as a result of his negative attitude towards his father he [Amenophis IV] had destroyed his father's cartouches in the steles, and that at the back of his great creation of a monotheistic religion there lurked a father-complex. This sort of thing irritated me, and I attempted to argue that Amenophis had been a creative and profoundly religious person whose acts could not be explained by personal resistances to his father. . . . At that moment Freud slid off his chair in a faint. . . . I picked him up, carried him into the next room, and laid him on a sofa. . . . I shall never forget the look he cast at me. In his weakness, he looked at me as if I were his father. (1961, p. 157)

About Freud's two fainting episodes, Jung commented that "the fantasy of father-murder was common to both cases" (*ibid.*), but he does not say whose fantasy it was. Nor does he mention the following:

Prior to the lunch where the above conversation occurred, Jung and Freud had reconciled their differences over the "Kreuzlingen

---

3. In his letter of Feb. 17, 1908 (McGuire 1974, pp. 119-20), Freud had changed his salutation from "Dear Friend and Colleague" to "Dear Friend." Jung had responded, "The undeserved gift of your friendship is one of the high points in my life . . . " and he asked Freud to "let me enjoy your friendship not as one between equals but as that of father and son" (ibid., p. 122).

gesture," but then at lunch Freud began to criticize the Swiss for omitting his name from their publications! He fainted when Jung went on to defend Amenophis' erasure of his father's name as a creative, religious act.

Jung reported that shortly after his own father's death in 1896, his mother commented: "He died in time for you" (Jung 1961, p. 96). Then he had a series of dreams in which his father returned, and in the dreams Jung was both confused about whether his father was dead or not and felt guilty for thinking he was dead and for taking over his room at home.

Concerning the "unusual activation of the unconscious," Jung comments that one fantasy kept returning again and again: Something is dead, but it is also still alive (Jung 1961, p. 172). Around Christmas of 1912 (one month after the Munich conference), Jung had a dream that he related to alchemy. It involved a female dove and a male dove busy with the twelve dead. The tension he felt, which he could not explain, was resolved by another dream, this time of sarcophagi, with the figures "curiously mummified" (ibid., pp. 172-73). The following connections stand out: Mummification is a way to keep something dead "alive"; mummies are Egyptian, as was Amenophis; Amenophis erased his father's name, i.e., killed or mummified him—as Jung denied doing to Freud—with the same guilty ambivalence Jung displayed toward his own father's death.

With regard to the mummified figures in the dream, Jung writes in particular about a dead crusader who comes to life (1961, p. 173). His next comment, seemingly incidentally, is about Freud, but Jung does not draw the connection. Rather, he claims, as in the case of the skulls, these dead that refuse to die refer to the still-living archaic layers of the impersonal psyche.

In January 1913, Jung received a letter from Freud breaking off personal relations. He responded on January 6, 1913: "I accede to your wish that we abandon our personal relations, for I never thrust my friendship on anyone. You yourself are the best judge of what this moment means to you. 'The rest is silence'" (McGuire 1974, p. 540).

Everything in the chronology so far points to the dangerous, aggressive impulses toward Freud that Jung, because of their destabilizing effect, must deny. In this letter, we see that Jung consciously expects the rupture of the relationship to deal Freud a mortal blow. But as his choice of quotation suggests, unconsciously Jung knows that it is he himself who is about to suffer the blow. "The rest is silence" is from *Hamlet*, V, ii. They are the Prince's final words after he has slain his stepfather, the King, and is himself about to die.

No further letters of a personal nature follow. There are a number of business letters concerning the International Association of which Jung was president, and the *Jahrbuch*, of which Jung had remained the editor. However, in October 1913, Jung writes to Freud that:

> It has come to my ears . . . that you doubt my *bona fides*. I would have expected you to communicate with me directly on so weighty a matter. Since this is the gravest reproach that can be levelled at anybody, you have made further collaboration impossible. I therefore lay down the editorship of the *Jahrbuch* with which you entrusted me. (McGuire 1974, p. 550)

His resignation effectively ended the *Jahrbuch*.

Jung writes of this time:

> Toward the autumn of 1913 the pressure which I had felt was in *me* seemed to be moving outward, as though there were something in the air. . . . It was psychic situation, but from concrete reality. This feeling grew more and more intense. (1961, p. 175)

Again, Freud is not mentioned, but the world political situation is. Jung then writes of that same month of 1913:

> In October . . . I was suddenly seized by an overpowering vision: I saw a monstrous flood covering all the northern and low-lying lands between the North Sea and the Alps. When it came up to Switzerland I saw that the mountains grew higher and higher to protect our country. I realized that a frightful catastrophe was in progress. I saw the mighty yellow waves, the floating rubble of civilization, and the drowned bodies of uncounted thousands. Then the whole sea turned to blood. (Ibid.)

This was the first of five world-destruction fantasies that Jung reported. This same one was to be repeated two weeks later. Again, Jung fails to mention the final collapse of his bonds with Freud, his resignation from the *Jahrbuch*, or the *Jahrbuch*'s demise. he decided that he was menaced by psychosis (1961, p. 176) but related it to no personal precipitants. Ultimately, he would attribute these fantasies to the outbreak of World War I nine months later.

In describing the increasing feeling of pressure that began around the time that Freud broke off personal relations with him, Jung comments (1961, p. 176) that "an incessant stream of fantasies had been released." This comment occurs after he describes the outbreak of World War I, and the casual reader is left with the impression that he is describing events that occurred only then, nine months after he resigned from the *Jahrbuch*. But as is clear from his later remarks (ibid., p. 179), he is actually discussing the inner events of June 1913, five months after Freud broke off personal relations and eleven months before World War I. Jung describes his state as follows:

> The dreams, however, could not help me over my feeling of disorientation. On the contrary, I lived as if under constant inner pressure. At times this became so strong that I suspected there was some psychic disturbance in myself. (Ibid., p. 173)

Jung relates that he went over his childhood memories, searching for the cause of this disturbance, but to no avail. He does not connect this state to the deteriorating relationship with Freud nor to his past anger and guilt toward his father. He then began "play therapy" and, enacting a memory from age 11 or 12, he began constructing a town out of stones. At that age he had grown increasingly isolated and he had spent much of his time playing with stones and blocks. It was this period of his childhood that could be diagnosed as a schizoid withdrawal, and which Winnicott (1964, p. 453) saw as masking childhood schizophrenia. In another place, referring to his state of mind in late 1913, Jung says: "I felt as if gigantic blocks of stone were tumbling down upon me. . . . Others have been shattered by them—Nietzsche and Hoelderlin and many others" (1961, p. 177). He is referring to the psychosis that destroyed these two men. A page later, he admits: "I was afraid of losing command of myself and becoming a prey to the fantasies— and as a psychiatrist I realized only too well what that meant" (ibid., p. 178). Nonetheless one paragraph earlier, Jung says: "From the beginning I had conceived my voluntary confrontation with the unconscious as a scientific experiment which I myself was conducting" (ibid.).

No further letters to Freud followed until April 1914. Prior to that, however, about five weeks after Jung resigned the editorship of the *Jahrbuch*, he recalled that:

> It was during Advent of the year 1913—December 13, to be exact— that I resolved upon the decisive step. . . . [B]efore me . . . stood a dwarf with a leathery skin as if he were mummified. I squeezed past him and waded knee deep through icy water. . . . At first I could make out nothing, but then I saw there was running water. In it a corpse floated by, a youth with blonde hair and a wound in the head. He was followed

... by a red, newborn sun rising up out of the depths of the water. ...
[T]hen a fluid welled out. It was blood. ...

At the end, the dawn of the new day should have followed, but
instead came that intolerable outpouring of blood—an altogether
abnormal phenomenon, so it seemed to me. But then I recalled the
vision of blood that I had had in the autumn of that same year, and I
abandoned all further attempt to understand. (1961, p. 179)

In spite of the direct line of associations running back to Freud
(the dwarf with the leathery skin, as if mummified), Freud is not
mentioned.

Earlier in his autobiography Jung recalls the following memories, which he does not, however, connect to the above fantasy:

The maid comes running and exclaims, "The fishermen have found a
corpse—came down the falls!" ... I quickly stole into the garden to
the washhouse. ... At the back there was an open drain running down
the slope, and I saw blood and water trickling out. ... I was not yet
four years old. (1961, p. 7)

In this connection, Jung recalls being ill at age three, which he
relates to his parents' separation:

My mother spent several months in a hospital in Basel, and presumably
her illness had something to do with difficulty in the marriage. ... I
was deeply troubled by my mother's being away. From then on I always
felt mistrustful when the word "love" was spoken. (1961, p. 8)

Later, he says:

These are my outward memories. What follow now are more powerful,
indeed overwhelming images. ... I remember pain and blood, a doctor
sewing a wound in my head. ... My mother told me, too, of the time
when I was crossing the bridge. ... The maid caught me just in time.
... I was about to slip through. These things point to an unconscious
suicidal urge or, it may be, to a fatal resistance to life in this world.
(Ibid., p. 9)

This material is so rich that it is not possible to interpret it fully
here. However, certain connections stand out starkly. First, Jung's
fascination with death, with "the imperishable world," and his "fatal
resistance to life in this world" (1961, p. 9) is intimately linked to
his experience of abandonment by his mother. Second, the images
from this period of his life recur in the hallucinations that begin as
the relationship with Freud deteriorates. Third, as is implied by the
Hamlet quotation, Jung cannot "murder" Freud without "killing"
himself as well. The blond youth with the head wound in Jung's
fantasy of 1913 (ibid., p. 179) is Jung himself. And, indeed, what

follows the "decisive step" referred to above is another dream in which, in the company of another strange man (linked to the dwarf with the mummified skin), "brown-skinned . . . a savage" (ibid., p. 180), Jung kills the blond hero Siegfried. The connection between Freud and both the brown-skinned man and Siegfried ("Sig. Freud") is clear. In describing his attempt to understand the dream, Jung has an obsessive thought that unless he successfully interprets it, he must shoot *himself*—presumably in the head (ibid.). The blond hero, linked to the dead blond youth of the fantasy, who is in turn linked to Jung's memories of his own head wound, is also Jung himself: "as though I myself had been shot, a sign of my secret identity with Siegfried" (ibid.).[4]

Jung feels that the tragedy being enacted here is that of the sacrifice of his Germanic heroism.[5] More to the point, this is the tragedy of Jung's "secret identity" with Freud, the man on whom Jung has had a "dangerous" "religious crush." It is an instance of the inherent tragedy of psychotic character. The aggressive derivatives of normal oedipal rivalry between people are too dangerous to be acknowledged and expressed because of the most typical feature of psychotic organization, the weakness of self/object differentiation (Bak 1954). Whether this is due to a defect or a defense, its presence makes abandonment intolerable, for abandonment by the other leads to death of the self. This makes discharge of aggression (murder of the ambivalently loved other) impossible, for that is tantamount to suicide. As did Hamlet when he killed his stepfather, so when Jung killed Siegfried did he kill himself.

The only remaining links to Freud and to Jung's identity as a

---

4. The conflation of both Jung and Freud in "Siegfried" is further suggested by the correspondence between Jung and Sabina Spielrein. It was Spielrein's persistent wish to effect a reconciliation between these two men, between whom she was (oedipally) entangled. She and Jung fantasized about having a child together, which they would call "Siegfried." It is hard to imagine that this would not have been a significant association to Jung's dream, especially given the connection to Freud and Jung's comments about "Germanic heroism": "Siegfried" was to be a child who would unify Germanic and Jewish traits, at least in Speilrein's wish, just as Freud and Jung were to be reconciled (Carotenuto 1982). Freud expressly chose Jung as his "crown prince" in part because Jung was not Jewish. After the break, Jung attacked Freud's theory, in part, for being Jewish. Thus, more abstractly, "Siegfried" may have been an expression of Jung's desire for a union with Freud on many levels. It was not only Jung and, for Jung, Freud, who died in the attack on Siegfried, but the bond between them died as well.

5. Jung, and later the Jungians, would interpret this collectively, i.e., as a culture-wide imperative for the sacrifice of the Western ego-oriented attitude.

psychoanalyst were severed in April 1914. Although he explained his actions as stemming from a difference of professional opinion, Jung wrote to Freud using a striking choice of words: "I can no longer consider myself a suitable personality to be president [of the International Psychoanalytical Association]. I therefore tender my resignation."

In an odd gesture for a formal letter of resignation, he wrote three crosses in pen at the end (recall Jung's letter of Nov. 2, 1907, referring to Freud's "dangerousness"). Ten days later he also re-signed his post as a lecturer in the medical faculty of Zurich University.

The same month, and, then again in May and June, Jung had a dream that recurred three times:

> In the middle of summer, an arctic cold wave descended and froze the land to ice. I saw, for example, the whole of Lorraine and its canals frozen and the entire region deserted by human beings. All living green things were killed by frost. (1961, p. 176)

Jung commented that:

> the third dream . . . had an unexpected end. There stood a leaf-bearing tree, but without fruit (my tree of life, I thought), whose leaves had been transformed by the effects of the frost into sweet grapes full of healing juices. I plucked the grapes and gave them to a large waiting crowd. (Ibid.)

This last image of the frost rendering healing powers to a fruitless tree strikes me as a symbolic representation of both the theory of homeostatic compensation Jung later elaborated and a reconstruction—in grandiose form—of the self. It hints at the resti-tutive phase ahead for Jung. Indeed, Jung considers the final end of his "confrontation" to have been marked by a 1927 dream in which a Mandala appears. It, too, contains "a single tree . . . in a shower of reddish blossoms . . . as though . . . the source of light. My companions commented on the abominable weather" (1961, p. 198). Concerning this dream, he remarks:

> Without such a vision I might perhaps have lost my orientation and been compelled to abandon my undertaking. . . . When I parted from Freud, I knew that I was plunging into the unknown. . . . It has taken me virtually forty-five years to distill within the vessel of my scientific work the things I experienced and wrote down at that time. As a young man my goal had been to accomplish something in my science. But then, I hit upon this stream of lava, and the heat of its fires reshaped my life. . . .

> The years when I was pursuing my inner images were the most important in my life. . . . It all began then; the later details are only supplements and clarifications of the material that burst forth from the unconscious and at first swamped me. (Ibid., p. 199)

Thus, Jung presents a picture of near-psychosis precipitated by the loss of a critical object relationship and subsequent restitution. The picture is drawn with the clarity and detail that only a highly gifted observer could provide, and the ideational system that results in the stability of the restitutive phase is a work of genius. Nonetheless, this ideational system contains the same defensive elements that one finds in less valuable and profound delusional systems. The presence of these defensive elements—wherein useful concepts such as the archetypes or the collective unconscious were utilized by Jung, and may continue to be utilized by Jungians, as a defense against object loss—creates the continuing conflict between the symbolic and clinical approaches.

## Conclusion

A vital aspect of Jung's self-cure was his elaboration of a set of ideas within which he was able to contain his otherwise overwhelming emotions. These ideas, in turn, are an elaboration of the personifications that both expressed the emotions that arose out of a profound experience of abandonment *and* substituted for the lost object.

The generation of such images (in the forms of dreams and hallucinations and fantasies) and their elaboration into a highly organized set of ideas is a predictable part of the restitutive phase of psychosis. As Jung points out, however, the death and rebirth phenomenon is not restricted to schizophrenics. When such decompensations occur to a psychotic or near-psychotic degree in average individuals, the restitutive ideational system tends to be highly idiosyncratic: It is uncritically substituted for reality, and it is of little use to anyone else. In Jung's theory, on the contrary, because of his enormous creative gift, the ideational system is of great general value. It contains, nonetheless, defensive elements that we can recognize as analogous in their function to the delusional ideas in psychosis and that stabilize the self by creating distance from threatening objects.

This defensive element may be expressed simply as an undervaluation of the object. Because of the relative lack of self/object differentiation, the normal need for others is, in the psychotic character, more threatening than can be managed. The solution to this "need/fear dilemma" (Burnham 1969) is distance.

Many aspects of Jung's theory are influenced by this underval- uation or lend themselves to it. For instance, one can mention the emphasis on factors in the psyche native to the individual, the relative down-playing of personal experience in shaping personali- ty, the emphasis on the collective dimension of the archetypes, and the assumption that archetypal configurations are not reducible, at least in part, to primitive object relations. On the other hand, there is no better description than Jung's of self-pathology as it is subjec- tively experienced and as it relates to the great cultural creations of mankind.

If Jungian theory is to reflect the clinical picture of psychosis and psychotic character, it must be altered in such a way as to preserve Jung's descriptive phenomenology while eliminating its explicit or implicit undervaluation of personal relationships in the past or present. I would like to conclude with an instance of such an alteration.

The idea that the archetype is innate and latent within the individual is consistent with its homeostatic function. How would we need to modify this idea in order to accept that it functions pathologically as a substitute for the lost object? The modification is deceptively simple. The archetype does not characterize an aspect of the individual psyche, but rather it expresses a relationship between people. The archetype is not "in" a person but "between" persons. What does this mean?

We are accustomed to thinking of the biological form of a plant or animal as the result of the evolution of that individual species as it adapts to its environment. We think, similarly, of the evolution of "organs of the mind," resulting in a heritable, archetypal predispo- sition to emotional, cognitive, behavioral, and imaginative response. However, implicit in this view is an assumption that simplifies our thinking about evolution and inheritance and is false. We are assum- ing that the environment in which the form has evolved is stable. In this view, evolution is a process of adapting to the environment.

In fact, biological entities are organized in systems. The so- called "stable environment" is not stable at all; it co-evolves with the species. The "eco-system" is as organismic as any single organ- ism. A shift in one element has a cascade of effects in all the others. It is the overall level of homeostasis that tends to be stable, barring a major shift in the external conditions (for example, a sudden change of climate). As a matter of convenience, we may speak of an animal adapting to its niche, but in fact the niche has also adapted to the animal.

This is equally true of the development of human emotional patterns in their environment, that is, the emotional responses of others. Put differently, the human instincts of sexuality and aggression develop interactively with their objects—other people. This is also true of the "instinct" for meaning. I do not believe that, as Perry put it, the sense of meaning is the same as the discovery of who I am, but rather that the sense of being someone and the accompanying sense of meaning occur when one is in a relationship. Archetypal images express patterns of human interaction and are more than just parts of the self.

We have learned from observation of infants that just as neither the mother nor the child is a *tabula rasa*, neither are they a predetermined lock and key. That is, the infant does not carry within an *imago* to project onto the adult, as we are accustomed to believe. Rather, in the course of maturation, interactions between the mother and child alter both of them. A fully developed pattern of behavior is not inherited, nor is it learned. Rather, certain primitive factors are inherited (very difficult to characterize, though attempts are being made to do so [Aslin 1981; Gollin 1981; Izard 1977, 1978]) and are ready to be triggered in both parent and child. The proper "fit" between responses alters each in such a way that a new set of interactive and altering responses is produced. This leads to the next set, and so on. Perfectly meshed with this sequential alteration in mutual response is the timed maturation of the nervous system (Parmelee and Sigman 1983).

Thus, what we witness in a four-year-old child as a highly organized archetypal fantasy or dream is not, itself, heritable. Rather, it is the end product of an extraordinarily complex relationship. The shaping, molding, projecting, introjecting, and reprojecting (Klein 1946) that occur in the early years of life, are so complicated that they preclude both the assumption of direct inheritance of archetypes and any certain separation in primitive fantasy material of subject and object representation. The archetypal images that appear in an adult mind as a consequence of regression equally depict primitive aspects of both the self and the subjectively experienced object.

A number of implications flow from the above conclusions.

First, archetypal images need to be understood as the epigenetic consequence of developmental processes, certain elements of which (as may or may not be evident in the final product) are inherited. These heritable elements are the subject of ongoing research that has already altered traditional psychoanalytic theory in the direction of greater appreciation of what is innate (Campos et al., 1983). They ought to alter Jungian theory in the direction of greater appreciation of what is not innate.

Second, archetypal images, traditionally thought of as the epitome of impersonality, must on the contrary be considered highly personal. That is, archetypal images carry the most primitive, emotionally overwhelming aspect of specific personal relationships. As was the case with Jung, they refer to critical relationships in the present and in the past. Their impersonal appearance does refer to what is common between human beings, but to treat them as impersonal is to utilize this commonality defensively to create distance from painful emotions in relationships. Synthetic understandings and interpretations that emphasize the collective dimension, while minimizing the personal referents, reinforce this defense. In certain circumstances, a reinforcement of this defense may be the best possible solution, and in the hands of creative individuals this may yield something of great value. But one ought to understand what one is doing in such a case, for it is a matter of clinical judgment and not of absolute truth.

What does it mean to take into account the personal referents of archetypal images? It means everything that we call by the pejorative term "reductive." Precisely the most archetypal images need to be understood in terms of events in specific personal relationships of both the present and the past. Thus, a seemingly impersonal dream will almost invariably contain important but unacceptable erotic and aggressive feelings toward the major figures in the patient's present life and from childhood. These figures will be current loves and hates (and, if the person is in therapy, the therapist) and early family members. That these feelings are expressed in mythological form should be an indication to the therapist of their subjectively dangerous nature, and, perhaps, of the patient's need, for a time, to keep distance from them by attending only to their collective meaning.

When we speak of psychosis, we think of extreme mental disorder. But since Jung, we can think of psychosis as an extreme version of a kind of mental functioning that, in milder form, is present in almost everyone. In this view, synthesis, upon which Jung based his theory, is the general equivalent to the resititutive phase of a psychosis. One might say that there is a primitive core to personality, and in some measure this core shows itself in everyone. Disruptions in the sense of self fuel creative, synthetic solutions. However, if it is also true that these disruptions of the self are directly related to disruptions in object relations, then we would have to admit that these synthetic solutions are also defenses. This does not mean that they are not necessary or valuable. But from the therapeutic point of view, synthetic interpretations exact a cost. This cost may be warranted or it may not be. The therapist, however, cannot afford the alchemist's delusion. Many wonderful things can be made of lead, but lead cannot be turned into gold.

## References

Abraham, K. 1908. The psychosexual differences between hysteria and dementia praecox. *Selected Papers on Psychoanalysis* 1:64–79. London: Hogarth Press, 1949.

Arlow, J., and Brenner, C. 1969. The psychopathology of the psychoses: A proposed revision. *International Journal of Psychoanalysis* 50:5–14.

Aslin, R. 1981. Experiential influences and sensitive periods in development: A unified model. In *Development of perception*, vol. 2. New York: Academic Press.

Bak, R. 1954. The schizophrenic defence against aggression. *International Journal of Psychoanalysis* 35:129–34.

Bleuler, E. 1950. *Dementia praecox, or the group of schizophrenias.* New York: International Universities Press.

Burnham, D. 1955. The restitution function of symbol and myth in Strindberg's "Inferno." *Psychiatry* 36:299–343.

————, Gibson, R., and Gladstone, A. 1969. *Schizophrenia and the need-fear dilemma.* New York: International Universities Press.

Campos, J., et al. 1983. Socioemotional development. In *Handbook of child psychology*, P. Mussen, ed., vol. II, pp. 783–915. New York: Wiley.

Carotenuto, A. 1982. *A secret symmetry.*

Erikson, E. 1968. *Identity: Youth and crisis.* New York: Norton.

Federn, P. 1952. *Ego psychology and the psychoses.* New York: Basic Books.

Ferenczi, S. 1913. Stages in the development of the sense of reality. In *Sex in psychoanalysis*, pp. 213–39. New York: Basic Books, 1950.

Freud, S. 1911. Psycho-analytic notes on an autobiographical account of a case of paranoia (dementia paranoides). In *Standard edition* 12:97–108. London: Hogarth Press and The Institute for Psycho-analysis.

————. 1914. On narcissism: An introduction. In *Standard edition* 14:69–102. London: Hogarth Press and The Institute for Psycho-analysis.

Frosch, W. 1983. *The psychotic process.* New York: International Universities Press.

Glover, E. 1961. Some recent trends in psychoanalytic theory. *Psychoanalytic Quarterly* 18:290–302.

Gollin, E. 1981. Development and plasticity. In *Developmental Plasticity*, E. Gollin, ed. New York: Academic Press.

Gruenberger, B. 1979. *Narcissism.* New York: International Universities Press.

Hartmann, H. 1952. The mutual influences in the development of ego and id. *Psychoanalytic Study of the Child* 7:9–30.

Hesse, H. 1929. *Steppenwolf.* New York: Henry Holt.

Izard, C. 1977. *Human emotion.* New York: Plenum.

_____. 1978. On the ontogenesis of emotions and emotion-cognition relation-
ships in infancy. In *The development of affect,* M. Lewis and L. Rosenblum, eds.
New York: Plenum.

James, W. 1901. *The varieties of religious experience.* New York: Macmillan, 1961.

Jung, C. G. 1909. The psychology of dementia praecox. In *Collected works,* vol. 3,
Princeton: Princeton University Press, 1960.

_____. 1911. Wandlungen und symbole der libido, I. *Jahrbuch fur psychoanaly-
tische und psychopathologische Forschungen,* III.

_____. 1912. Wandlungen und symbole der libido, II. *Jahrbuch fur psychoanal-
ytische und psychopathologische Forschungen,* IV. [These 1911 and 1912 articles
have been translated as *Psychology of the unconscious* (New York, 1916; London,
1917). An extensively rewritten version–with most of the passages quoted herein
deleted–constitutes vol. 5, *Collected works* (1956).]

_____. 1916. *Psychology of the unconscious.* New York: Moffat, Yard.

_____. 1919. On the problem of psychogenesis in mental disease. In *Collected
works* 3:211–25. Princeton: Princeton University Press, 1960.

_____. 1921. *Psychological types.* In *Collected works,* vol. 6. Princeton: Princeton
University Press, 1971.

_____. 1936. Psychological factors in human behavior. In *Collected works,* vol.
8. Princeton: Princeton University Press, 1960.

_____. 1939. On the psychogenesis of schizophrenia. In *Collected works* 3:233–49.
Princeton: Princeton University Press, 1960.

_____. 1952. Religion and psychology: A reply to Martin Buber. In *Collected
works* 18:663-70. Princeton: Princeton University Press, 1955.

_____. 1957. Letter to the second international congress of psychiatry (sympos-
ium on chemical concepts of psychosis). In *Collected works* 3:272. Princeton:
Princeton University Press, 1960.

_____. 1958. Schizophrenia. In *Collected works* 3:256–70. Princeton: Princeton
University Press, 1960.

_____. 1961. *Memories, dreams, reflections.* New York: Random House.

_____. 1973. *Letters: 1906–1950,* vol. 1, G. Adler, ed. Princeton: Princeton
University Press.

_____. 1975. *Letters:,* vol. 2, G. Adler, ed. Princeton: Princeton University Press.

Kohut, H. 1971. *The analysis of the self.* New York: International Universities Press.

_____. 1977. *The restoration of the self.* New York: International Universities
Press.

_____. 1984. *How does analysis cure?* New York: International Universities
Press.

Kraepelin, I. 1919. *Dementia praecox.* Edinburgh: Livingstone.

Langer, S. 1953. *Feeling and form.* New York: Scribner.

Levene, H. 1982. The borderline syndrome: A critique and response to recent
literature on its etiology, dynamics and treatment. *Modern Psychoanalysis* 7/2:165.

McGuire, W., ed. 1974. *The Freud/Jung Letters.* Princeton: Princeton University Press.

Miller, F. 1906. Quelques faits de l'imagination creatrice subconsciente. *Archives de
Psychologie* V:36–51.

Pao, P. 1979. *Schizophrenic disorders: Theory and treatment from a psychodynamic
point of view.* New York: International Universities Press.

Parmelee, A., and Sigman, M. 1983. Perinatal brain development and behavior. In
*Handbook of child psychology,* P. Mussen, ed., vol. II, pp. 95–156. New York:
Wiley.

Perry, J. 1976. *Roots of renewal in myth and madness.* San Francisco: Jossey-Bass.

Satinover, J. 1980. Puer/puella: The narcissistic relation to the self. *Quadrant*
13/2:75–108.

_____. 1983. Jung's lost contribution to the dilemma of narcissism. *Yale Psychi-*

*atric Quarterly* 6/2:18–20 (Abstract); *Journal of Psychoanalytic Association* (in press).

————. 1984. The mirror of Doctor Faustus: The decline of art in the pursuit of eternal adolescence. *Quadrant* 17/1:23–38.

Van der Waals, H. 1965. Problems of narcissism. *Bulletin of the Menninger Clinic* 29:293–311.

Winnicott, D. 1964. Review of C. G. Jung's *Memories, dreams, reflections. International Journal of Psychoanalysis* 45:450–55.

# Some Dream Motifs Accompanying the "Abandonment" of an Analytic Practice

## Patricia Berry-Hillman

I recently left my practice in Texas to move to northeastern Connecticut. Although I had announced my plans ten months before my actual departure, many of my analysands would maintain I not only left but abandoned my practice and them. These ten months preceding my leaving were difficult. Persons who had long since terminated their analytical work now wanted to return. New ones wanted to begin—particularly, I suspected, because there was a limited time remaining. During these months there were major upsets in the life situations of many of these persons—financial collapses, divorces, accidents, lost jobs—the kinds of life crises that generally bring people into analysis, hardly material for its conclusion.

I had not experienced this difficulty in separation before, and had on many occasions left my practice regularly for extended periods each summer as well as various times during the year. Everyone who worked with me knew this pattern to be a condition of the analysis and generally their psyches had responded appropri-

**Patricia Berry-Hillman,** Ph.D., is a member of the Inter-Regional Society of Jungian Analysts and author of *Echo's Subtle Body* (1982). She is a Fellow of the Dallas Institute of Humanities and Culture and is a practicing Jungian analyst in Thompson, Connecticut.

ately, winding down and resolving whatever problems were being worked on before separation, not bringing up what could not be dealt with in the time allotted.

But on this occasion things were different. Problems appeared that seemed inappropriate to go into in the few months remaining. My concerns about separating in the "right way"—i.e., to separate without abandoning—came to little result and only served to increase my guilt. Something appeared out of order in the psyche's clock—theirs or mine—as though we shared some mis-chronicity. It seemed I could do little more than trail along behind the psyche's processes as they occurred.

Peering back, I would like to discuss some of the dreams and dream motifs that occurred during this period. Since I have now the advantage of a certain distance (as well as the advantage of knowing the end of each story before I begin it), these dreams make more diagnostic and prognostic sense than they did at the time. That is to say, the deconstructive, deintegrative experiences these analysands seemed to be going through now appear strangely fitting, and perhaps even necessary, to the psychological situation.

The most disturbing and dramatic dreams were those that involved motifs of annihilation. One such dream, dreamed by a young man three months before the analysis was to end, went as follows:

Dream: *I am coming out of the woods into my childhood neighborhood. The area is crawling with cops. I am leery, afraid of getting caught. It is the last day—the bomb will be dropped soon and all the people are evacuating their homes. . . . It is silly to run because there is no escape and they all know this. I start walking like I know what I'm doing, pretending the police don't bother me. I go into my garage and see some of my old toys on the shelf. I begin taking them off to give to all the little kids. There are a couple of things I am attached to and decide to keep. There are also a couple of caps I must keep, and I put both on my head—one a light blue and white cap like a sea captain's. I am anxious to get all this stuff down to give away. It will fall soon—it is already incredibly bright outside. It is 11:00 and we only have until 12:00 when it will fall.*

This dream appeared at a time when, according to the dreamer, "nothing much was happening" in his life—except that the analysis was ending and he did not know what his life would be like without it. However in the dream we see that he is not only facing a separation (in fact, there are no actual images of separation), but an annihilation. In one hour the bomb is to fall and "there is no escape."

Now what is the bomb? Since it is difficult to determine what anything in a dream means for certain, rather than thinking definitively about the dream and its symbols, I tend to proceed more pragmatically, looking to the particular effects and constellations (i.e., associations) within the dream itself.

Whereas one would expect "annihilation" to be a completely destructive horror, here we find that it is associated with light. "It is incredibly bright," and the fall of the bomb is to occur at noon (presumably when the light of the sun is at its height). The consciousness implied by this light is further emphasized in the movement "coming out of the woods."

As the dreamer emerges from the woods, he finds himself in his childhood neighborhood, which is now "crawling with cops." Though one would think "the cops" to be a welcome presence at the scene in which a catastrophe was about to occur, for this dream ego they are threatening—as threatening (judging from his preoccupation with them) as the bomb itself. His manner of evading (defending from) this threat is to pretend he is not bothered and knows what he is doing ("I start walking like I know what I'm doing, pretending the police don't bother me"). He then proceeds to his family garage, takes some toys down off a shelf, and gives them away.

On the basis of these images I saw the therapeutic task, despite the obvious horror of the image of annihilation, to be that of supporting the dreamer through the experience by helping to dismantle his defenses against it, that is, to aid the inevitable (in the dream there is no way out).

But to what extent, I wondered, did the portended catastrophe involve not only the end of an aspect of the dreamer's *Weltanschauung* (the world with which he identified) but also the end of a reality in which the analysis had been participant? After all, was not the analysis the matrix that had supported the world of the analysand and myself? And was not that shared world the reality that was to terminate?

Whereas issues of separation can be managed more or less effectively on an interpersonal level, the termination of the analysis itself seemed to be controlled by overpowering forces beyond personal control. As to how these events would proceed I could only speculate, though the activity of play, as hinted at in the dream, seemed to provide an opening of sorts.

In the dream we find the dreamer, in preparation for the anni-hilation, taking down the childhood toys with which he had played. He then gives these toys to little children. Whether we regard these children as existing externally in the dreamer's world, or subjective-ly as the child-like parts of the dreamer's personality (sources of delight, imagination, and carefree irresponsibility), in either case there is a coming down of play (the toys taken down off the shelf) out of familial storage and a disidentification with them.

One would expect this movement (taking down and giving away) to detach the dreamer from certain childish identifications, freeing him from his family garage as source (storage place) for his childhood things, as at the same time allowing more access to his child-likeness, since it is now distributed among the children of his psychic neighborhood. The shift is from the childishness of secret attachment to the openness and opening out of the child-like.

Neat dream interpretations, such as the above, never come out quite the way they ought. The psyche is endlessly clever in its ability to turn events so that their shadow possibilities have play as well. In this situation, for example, giving away one's childish things is subtly close to getting rid of these things onto others, i.e., project-ing.

With this dreamer, such was the case. He began to view friends and associates as immature, childish. As he withdrew emotionally from them, he felt himself an "adult," superior to their foolishness. Though in the dream there was no need for him to lose touch with the child-like, in life the shadow of the situation was lived so that projection became his way of getting rid of childish things.

The dreamer's fear of being caught by the cops is a more obvious shadow motif. Since the dream is about the threat of anni-hilation, one wonders if the police (superego forces? social respon-sibility? collective psychic order?) do not have something to do with this threat. Are not the actions of "coming out of the woods" and giving away childish things presentiments of what is to occur, and hence apotropaic gestures to mitigate its inevitability?

At this point, however—it is still only 11:00—the dreamer is still able to avoid the police, as he has also managed to keep a few toys he "feels attachment to" and a couple of caps, which he places on his head. His attitude is to "start walking like [he] know[s] what [he] [is] doing."

Whereas these actions are ways of keeping attachments and defending against the wipe-out of annihilation, they may have purposive value as well. The attachments keep him connected with objects of sentimental value, and the caps give him persona orientation, headgear for making his way through the ordeal. The cap he mentions is a captain's hat that matches his baseball jacket. One might expect that he will appear in charge, captain of his ship, capable of determining his course, but this cap too, we must remember, was on the same shelf as his toys from childhood.

This image leads one to expect the dreamer to adopt a somewhat juvenile, but also heroic, manner of orienting. So too with "walking like [he] know[s] what [he] [is] doing." However, if the police have to do with social responsibility, as we supposed above, then this persona capping in preparation for the role may be more fitting than the exaggerated pretense it at first appears to be. He may need something of the self-determining attitude this cap implies, though he may also be required to sacrifice his adolescent identification with it.

Since the heroic child appears to be a dominating element in the dreamer's sense of identity—the captain's cap, pretending he knows what he is doing—one might also expect periodic crashes (down off the shelf), annihilations, incapacitation. Indeed this man frequently reported himself lost and unable, feeling as though he lived in a world to which he did not belong.

This brings us to another complexity of the child—it is both special and bereft. Archetypally the child is both hero and orphan. He is a hero in that he experiences his parents as divine and his purpose as divinely meant. Yet these divine parents are inhuman, leaving him unparented—i.e., orphaned—in the mundane world. (Myth shows often enough the orphan nature of the hero and the heroic nature of the orphan.) In human life this identification is accompanied by a necessary interpenetration of inflation and deflation, a feeling of being divinely claimed, far above the ordinary and at the same time abandoned, bereft, and worthless. The orphan is both too good and not good enough for life in the actual world.

The end of the analysis and my leaving were felt as abandonment specifically, I believe, by this divine child aspect of the personality—not only in this particular analysand, but in that archetypal figure/element as it was also experienced by others. The divine child felt abandoned by the inevitable termination of analysis, an end not seen as fulfillment of the child's desire to grow and accomplish, but an end seen as being cut off by the gods or fate. (That this "fate" was no more than my mundane reality—a person who, after a long-announced forewarning, was moving—was incomprehensible whenever this archetypal constellation dominated. For the child, ending was abandonment, and abandonment was cosmic.)

But does not analysis invite this situation? As a constructed, artificial containment, a *temenos* apart from the ordinary world of everyday contingencies, analysis is where gods and goddesses thrive and passions work powerfully enough to change life. The effectiveness of analysis has at least in part to do with the specialness of this situation and the exaggerated emotions it creates. Also it is a place, par excellence, for the child. Where else can the child speak of its concerns with such abandon—concerns involving parents, siblings, hurts, needs, and fantasies? Where else can it be favored by this special quality of loving attentiveness?

What I am suggesting is that there is something about the nature of analysis per se, the secret of its power, that also inadvertently, despite its best intentions and all its efforts to the contrary, supports the divine child. So too abandonment, experienced as an archetype in extreme, mythical form, is always close by—the more particularly so the more this special child with its more than human needs is constellated.

\* \* \*

Let us turn to another annihilation dream, dreamed by another dreamer about the same time, that is, a few months before my leaving.

Dream: *There was a . . . clearing-out of a certain place with the realization I'd never see it again. Time was bearing down on me. I understood this was the end. I knew we were all going to die. I went to a barn or shed of my husband's to put a few things there to be kept safe, but there was nothing left but a shell, a skeleton-like foundation and some upright boards rising to a triangular shape at the roofline. Already it had been taken apart in preparation for this rapidly approaching finality which seemed more and more to be an annihilation of all there was. My husband, who seemed my last hope, was in the dying and decaying process, not with his body, but with his belongings. Some boards he had been storing were cut short and uneven, no longer usable. I recognized that there was no more running,*

*no more trying to find some place to wait out this death sen-
tence that was on us. Very soon we would all be extinguished.*

In this dream the threat of annihilation is accompanied by a
"clearing out of a certain place." When the dreamer goes to her
husband's structure in hopes of keeping a few of her things "safe"
there, she finds this shelter no longer viable. Boards he has been
storing have been "cut short" so that they are unusable. All that
remains is a "triangular shape at the roofline."

Whereas for the previous dreamer the annihilation entailed a
collapse of the childish (bringing the toys down) and an emphasis
on structure (the police), for this dreamer the situation is the
contrary in that her structure collapses and what remains is high
up—a triangular shape at the roofline.

If the annihilation parallels the end of analysis, then we must
assume that the analysis in some way or other may have helped to
support these husbanding structures (along with something she has
now been forced to clear out). Was this protective frame the frame
of the analysis itself? Since her husband's sideburns have been cut
short and uneven, has the length of the analysis and its regularity
served to shelter her? Since time is now "bearing down" on her, has
the analysis helped her evade the demands of living in time?

Etymologically the word *abandon* (Latin *ad* + OF *bandon*) has
to do with the giving up of control or order. Certainly the analytical
frame is an ordered situation in that sessions of a particular length
are held at regular times in designated places, and there are certain
conventions accompanying these meetings.

But within these boundaries, the actual work of analysis is
frequently deconstructive. Analysis is as involved with dismantling
defenses and taking things apart as it is with putting them together.
Perhaps more so. How this animus construction of the analysand's
psyche could be paralleled with the work of the analysis is difficult
to imagine. Certainly this is not the intent of analytical work, and yet
the dream suggests that somehow it must have been going on
despite my analytical, deconstructive intentions.

Whereas the first dreamer, as we saw, was able to save something
of his childhood (the captain's cap that matched his baseball jacket), for this dreamer all that is left is a "triangular shape at the
roofline." This upward-pointing triangle hints at an orientation
perhaps more spiritual in its direction than was the captain's cap for

the previous dreamer. If the captain's cap served as a defense (a heady attempt at being in charge), the upper triangle might serve a similar purpose in terms of spirituality.

In Jung's work on the Trinity he noted the importance of a missing fourth: the rejected shadow and the feminine body. Hence with this dreamer we might expect spiritualization as her style of defense, cutting her off from lower, more embodied realms. At the same time, however, we must recognize the purposiveness of this defense. The triangle pointing upward toward the beyond also indicates this direction to be the dream's *telos*, implying that a spiritual attitude is genuinely needed.

There were long periods in working with this analysand in which I felt cut off and excluded from her psychic life. My reactions had little influence on the negativistic structures and litanies she reiterated to prove her life was hopeless. Her sins had been too great and fate too cruel for a possibility of more positive develop-ment. Life itself did not matter so much as her ideas about life. The fact that I was present physically, bodily with her, did not matter, only that I would eventually be leaving. She felt abandoned by me, and I (I must admit) felt abandoned by her, excluded by her structures such that I could no longer share in her emotional life.

Around this time she dreamed she had an image of an eagle on her pillow. She then reflected in the dream that this eagle was what I (and my husband) could not understand. This assumption was correct in that I viewed the eagle as the high-soaring, solitary, spiritualized attitude by which she cushioned her head to sleep. My own animus (perhaps imaged here as my husband) was psychologi-cally critical and unresting in its attempts to get this dreamer out of the tree tops. As a result we missed each other. She felt unappreciat-ed and I became impatient.

She then dreamed that she had gone to another analyst, whom she had asked not to tell me of her visit but to keep it private. In this analyst's office she sat in a purple chair that was unstable and "tippy." The analyst asked her about the purpleness of her chair and insisted that she tell me of her visit.

When we worked on this dream, we took the analyst to whom she had been talking as an internal figure who drew attention to her purple position (which I took as spiritualized constructs) and ob-jected to her psychologizing self-sufficiency. She explained that she had preferred to work on these problems by herself rather than bringing them to me, because she did not wish to depend on me for support.

This theme of independence versus dependence (becoming in its more radical forms self-enclosure and isolation versus interconnection or relationship) was a common theme for many of my analysands during this period. Another such theme, as mentioned in the previous case, was the coupling of inflation with deflation and meaninglessness. For both these themes the child played a central role.

There were other dreams involving the child or the childish. One dreamer had a series of vomiting dreams in which she or other figures in the dream vomited a pink liquid. This pink liquid, apparently ingested (introjected) by the analysand, needed to get out so that something not pink—in this case, anger—could be expressed.

Another dreamer had repetitive nightmares of her daughter leaving her. For this particular analysand there was ambiguity between leaving and being left which showed in dreams in which I would be leaving, and then the dream would switch and she would be leaving, etc. This theme showed also in her dreams of her daughter. There was a whole series of dreams in which her daughter was suddenly missing, had gone to live with other parents, no longer wanted her mother's nursing, was being nursed by someone else, and so on. These dreams were extremely upsetting to the dreamer for it seemed to her that without her daughter she could not survive.

In this case, the daughter was the divine child with whom the dreamer in the guise of mothering remained attached. For several years this daughter had been a helpful figure in the analysis, showing a healthy instinctuality that the dreamer lacked in her conscious personality. This child served as a kind of Self figure, orienting the dreamer toward what was of value in her psyche. The child was the pearl of great price.

In the last months of the analysis, however, something changed, and this child began to reveal another side; she became magical, overly precious, and jealous concerning her mother's attentions.

In one such dream, the dreamer had become involved with a male figure—who, because he was "fleshy," seemed at first repulsive to the dreamer. Once she had made love with this man, however, the horizon changed and the sky became "hauntingly lovely." Moreover, she found that the man was extremely loving, kind, and tender.

But her daughter Jilly became jealous, not wishing to share her mother with this man. In an effort to propitiate Jilly, the dreamer took her to a magic store. But "magic no longer pleased Jilly" if her mother was to be involved with this man.

I regarded this fleshy man as bringing the "body," the flesh this dreamer was in need of. As a magical, special child, Jilly, however, resisted this loss of her mother to a more substantial partner. Jilly insisted on remaining the divine child and the sole focus of her mother's attentions.

In this relation of the dream ego with the divine child, two aspects of the child were expressed. The child wanted to leave the confines of her mother's identification—the mother/divine child syzygy the dreamer had been living. But the child also resisted the loss of power created by this separation.

Early on we saw how another dreamer managed at least a temporary separation from the child by giving to the child (children) things to carry for him. By giving his childhood toys to the children, the dream ego was able to separate from his childishness without repressing it completely.

The analysand with whom we are now concerned, however, had a slightly different problem and dynamic. For her the child was clearly an "other"—i.e., Jilly—to whom she was mother. The problem was to recognize that this divine child was herself as well, and that in fact she lived this child out in all sorts of unconscious ways— as in her tendency to magical thinking, her feelings of entitlement and preciousness, and so on.

Leaving and being left were curiously interrelated in this woman's psyche, because for her the problem was one and the same: If she could leave (separate from) the divine child, she could also allow it to leave her. And vice versa: If she could let the child leave, she could also separate herself from an unconscious particpation with it.

* * *

Let us return to these cases now with a word concerning how each worked out.

The man who evaded the annihilation by doffing a captain's cap and giving away his childhood toys was eventually brought up short through legal difficulties with the "police" in the form of auditors. He was found to have been negligent with funds at the agency where he worked. He had gone too far with his captain's cap, claiming rights and powers that were not his to wield. Alongside this rather severe external limitation brought about by the auditors, the analysis focused on the task of differentiating his many police. In fact, he was surrounded by superego forces of so many sorts that his escape had been either to ignore them completely by retreating into childish abandon or to be crushed through self-criticism. This massive and indiscriminate criticism had served to keep him fleeing into childhood as a means of escape.

We made some progress, though not as much as I would have liked, on his tendency to isolate himself emotionally by seeing others as inferior and childish. He did, however, begin parenting his inabilities and weaknesses in manners that were more frequently appropriate, rather than resorting to the extremes of either unmercifully condemning himself (psychologically beating himself) or allowing himself the utter freedom of childish inflation.

In the case of the religiously inclined analysand, the one who sat in a purple chair and spoke with a secret analyst, the themes of the last month of the analysis were of a predictably religious nature, but in such a way that the connection between us was reopened and deepened.

In one dream she gave birth to a son, in honor of which my husband and I set up a Christmas tree on what had been a children's swing frame. In another, her father died and an image of the cross appeared in his stead—a cross which in the dream had to do with the "raising of children." She was also able to express more directly her needs and fears concerning my leaving. A horse in the sky now fell to earth. A structure was discovered which had movable walls. Young people wanting to party interrupted her from writing her dreams. A final image involved a communal religious gathering in which the dreamer sang and worked together with others.

The woman who had vomited pink liquid dreamed toward the end of the anslysis that she was in a native village. A nurse in the village gave her a container, instructing her to spit into it. As she spit, a bloody phlegm gushed from her mouth. Later she walked among the natives feeling "really close to them," learning that "they had had a sadness in their lives too" which involved "the loss of a precious child."

This movement toward community through suffering was evidenced also by the woman who had lost her magical daughter. This woman realized in a dream that her breasts were aching with the need to nurse, but that since her daughter was now gone and no longer needed nursing, she would feed others who did. In one dream she was given an amulet of a divine cow with "mankind" hanging from its udder. In yet another, the final dream of the analysis, "Pat" had lost her crystal goblets and, though try as she might, the dreamer could not retrieve them for her.

These dreams each showed movements from the dreamers' concerns with personal losses and sufferings to a larger community in which this suffering was shared, or, as with the last dreamer, even used to nourish others. I wonder if this theme does not correspond with a movement out of the closed personal containment of the analytic vessel, i.e., "Pat" and her crystal goblets.

In *Mysterium Coniunctionis* (1955, p. 18) we read that the orphan must be "slain at the beginning of the work for purposes of transformation." Since, in a sense, the work is always beginning (inasmuch as transformation is always beginning), this being slain that the orphan experiences would seem an archetypal necessity all through analysis, not only at its end.

Often abandonment is powerfully literalized during termination. Yet abandonment need not be equated with termination, since this equation reinforces the illusion that abandonment can be terminated, worked through—as though it were an experience to be got over. More important is its deepening as a deepening of the child, or maturing of the child, into the archetypal nature of orphanhood. Here the archetypal has the therapeutic effect of grounding and collectively humanizing, thereby allowing personal disidentification.

For the orphan there are no adequate parents, and attempts to find them result in little more than temporary arrangements, illusionary fantasies of containment. I believe analysis is one such illusionary containment, which in its ending constellates the experience of abandonment necessary for slaying the identification with the orphan.

Mankind is an orphan were it not for God, according to St. Augustine (Jung 1955, p. 22). Psychologically translated this would imply that for the abandoned child there are no "good enough" parents and that analysis, insofar as it inadvertently sits in for these parents, is furthering a secular illusion that only through its dissolution may be finally redeemed. We are indeed all, in part, orphans, and it is through the suffering of this archetypal fact of abandonment (and abandoning) that we can join together in community. This communal feeling, based on a recognition of our mutual aloneness and suffering, is a religious emotion, an existential reality, and a return to the world with a recognition that the world is all we have, and that maybe it is "good enough."

## Reference

Jung, C. G. 1955. *Mysterium Coniunctionis.* In *Collected works*, vol. 14. Princeton: Princeton University Press, 1970.

# Perilous Beginnings: Loss, Abandonment, and Transformation

## Harriet Gordon Machtiger

For many people, coming to selfhood has a perilous beginning. It is a journey fraught with physical and psychological traumata centering on the theme of loss and abandonment. For them, life is a constant preoccupation with survival. Though the psychological effects of childhood trauma may only become apparent in later years, the actual damage to the personality has been there since childhood, even though it may be masked by a superficial adjustment.

Most of the clinical literature, except for the work of Bowlby (1960, 1961, 1979, 1980) and Engel (1961), makes no mention of loss and mourning as processes of normal development. The major emphasis has been on the role of separation, loss, and mourning in depressive illness. These losses all involve the death of a significant person. Engel (1961) reports that the loss of a beloved person is as traumatic psychologically as being wounded is physically. He likens the process of mourning to the processes of physical healing.

**Harriet Gordon Machtiger**, Ph.D., is a Jungian analyst practicing in Pittsburgh, Pennsylvania. She received her Ph.D. in psychology from the University of London and is a member of the New York Association of Analytical Psychologists. She is the author of "Countertransference/Transference" in *Jungian Analysis* (M. Stein, ed., 1982) and "Reflections on the Transference/Countertransference Process with Borderline Patients" in *Chiron: A Review of Jungian Analysis* (1984).

In the Jungian literature there is little mention of separation, loss, and mourning. Yet a large part of the material we deal with in the analytic work is concerned with these recurrent themes. There is only one mention of mourning in the entire *Collected Works* of Jung. In a paper entitled, "General Aspects of Dream Psychology" (1960, par. 456), Jung states that "the purpose of ostentatious mourning is to arouse the sympathy of others." Jung did take note of the importance of separation for the individuation process and drew parallels between the relevance of the *separatio, divisio,* and *coniunctio* in the alchemical process for understanding the development of the psyche.

The majority of the losses sustained in life, however, are intrapsychic and not because of the physical death of a loved one. Loss is a normal developmental phenomenon closely connected to the separation entailed in the archetypal unfolding that is inherent in the individuation process. Strauss (1962) calls our attention to this in her work on the relevance of the archetype of separation. Loss in infancy and early childhood occurs for physical and psychological reasons. Bowlby (1960) notes that early loss is an event of highly pathogenic potential since the processes of mourning in the young child all too readily take a course damaging to healthy personality development. Mourning, however, is an integral part of coming to terms with loss. It allows for transformation and healing to take place. The capacity to mourn and deal with separation and loss is built up in a relationship with a mother who assists her child in coping with the problems engendered by separation at the various stages of development.

In the mother-child dyad, all the feelings, perceptions, and behavior surrounding the archetype of separation are constellated within the child's psyche. The child's contact with the personal mother determines the outcome of the encounter with the mother archetype. The child must successfully separate from the parental archetype as well as from the actual parent. In the situations where the archetypal intent has been thwarted or injured, a loss complex is constellated. The conflicting wishes for union and separation cannot be resolved. This complex interferes with conscious performance and has a life of its own.

In healthy mourning, the libido gets transferred and reinvested in new images or objects. In unresolved mourning, these processes have been interfered with. The libido is still bound up in the old imagery, and the experience of loss is an etiological agent with implications for the formation of neurotic and psychotic psycho-pathology. There is a repressed yearning for the lost object, and there are feelings of anger and reproachfulness. Examples are individuals with *puer* psychology or narcissistic personalities who have a good deal of difficulty tolerating loss, anxiety, frustration, or depression, with a consequent inability to mourn.

The individuals that I am going to discuss in this paper all experienced some form of early loss. They sustained damaged body images due to a physical handicap, suffered a chronic illness, experienced the death of a parent, and tangentially suffered from inadequate parenting. Their physical problems and attendant psychological problems were confounded by a predilection for dissociation or a loss of contact with the body. Their mothers' inability to accept and fully love their handicapped child contributed to difficulties in the relationship between ego and self, as well as in the ability to accept their physical limitations and their own reality. Damaged body images are injured self images.

Looking at individuals who have sustained wounds in childhood contributes evidence for the existence of a loss complex. The capacity for attachment and affectional bonding originates in the reciprocal interaction between the infant and its primary caretakers. The infant needs to be engaged with the mother across the whole spectrum of emotional possibilities.

The putative experiences of rejection in childhood impede the acquisition of the ability to deal with loss. The lack of this capacity coincides with the development of a false self or a persona wherein feelings are bottled up. Borderline and narcissistic features predominate and interfere with the maturational process. Where there are these impairments in the flexibility of the personality, under the stress of separation, clinging patterns, obsessive-compulsive concerns, hysterical symptoms and patterns, and a tendency to externalization often result. These distortions of character serve as protection against experiencing feelings of anger and intimacy.

The failure to mourn and work through archetypal separation results in a developmental lag which leaves the person stuck in a state of disequilibrium. The specific problem is manifested and reflected in an inability to make optimum use of the transcendent function and symbol formation. In Jung's words:

> Archetypes were, and still are, living psychic forces that demand to be taken seriously, and they have a strange way of making sure of their effect . . . their violation has as its consequence the "perils of the soul".

. . . Moreover, they are the unfailing causes of neurotic or even psychotic disorders, behaving exactly like negative or maltreated physical organs or organic functional systems. (1940, par. 266)

When the archetypal development is interfered with, as in the case of unresolved mourning, a loss or abandonment complex can result.

In the therapeutic experience, healing and transformation take place when a more cohesive self coalesces through the *participation mystique* with the analyst-parent through the experience of the transference/countertransference. The analysands who are the focus of this paper were imbued with fears of disintegration and needed the presence of another to feel alive. Actualization of the transcendent function is always in the context of the body and in relationship to other people. Therapy provides the opportunity to rework the earlier traumata.

### Loss and Abandonment

One of the most common fears is that of being abandoned. Abandonment is a dominant theme in child myths (Jung and Kerenyi 1969). In ancient Greece, and in some far-off cultures today, abandonment, filicide, and infanticide were not uncommon fates. Abandonment has been associated with the terrible mother, the savage goddess, the witch, the hag. The archetype of abandonment is associated with death, suffocation, stagnation, symbiosis, and the fear of incorporation.

Change and growth, however, always entail loss. In an assault from without, the self is threatened and anticipates defeat or annihilation. In an assault from within, the integrity of the self comes into question. The growth and differentiation of any new parts of the personality entail mourning for what will no longer be. During this process, the individual moves from periods of calm to periods of unsettling oscillation. These developments are simultaneously affective and cognitive. The pain of loss brings growth, transformation, and renewal in its wake. Each new stage of life necessitates a separation from the previous stage through mourning. The mourning itself has historical antecedents in the individual's characteristic or stylistic way of responding to loss.

Most psychologies depict the process of human development as a move toward differentiation. With each increase in differentiation, a loss is sustained. The infant's first task is to differentiate between self and environment, to discover that being is the opposite of non-being. Biological growth and sensorimotor experiences play an important role in facilitating the intrapsychic differentiation of self and other (Piaget 1954). All behavior is the product of an epigenetic course of development of intrapsychic components which are regulated both by the inherent archetypal predispositions and by cumulative environmental experiences. The self and the other complement one another in a dynamic, mutually integrative relationship in which connectedness and separateness interact to create a transforming amalgam of a shareable experience.

The ego of the child is aware of its dependence on the external world and experiences helplessness when needs are not met. When help is not forthcoming, there is a sense of loss and a psychic awareness of self as a separate entity. Despite fluctuations in bodily feelings and emotions, as well as changes in external development, self imagery is constantly deintegrated and reintegrated by use of the symbolic process (Fordham 1957).

To experience loss is to have achieved a certain level of psychological attainment in object relations; one can only lose what one believes one has previously possessed. Without an awareness of self, the child cannot conceive of separation. The most fundamental, basic anxiety stems from the threat of loss of self. To remain embedded in another subjects us to the greatest peril of all, the loss of oneself. According to Strauss (1962), the experience of separation plays an integral and necessary role in the process of ego development. It is a recurrent stage in self-realization as well as in individuation. Permanence has no meaning without the concept of disappearance.

Separation refers to the child's movement away from fusion with the mother. Individuation is concerned with the development of one's own unique personality (Mahler 1968). In order to manage this, one must have the capacity to retain an internal image of self and other. The conflict between the wish to restore the primary union and the need to separate oneself from the predifferentiated self is basic to the individuation process. The result of the extrication or disembedding is the sense of unrecoverable loss.

We can therefore postulate that separation anxiety is not only concerned with fears of the loss of the other, but is additionally engendered in fears of losing the sense of self. As long as the child is embedded within the matrix of the primary union or in the other, this specific distress does not exist. It is only after the wrenching experience of differentiation from the other that fear of losing one's own center occurs.

A sense of abandonment does not always go back solely to these beginnings; it is closely connected to concerns regarding object constancy as well. If there is nobody present to relieve the discomfort and frustration, a sense of object loss emerges. It appears that loneliness, isolation, or separation can only be tolerated for limited periods of time without evoking profound psychic changes. The object constancy attained in childhood is the precursor of the capacity for separation at later times in life. The conflicts over dependence and abandonment, as well as the failure to attain an adequate level of object constancy, reflects developmental lags in the area of separation and individuation.

In Fordham's view the experience of oneness in symbiosis and regression is instrumental in reaching the area from which symbol formation derives.

> It will be apparent by now that symbolization may be related to the absence of an object, and may be important in periods during which a valued object is lost. The affect associated with the loss of a loved one is mourning. (1976, p. 21)

The bereavement process of mourning can be seen as synonomous with ego development and the differentiation of the psyche. The symbolic attitude emerges only after this psychic differentiation has occurred.

The failure to navigate the earlier developmental phases generates continued dependency and fears of abandonment, separation, anxiety, and the loss of love. Childhood narcissistic trauma may produce a state of affairs in which sadness and grief cannot be tolerated. There can be hypochondriachal concerns, mood swings, persistent yearning for the lost object, guilt feelings, and difficulty with commitment and interpersonal relations.

## The Impact of Handicaps

The diagnosis of handicap, or chronic disease, can be experienced as a threat and a trauma that produces psychological changes in both the child and the members of its family. The reactions of the parents will closely follow those we associate with loss, death, and dying.

Psychological preparation for a birth normally involves the wish for a perfect child as well as the fear of having a damaged one. When the child is defective, the discrepancy between the mother's wishes and the actuality is too great. The irretrievable nature of the defects can lead to feelings of ambivalence. The mother may have a guilty and depressed attachment to the child, or she may experience a narcissistic injury and identify with the child. The child may be overprotected and infantilized.

There may also be overt rejection and a failure to bond. When the capacity for differentiation is undermined by an overly intrusive or overly withdrawn environment, the growth-inhibiting world of the child may be incapable of tolerating assertiveness, dependency, curiosity, and negativism. There may be a failure to respond to the developing uniqueness of the child. The loss of the ideal child is mourned. If this fantasy attachment is not relinquished, the mother may remain unattached to the actual child. If the bereavement response is not worked through, the grief may be introjected as guilt, or projected outward as anger.

When illness becomes an important aspect of personal experience, people create unique images in their efforts to attach meaning to it. Different kinds of illness experiences evoke different archetypal constellations, which affect the adaptation. Illness threatens one's sense of identity and continuity, bringing uncertainty, anxiety, anger, helplessness, depression, and isolation. The anxiety-laden images contain fears, threats, worries, and unpleasant feelings. Bodily damage and helplessness are frequent concerns. The threat to identity may be reflected in paranoid delusions, but some of what is labeled paranoia in the visually handicapped may in fact be normal reality-based responses to life in a blurry world. The person may feel maimed, damaged, deformed, and ashamed. There is the anticipation that others, too, will see him or her as different and less worthy.

Hospitalization is a major loss experience, particularly if it takes place when the child is in the midst of struggling with total dependence on objects and making self-other differentiations. Some children experience hospitalization as punishment. They will say, "Take me home, I'll be good." The experience may have an impact on specific fears and fantasies focusing on a specific cognitive content, such as school performance.

Individuals with a visual handicap have to deal with specific issues related to the importance of vision in organizing the psyche temporally and spatially. Vision is the most important modality for interaction. The deprivation of visual experience leads to autistic syndromes.

Eye-to-eye contact is one of the essential elements in human encounters. Mythology, folklore, and colloquial language stress reciprocal eye contact in a direct, interpersonal or metaphorical sense. The killing face of Medusa, the evil eye, Tiresias, Oedipus, and Cyclops all attest to the powerful effect of vision or the devastation of losing it. We speak of "love at first sight," "if looks could kill," and "seeing eye to eye."

Eye contact, or the mutual gazing of mother and child, is an important ingredient in the forging of preverbal affective ties and contributes to the development of emotional reciprocity and attachment formation. It also has ramifications for the mother's own emotional state. She is influenced by the infant's response to her. In the event of visual problems, mother and child cannot make an appropriate accommodation to each other. It is through the interchange of glances that we send and receive emotional communication. We use visual images of self and other, inner and outer, to delineate our world.

The visually handicapped child has to build up its world without relying on visual impression. Burlingham (1965) maintains that this leaves a gap in the child's involvement with the external world and increases its involvement with its own body. With the greater egocentricity, the body becomes the source and object of stimulation. She notes that vision keeps the mind more firmly tied to external reality, whereas hearing is more closely linked to the internal world. Visual deficits lead to more introversion.

The difficulty in constructing a concept of self when one has a visual handicap causes a delay in acquiring a stable self-image. Fraiberg (1979, p. 268) states that the "child must find a path to self representation without the single sensory organ that is uniquely adapted for synthesis of all perceptions and the data of the self." Nagera (1965) views the visually handicapped as having a more marked and longer period of dependency on the external object world. There is difficulty in maintaining self-esteem and a tendency to inhibit overt expression of aggression against the people on whom they are dependent. There is an alertness to external dangers, and events are often wrongly interpreted. Withdrawal into fantasy becomes a source of safety and gratification. Visual handicaps intensify issues of separation.

## The Effects of Handicap on the Body Image

The development of a basic awareness of oneself as a distinct and separate physical being is a major developmental accomplishment of early childhood. The psychology and physiology of the newborn child cannot be separated. The body image is a hypothetical construct of usually unconscious images, along with preconscious and conscious endopsychic representations regarding the shape, appearance, position, and organization of the body and its immediate surroundings. Jung (1939) speaks of the reality of being embodied and tells us that the self is both body and psyche. The center of our system of valuables is our own physical self.

Every child, handicapped or not, must structure its world and integrate a world image with a body in order to know who and where it is. It is a world we half create and half perceive. The infant's world is a mother-body world. The sensations and awareness of interactions with the mother contribute to the formation of the body image. The somatic, sensory, and motor functions of the body are important for the continued differentiation of the bodily self and its psychic representations from that of the external world.

The demarcations of the body image initially take place within the symbiotic matrix. The body ego contains two types of representations: an inner core with a boundary that is turned toward the inside of the body, and an outer layer of sensoriperceptive engrams that contribute to the body self. Health problems affect the child's developing image. Its ideas about bodily functioning and the origins of discomfort may be unrealistic. The child may feel responsible for the illness. For example, a child may attribute its diabetes to eating too much candy.

The painful distortion of one's body image can lead to bizarre misstatements. Fisher and Cleveland (1968) propose that disturbances of body image include: gender-identity issues, concerns focusing on body integration and deterioration, feelings of depersonalization, and a sense of loss of body boundaries. They postulate that the body is a psychological structure that separates and protects the self from the environment.

Barton and Cattell (1972) found that children with chronic physical problems were weaker in ego strength and less emotionally mature than their peers. Their traits reflected greater dependency and overprotectedness. Five years after the initial study, there was still a marked failure to progress, and they appeared even more insecure, apprehensive, and troubled. Illness or handicaps have profound effects upon the internalized self-image. For some people, these deficits can never be fully overcome, and the capacity to separate self-image from actual appearance remains permanently impaired.

## Clinical Material

The purpose of presenting this case material is to elucidate further the impact of wounding on the development of the self in some visually handicapped individuals and to illustrate two main issues. First, that the origins of the analysand's problems lay in the wounds and deficiencies of the persistent emotional atmosphere of his or her childhood environment, and that this algorithm led to the formation of the loss complex and preoccupation with abandonment. Second, that the wounding and the transformation of needs were worked through in the transference, and a more stable sense of self was achieved.

In the analysands I am going to discuss, the pathological mother-child relationships impeded attempts to separate and had adverse effects on the individuation process. These analysands displayed the low energy, damaged body images, depressive undertones, faulty self-esteem, and grandiose self expectations that have been mentioned. Sexual acting-out was common. In some instances, narcissistic parents invaded and took over the self. The patients had to reconstitute the sense of self in therapy. The major focus of treatment was on separation anxiety, which constantly threatened the analysands with regressive merger and loss of identity.

The therapy served a developmental function by providing a secure base and a containing function. The therapist needs to supply the qualities which were lacking in the relationship with the parents, and which, *in loco parentis,* influence the acquisition of a secure attachment in the analysand and which enable further growth. Attachment has relevance for the development of the therapeutic alliance and enables the work to continue despite transference feelings. The therapist must be experienced as real, concerned, and in touch with the patient's distress and nonverbal communications.

One of the values of the psychotherapeutic experience is the progression from monologue to dialogue. This can only transpire after the gaps in maturation are filled in. Rapport needs to be reliable and unconditional if we are to create a therapeutic milieu that affords a new opportunity for parental responses to correct many cognitive misperceptions and distortions and make pathological responses less necessary. Only then are new developmental responses possible. The tasks of separation need to be reenacted within the analytic experience. The analyst functions as part of the psychic structure of the analysand and as a parent as well, providing calm and subtle mirroring of the child's original environment. The interpersonal relatedness is essential for movement away from enmeshment in a uroboric mode of being. The transference-countertransference is a reenactment of the unconscious drama of childhood. Volkan (1976) has referred to therapy as "re-grief work."

In the analytic work, the role of the analyst is to mediate the transcendent function for the analysand, until such time as the analysand has developed sufficient ego strength. Very dependent analysands perceive the analyst as a magician who will lead them to a clear and conflict-free future in a promised land. When the analyst cannot fulfill the profound needs of these patients, intense rage and disappointment, with concomitant disillusionment, make it difficult to sustain the therapeutic alliance. Clinging behavior is prominent in the endless attempts to assuage the inner emptiness. Any criticism, real or implied, any failure in comprehension on the part of the analyst, evokes fear of abandonment in therapy. The sense of disappointment and conflict is ever present.

Treatment reveals a deep sense of loss and rage. Separation anxiety and loss and abandonment complexes are manifested at the ending of sessions and at vacation times. It is important that the analyst remain undamaged and survive the analysand's destructive fantasies and impulses. There may be unceasing efforts to merge with the analyst in an effort to ease the pain of separation. There is a need to develop a better ability to differentiate, in a relative sense, self from non-self, thus facilitating a better consolidation of object constancy. Therapeutic change comes about when the analysand has worked through the pain, rage, depression, and guilt and is able to bear loss.

*Case #1—Ms. Z*

Ms. Z is a visually handicapped, divorced woman with one child. She works part-time as an educational program administrator. We began twice-a-week psychotherapy for what she described as some painful current issues. Her intellectual assets were evident, and from time to time there was a glimmer of charm. Her father had been a minister who had died suddenly of a coronary when Z was nine years old. The mother kept the household going by giving piano lessons. The analysand felt she had decathected life at the time of her father's death.

Z's major problems had their roots in experiences of abandonment intertwined with conflicted love. She was unable to trust anyone and had low self-esteem and little capacity for relationships. She would speak of wanting to be close to people, but when the opportunity did arise she was too terrified to make use of it. Often she was consumed with suicidal ideation. For her, life was a succession of abandonments. Each occurrence left her angrier and more immersed in a sense of futility. Z had been badly neglected, both physically and emotionally. There was no structure or predictability within the family of origin. She felt as if she had a masochistic child within her who evoked anger and engendered painfully tormented and hateful feelings.

The mother had reacted with disappointment at having a visually handicapped child. She did try to breast-feed her but found it painful, and the infant was abruptly weaned at the age of three weeks. The mother herself had experienced early deprivation and unmet dependency needs in her own childhood. Consequently, she wanted her child to be totally independent and immune to loss and trauma. This promoted the development of a pseudo-maturity and precocity, wherein the analysand could protect her fragile ego functions through pseudo-mastery.

When she was in first grade, Z developed digestive disturbance symptoms. The parents reacted as if she were a malingering school phobic. The condition eventually required hospitalization, which she experienced as an abandonment. She had several other hospitalizations in latency.

As a child, Z was inundated with persistent fears that her parents would go off and leave her. At the same time, she hated to be a passenger in the family car and described feelings of being kidnapped, imprisoned, and utterly alone. Ms. Z lacked basic trust and needed to be in control.

Her visual handicap led to a comparative lack of stimulation which tended to exacerbate feelings of isolation. She lacked the psychic structures necessary to regulate tensions and establish containment, to sustain feelings of contentment and well-being. Reflective self-awareness was minimal. At the same time, Z was well aware that her frequent dark moods, low self-esteem, and predilection toward self-destructive actions hindered her.

Z's mother appeared to have been oversensitive in regard to her own capacity for fulfilling the function of motherhood. Every indication or reminder of the child's difficulties engendered feelings of inferiority in her and created tension and depression. The child's reported difficulties with colic and lactation may have been due to this underlying tension between them. Sometimes somatization was used to obtain release from duties and responsibilities. Her disproportionately large number of illnesses suggests that either by chance or by constitution she was unusually prone to disease processes, or she repetitively somatized. Illness was a way of life. The sick role exempted her from the usual domestic obligations. While her father was still alive, he often took over the running of the household. The parents were social isolates who tended to be hypercritical of others and to experience people as abusive and attacking.

In therapy, Z recalled with chilling detail the anxiety and sense of terror that accompanied the actual abuse she experienced as a child. One of her mother's most severe punishments was to have her kneel on uncooked rice grains for hours. At other times, food provided the arena for sadistic interaction. A feast-or-famine atmosphere would prevail. Deprivation of food and overrigidity regarding diet were followed by a period of overindulgence, a vicious cycle wherein Z would get caught up in a self-restrictive diet, followed by eating binges that resulted in intense guilt.

As an adolescent she was terrified of putting on weight and had a compulsive commitment to physical exercise. There were constant battles with her mother over bathing, eating, curfews, and whether she could be allowed to stay home alone when her mother was unable to be present. Additionally, there was confusion about gender identity. Z was predominantly heterosexual but participated in homosexual opportunities. After an adolescence marked with episodes of promiscuity, she married a fellow student in her junior year of college. The classmate was from the same neighborhood, and she had known him slightly from the time she was in elementary school. The marriage lasted six years and one daughter was born. She described her former husband as solid, well meaning, and boring. Several years after the birth of the child, he fell in love with another woman and left. Z was bereft. Her interaction with her own child appeared to repeat the pattern of her own childhood. She felt overwhelmed by domesticity and the responsibility of motherhood.

She still needed a mother herself. Like her mother, she was afflicted with headaches and backaches and would somatize the stress reactions.

As therapy continued, a picture of the parental psychopathology emerged. When encouraged to describe her childhood, Z revealed a self-image of an unwanted child who could never do anything right. The more she shared, the more I reacted with an urge to rescue her. The pressing need to unburden herself made her an eager patient. Together we unraveled a veritable cat's cradle of memories and feelings.

The focal point of the work centered on her father's death. Her mother had withdrawn into her own grief, leaving Z unable to develop reasonable, age-appropriate responses and methods of behavior. Instead of comforting one another, they became strangers. The mother was remote and unresponsive. Other relatives were unavailable, and the patient concluded that they did not love her and that the reason for this was that she was not lovable.

Despite the father's religious vocation, the mother was not a particularly religious woman, so religion offered no comfort. There were no factual explanations either. When the child asked where her father was, she was told that he was in heaven. Beyond that the mother could not be honest or realistic. It was a time of great confusion. Z shared poignant memories of looking for her father in the streets and on buses. She withdrew from the outside world and made use of her own body to console herself in her isolation. There was literally nobody to turn to. Although mother and child each suffered depression, the mother was unable to help her child to mourn.

For Z the father's death implied desertion and separation. Too much of her total capacity for relationship has been invested in him. When he died, part of the child died too. The deprivation of parental bereavement is overwhelming. In this instance, the surviving parent could not take on the enormous burden of helping the child deal with the loss. Reality testing had long been an issue for the whole family. Now the narcissistic mother and the patient joined in externalizing each other's projections. Mother and daughter would get embroiled in battles as to "who is right" rather than "what is happening." They manufactured a reality for each other to share. Terror was transmitted. The mother's expectations and fears of abandonment had materialized and had been validated in her husband's death. She now simultaneously clung to her child and pushed her away, handling her own terrors as though they all existed within the child. Curiosity was curtailed: reaching to discover the unknown was penalized. Z was specifically trained not to find her way beyond the family circle.

Evidence of pathological mourning was present. Z felt responsible for her father's death. Her closeness to him and her intense unresolved oedipal feelings were accentuated by the mother's frequent illnesses. Previously, when her mother had retreated to bed, the child had spent time with her father. Father's relative permissiveness and mother's punitiveness led to an uneven distribution of parental functions. Father's death seemed to be one more of mother's punishments.

From time to time I would feel helpless, inept, and inadequate to the demands of the treatment. Z's clumsy gait, visual impairment, incessant oral needs, and difficulty in functioning in a truly independent manner could be overwhelming. Her unintegrated body schema caused her to lurch when she walked. Stereotypic motility, swaying, rocking, and shallowness of human communications were at times almost too painful to witness. There was a gross discrepancy in her capacity to deal competently with some areas of life and her incapacity for intimate relations.

Any interpretation I made, no matter how gentle, was experienced as a wounding criticism that further intensified the misery of her life. As ambivalence and fear surfaced, I incarnated the powerful mother who had the potential to rob her of her independence. Whenever I could, I would attempt to help her reduce her idealization of me to life size. The attempts to provoke me into being a disapproving mother were syntonic at times. During vacation breaks, Z would act out by stuffing herself with food, indulging in promiscuity, and being preoccupied with hatred.

Z needed to develop a sense of her own identity over against an image of a damaged mother with whom she had previously been unconsciously identified. I needed to enact the analyst-mother who could accept her in spite of her imperfections and help her mourn the loss of her ideal self. I provided the strength that allowed her to withstand the self-hatred and propensity for sadomasochism. The reliving of the relationship with the mother in the transference alternated between exaggeratedly fearful compliance and indirect, rebellious defiance. She identified with her mother's victimized pattern of long-standing suffering and actively reproduced the misery and fear of her childhood. Sometimes I would feel worthless, scorned, and helpless. Often there was a thrust to merge and be at one with me in order to escape her underlying depression. But I also became a constant stable force in her life. Her autonomy was always respected and encouraged, and this provided the opportunity for growth. In an early dream, an older woman is helping her retrieve and put back into a basket a collection of items that had fallen out and were strewn about.

She expressed wishes to be held and cuddled. She would hold a pillow at home and fantasize that she was talking to me. In our sessions, supportive comments and empathic measures were offered and responded to. As Z began to have a more realistic picture of herself in relation to the world, the underlying sense of omnipotence abated. As this transpired, fearfulness, anxiety, demandingness, and clinging surfaced. Gradually she began to explore the possibility of being more open, clear, focused, and articulate in the communication of angry and resentful feelings. She began to differentiate between "can't" and "won't." At times she still became depressed, but the depression was no longer a low-grade, steady state of mind.

In the early phase of treatment, the form of communication had been a forced intellectual style, filled with self-pity and tinged with veiled antagonism to her mother. Prior to therapy she had felt detached and wondered if she were really capable of loving anyone. During therapy she began to realize how deeply she longed for love and care, how not getting it induced anger, and how she responded to loss with deep affect. She needed to weep and grieve for her injured and damaged child. As a result of the intense pain of the early years and the repeated frustration of her attachment behavior, she had become numb. After sharing her pain, she began to develop a respect for me and to express and experience real feelings of her own. Her anger at me lessened as she felt that I would be accepting regardless of what her feelings toward me were. Angry and hostile fantasies and thoughts did not result in losing me or destroying me.

Changing reactions to my absence during vacation or illness were a reflection of her growth. Initially, every separation meant abandonment. Now she could cope with increasing ease, using her own resources to sustain herself. Finding out that our relationship continued and that neither one of us was annihilated was a major discovery.

The consistency in the analytic attitude indicated to her that I could tolerate her dependent yearning, the accompanying anger, and the incessant demands. Her states of depersonalization and estrangement lessened as the developmental impairment in self-object boundaries was healed. Her ability to tolerate and deal with a wide range of internal and external experiences improved dramatically. Z can now recognize and ask for what she wants in a more vigorous and more deliberate and open manner.

*Case #2—Ms. X*

Ms. X entered twice-a-week therapy at age 26. A school teacher in a parochial school, she was born with a visual handicap that required numerous surgical corrections. Her parents were a prosperous professional father and an attractive, much younger mother. The mother's family was wealthy and "socially superior" to that of the father. The mother often deprecated his family. The patient grew up in a major city in relative affluence but with emotional deprivation. Although the father was often away on business trips, X was more deeply attached to him than to her mother. She was awed by her father.

Initially, sulkiness and skepticism about therapy predominated. Never having been listened to, never having felt valued or cared for, she was having an entirely new experience. X's history of early, unavoidable illness and pain had been compounded by maternal inadequacy in partnering at a crucial phase of development. Both phenomena contributed to a precipitous deflation of omnipotence. The circumstances that led to a too-abrupt deflation of a sense of her omnipotence fostered an angry dependency on the parents, along with an attitude of ambivalence. The unavailability of the mother during the child's early hospitalizations highlighted her lack of omnipotence.

Childhood was characterized by an overconcern with the mother's whereabouts. She would panic if the mother was not at home. There were physical and emotional clinging and temper tantrums. At times the father was so withdrawn and emotionally unavailable that he was experienced as nonexistent.

The analysand lived in a constant nightmare of a tenuous, unstable, and unpredictable world. The mother's constant threats that she would abandon her exacerbated her severe separation anxiety. An inner image of death and stagnation permeated her life. Threats such as "You will be the death of me," or "I'll kill myself" were made. At the same time, X's mother sought to control her life, and she consistently overprotected her from real and imagined dangers.

Initially, we needed to recognize how the mother's disturbance contributed to the turbulence of the early life experience which had been imbued with overwhelming rage, anger, deprivation, frustration, and helplessness. The mother vacillated from mild narcissistic behavior to psychosis. X recalled her mother's pushing her under water in the bath. She experienced herself as the center of her mother's universe. When seen for treatment, she exhibited multiple phobias, such as being afraid to eat in restaurants along with severe depression.

The mother's push for premature independence while at the same time clinging to her daughter, led to an upset in developmental balance. The mother seemed to be afraid of the intimacy the child offered and of merging and losing herself in the child. She had been so vulnerable and unprotected in her own childhood that she still needed to protect herself. In order to make developmental progress, X had to resort to compensatory efforts to achieve a modicum of equilibrium. Although at times these efforts can sustain a child, they eventually lead to developmental distortions. The patient needed to pretend to herself and to everyone else that she was "tough" and would act accordingly.

Her precocity led to an attitude of vigilance toward the possibility of loss and an intensification of separation anxiety. There was a tendency to mother herself, and a persona or false adaptive self emerged. Too often the mother's actions and reactions were based on her own needs and moods. That the analysand had a mind of her own was experienced as a personal rejection. The child was requested to rest in bed with mother when mother had a headache. Illness was shared, binding the two together in a common suffering.

In response to feelings of bodily impairment and subsequent inadequacy, X would overcompensate in the area of intellectual and educational endeavor. She initially had a predisposition to constellate the archetype of injury, deformity, and helplessness. The physical handicap was perceived as a punishment. Hysterical symptoms, images, and fantasies were acted out in physical symptoms until a sense of inner psychic reality could emerge.

Although X could negotiate the world with her pseudo-independence, at home she tended to be overly attuned to the needs of the parents. A sense of feeling needed provided her with a sense of security and lessened the fears of abandonment. She reported a great feeling of separation from other people, a loss of emotional contact with them, and a sense of loneliness and utter isolation prevailed. In addition to a loss of interest in what was going on around her, the world appeared to be dull, drab, dead, uninteresting, and unexciting. On the surface she related well to people, but underneath she was consumed by obsessive derogatory thoughts and envy. Feelings of weakness, smallness, helplessness, and inefficiency predominated. Everything required a major effort. Her concentration was poor, and her thoughts were imbued with gloom and melancholy. She spoke in a sad and plaintive tone of voice, and would tearfully report hollowness, worthlessness, shallowness, and the feeling that she had lost a part of herself. X would seek food and ask to be given a cup of coffee in her sessions. She felt trapped in conflict and suffering. The central analytic themes were separation and guilt. Her distorted body image was evidence of the insufficient mirroring by the parenting figure. When her mother was physically present but psychologically inaccessible, X turned to school work and comforted herself with food and autoerotic practices.

Her memories of hospitalization were bitter. She described being strapped down in bed in darkness with bandaged eyes, terrified and lonely, needing to hold her fragmenting self together with the imagery in her head. Any approaching footstep in the corridor would encourage her to think that her endless abandonment and isolation were coming to an end, but her parents did not visit frequently enough for her to derive much comfort from their existence.

According to X, abandonment was her karmic fate. She could not form satisfactory attachments and lacked close friends. When she met someone and became involved in a relationship, her reservoir of unmet dependency needs would well up and the other person would flee in self-defense. Or, if she got angry with someone, her first thought was to run away. Only when increased reality testing was promoted in therapy was X able to see that it was her own fears of abandonment that led her to run away. It was easier to leave and abandon the other than to be abandoned herself. She was eventually able to connect this with her mother's tendency to withdraw, as well as to her own early efforts to shut her mother out.

As alluded to earlier, the concerns, conflict, and resolutions around the theme of abandonment were predominant from the first analytic session onward. The initial account of the parents was that they were authoritarian and devoid of affection. The patient would get caught up in a litany wherein she was prone to disparage a world populated with people who would use her and then discard her. Implicit was the fear that I would join their ranks. All of her deep wounds were acquired when she had been enticed into relying on others.

In a moment of intense self-loathing, X shared that she was the most despicable of all the vile, disgusting people in the world.

> "I am still invested in hatred. I don't want to hate you but it is the only way to make sense. The hate is what I can't let go of. It is what I need to return to when all else fails, and everything else does fail eventually. I could not come to hate you today. Yet I can't let go enough to just be with you. You'll kick my teeth down my throat as sure as I sit here."

Her visual handicap contributed to feelings that at times the analysis was a lengthy chain of encounters with an invisible opponent or partner who was out to get her. She would project her aggression and experience it in terms of frightening fantasies of being attacked, engulfed, and swallowed up. At other times she would project her own feelings onto me, and she was unable to distinguish who was going to hurt whom. She would ask, "What is going to happen?" or she would say, "You are attacking me." At some points the disarray in the therapy resembled an opera bouffe. The patient would then see me as an impediment to her progress and assert that she did not need me.

Sexuality and gender identity were ever-present concerns. Both of the parents communicated that being female meant being an inanimate substance suitable for use or exploitation. The household atmosphere was such that sexuality was used not only as an undercover language for affection, but also as a vehicle to communicate rejection, denial, and coldness. The father made sexual approaches to her up to adolescence when the patient told him to stop mauling her. Whenever she was later in a situation of warmth or affection without sexual overtures, she panicked. I had the feeling that no one had allowed her to snuggle closely, or had sat patiently by while she played in childhood. Her severely constricted capacity for relationships was reflected in the strangulated ties to her parents. She could now admit to me that she was often frightened and confused.

X would complain that she had no energy to pursue any activity and had no interests in life. She was constantly searching in anticipation of other people's expectations of her responses to them. She

would speak of what she was "supposed to do." Her own perceptions were not to be trusted, and there was a naiveté about the basic
aspects of life and about the world. We were frequently dealing with
basic reality-oriented facts of day-to-day existence. Life was a quasi-
constant state of psychic unease in that the existence of external
reality and the demands of other people left her powerless and were
experienced as a continual and potentially traumatizing threat to
her psychic equilibrium.

X had to disidentify with the archetypal image of the great
mother before her individual identity could begin to develop. In
order to demolish the mother's omnipotent hold on her psyche, I
had to piece together the bits of information and confront her with
them. During this time, she dreamed of a blind old man who told
her that it was okay to bump into things.

In the transference, she distanced me as much as possible.
There was an underlying attitude of idealization and denigration.
She would bombard me with rejection, contempt, and reproach, and
lash out at the inadequacies of my methods of therapy. The day she
was angry with me for noting her insatiability, she had a dream of a
combination cemetery/mental hospital/house that was full of dogs
and sharks. Throughout the therapy she experienced fear of becoming too dependent, and yet at the same time she would request extra
sessions. My voice on the phone would confirm that she really
existed.

A major grudge was that with two such needy parents, she had
never had a childhood. She had experienced unpredictability in
nurture and witnessed great rage between her parents. She was
constantly trying to please them and make them love her. However,
she could never figure out what the rules of the game were. The
parental communication was, "You can't do it." If she did initiate
action, the rewards were slim. If she failed, her ineptitudes were
greeted with derision and "I told you so." She shared that she could
see and hear good things and people "on the other side of the
chasm," but the effect of that knowledge was negligible next to the
deafening roar of a hateful world screaming in her ears on her own
side of the gap. Isolation and defeat were ever present.

During the course of therapy, the ogre parents gradually
emerged as sick but almost human. She could now believe that her
parents, who were raised never to question authority or to disobey
overtly, had been subjected to harsh physical discipline themselves
as children and were unconscious of what they had done to her. It

was only after she had faced their dreadfulness that the patient was able to recognize the existence of previously unmentioned benevolence in the past.

Despite the high level of psychological-mindedness and good motivation, the years of early trauma left a heavy residue of armor to which she clung relentlessly. X could describe a void so deep that no one could fill it. It hurt to know that it could not be filled. The chasm of her loneliness could not be completely bridged. At times, sex was used to try to fill that void. Once she reported that she felt so alone at night that she would imagine that I was holding her quietly, not talking, the way one would hold a baby. She would open her eyes to look at me and feel content.

An ever-present question was whether I liked her or not. The real question was whether I could like her. She would come in impossible weather and even when she was ill; her fears of rejection and ejection terrified her more than illness or climatic conditions. It took years for her to realize how the pervasive fears of abandonment were part of her early heritage. After this, cancellations for valid reasons became possible.

Initially my leaving for vacation or to attend a meeting evoked fury. No matter how much advance notice was given, she would revile me and obsess and brood over it. Eventually we reached a point where she could recognize that I was present for her at appointment times, that I returned from vacations, and that I was unfailingly accepting of her and what she was feeling. Suspicion turned to wonderment and then acceptance. Her most scathing epithet was that I was an incompetent who would ultimately lead her down the path of disappointment and desertion once more. Trust built very slowly, and the ghosts of earlier abandonments gradually faded. She began to feel alive for the first time.

Eventually she could consider that possibly the world was not completely populated by people similar to those who shaped her idea of interpersonal relations. The day that she could say that she loved me brought a new and frightening experience for her. In the matrix of therapy, the analysand developed some capacity for relatedness. X could accept that the past was gone, and she was finally able to face what she could not face before: that she had been rejected as a child. As we spoke together about the content of her fears and angers, memories of the past were revived and connected with the present. The adaptive or nonadaptive nature of her responses, the function they had served in the past as well as their appropriateness in the present, and how well or badly they served her in her current life were thought through together. The therapeutic interaction increased the patient's freedom to express openly a widening range of thoughts, feelings, and impulses.

*Case #3—Mr. Y*

   Mr. Y, a diabetic and visually handicapped young man, began therapy at the age of 27. Before this he had participated in approximately five years of psychoanalytically oriented intensive therapy with several analysts. His experiences with the prior three analysts were unfortunate. One had died, one had relocated, and the third was not a good match. The shadows of the previous therapists were cast in the early months of our work together on the abandonment and loss motif. According to two of these therapists, Y was not a suitable case for classical analysis, an assessment which left him feeling rejected. My initial fear was that I was dealing with a therapy junkie who went from analyst to analyst seeking a magical cure. The last analyst interpreted his termination and wanting to work with me as a flight into the arms of the good mother and a manifestation of a transference psychosis.

   In our initial sessions, he shared having gone through many years of "supposed" analysis without being able to, or being allowed to, explore the things that he felt were important. Instead he was stuck in a good-and-bad-mother morass, and a good-and-bad-child morass, with which he was unable to do anything. He wanted to know if all of the past would go away and if his life was permanently ruined. "I need to go through all of this in a different way. Will you help?" he asked. In his estimation, either he was hopeless or his previous analyst was inept.

   Painfully self-conscious and self-critical, he was crippled by intense doubts concerning his competence. He would approach every task with dread, certain that he would be incapable of performing it. He had a basic depressive affect, low self-esteem, low vigor, and little long-term investment in goals and ideals. Y was tormented by a sense of badness and weakness, suffered great loneliness, and literally felt isolated. He lived in a continual state of internal chaos with no idea of where he ended and other people began. The sense of what is self and what is other was shaky. This confusion between subject and object belongs to a very primitive level of psychological development in which there is little awareness of what is inside and what is outside. The extent of his projections constantly left him feeling depleted and unable to react to the life that was taking place around him. He had little capacity for symbolization, and his thinking was of a concrete nature. Acknowledgment of his needs led to the evocation of rageful and envious affect. A stance of passive compliance was utilized, as assertion and aggression led to a loss of a sense of control.

At the start of our work together, he evoked warm maternal feelings in me. He appeared to be an appealing young man who was seeking to work on his problems. As our work progressed, I found myself feeling increasingly irritated and helpless. He lived in a milieu of constantly shifting part-objects, which would leave both of us feeling confused and disoriented. Life was a kaleidoscope of shifting sands. His dreams were of meandering through jungles, natural catastrophies, and wars.

During therapy, the analysand developed severe depressive episodes, along with a quiet somberness. Y was often stubborn but never defiant. He could behave as though I did not exist. He recalled childhood as a continuous barrage of verbal attacks by a mother whose anger seemed to increase with each assault. She would periodically withdraw into a depressive state that sometimes lasted for months at a time. During these episodes, she neglected her appearance and ceased caring for the home. The father would bring food in, while the mother remained in bed, announcing how worthless she was. The parents battled a lot, with the mother consistently hostile to the father. Periodically, she would threaten to send Y to live with relatives in a distant city.

From the age of three to eighteen months, the analysand wore Deney-Brown splints to correct a tibial torsion. Movement was impeded during the two prior months as well, when the infant was in a cast. Difficulties in assertion and aggression, plus concern with abandonment, may have originated in an Oedipus-like affliction. Mother added to the difficulty, since her problems in setting limits ended in her being too controlling. There was a mutual difficulty in expressing affection.

The relationship with the father was better, but he was often unpredictable. He was a self-centered man, an engineer, who was supersensitive to slights and given to depressive mood swings. Yet he was the more dependable of the two parents. In childhood photos, Y looked morose and dour. In several of them he had raised fists, indicating the noted ambivalence and marked anxiety of aggression. From the age of two there were asthmatic episodes. An early memory was of checking to see if his penis was still there. When he was four years old his mother ran away with a man ten years her junior. Y could not hold onto her image while she was gone. She sent gifts and eventually returned home eighteen months later, at about the time the patient's diabetes was diagnosed. During the mother's absence, the father and grandparents spoke disparagingly of her. When he was seven, the father was hospitalized for ten months. He returned home debilitated, and the mother was overtly depressed.

The analysand remembered refusing to go outdoors to participate in activities with other children. His additional recollections included his being whiny and demanding. Shoes and pencils had to be kept in a certain order, and any change threw him into a temper tantrum. When he made demands, his mother would lock him in the room as a punishment. He would cry until he fell asleep exhausted. At these times he felt abandoned by her.

Y lived in a world of blurry shapes and outlines. His childhood was populated by black monsters who were projections of his own angry feelings and an inability to deal with intense anger. Insulin injections were persecutory and terrified him. At school, the diabetic illness and the visual problems interfered with his need for conformity and acceptance. He was fearful that other children would see him as weird, particularly with the obvious dietary restrictions of diabetes. It was hard to be different, and he was avoided and teased. There were delays in growth and sexual maturation.

What emerged in the transference-countertransference was a portrayal of the early experience of maternal impingements and abandonment. In effect, he needed the psychic sustenance of optimal understanding and responsiveness that had been sorely lacking in crucial childhood years. As therapy progressed, the patient was able to relax more in the sessions. He would see me as needing to conduct my "magic analysis" while he was passive and contributed little input to the sessions. The first time he shared this, I was rather shocked: I had perceived his attitude to be just the opposite. What it accentuated was the extent of the powerful projective identification that characterized the mother-child dyad. In that relationship, the analysand needed to be the embodiment of his mother's projections. If he failed to do so, he ceased to exist for his mother. Projective identification was the principal form of linkage between the analysand and his mother. Many dreams contained imagery of intercourse with his mother, castration by his mother, and annihilation. They were comments on his longing for her and yet his fear of her as a potential depriver of his masculinity.

When I felt that I understood some aspect of the transference, or some part of his communications, I would venture an interpretation. These interpretations were met with indifference. Any attempts at interpretation were useless, and at best my comments were experienced as intrusions and impingements. The disconnected affects and depressed mood, the minimally stimulated rages, were linked to the traumatic experiences of childhood and the here-and-now transference manifestations.

From time to time the analysand would repetitively describe episodes and events from the past with the animation of a cow chewing its cud. Y would comment on my patronizing attitude as he delivered his monologue. All my efforts to interact with him were aborted, and I felt excluded by his solipsistic mode of communication. During some of the detailed monotonous descriptions, sadistic fantasies would come into my mind. Frequently I would become sleepy. At first I would become distressed, then I recognized that I was responding to his need to neutralize me and make me the impotent one. There was a need to control the therapeutic session omnipotently and indulge in the fantasy that he did not need me. At other times I was aware of being tested for endurance, and for assurance that despite his behavior I would not abandon him.

The chronic anxiety associated with the unconscious infantile fears of being overpowered, injured, and abandoned because of hostile rebellious strivings was a focus of our work. Y had to learn that his own anger did not frighten the world or cause it to fragment. The patient's strong feelings were no more dangerous to himself than they were to others. He had a need to be taken care of, and his demands for attention and love were out of all proportion to the realities of adulthood; consequently, they could never be adequately satisfied. Y could also get caught up in altruistic surrender when he felt that his assertiveness could damage loved ones. In the transference I was often the narcissistic mother, primarily interested in the gratification of my own needs.

As a result of his need to discriminate his own feelings, thoughts, and body, Y exhibited the characteristics of the grandiose self. There were a number of episodes of acute narcissistic rage and ambivalence between the wish to merge and remain within the protective orbit of the mother and the wish to exercise autonomy and stave off

engulfment by her. When attempts to mediate between these com-
peting needs failed, separation anxiety and the loss complex were
activated. When the boundaries and the sense of self were more
consolidated, a more stable self emerged. Y experienced anxieties
in connection with masculinity and femininity on the one hand and
heterosexuality and homosexuality on the other. Prior to therapy, as
soon as the possibility of intimacy with a woman appeared on the
horizon, he would break off the relationship. About midway in
therapy he was able to sustain a relationship with a young woman.
As his social circle of friends broadened, he was in reality less
dependent on me. The analysand had learned to evaluate his
strengths and weaknesses with some precision. His self-esteem grew
with his increasing mastery of life.

As his interpersonal relationships improved, his growth was
demonstrated in the dream content. There were fewer calamities
and catastrophes, and more dreams about ordinary human situations. I started to appear in some of the dreams. In one dream we
were traveling together in a foreign country. Through therapy, Y
changed and came to see himself in more imaginative, flexible, and
reliable ways. As the patient internalized the analyst's flexibility, the
more stable self was able to emerge. His tolerance for frustration
increased and his aggression was redirected away from the self. With
self boundaries more secure, life was perceived in terms of equality
and mutuality.

## Conclusion

The transformations of early childhood, with their ever-present
themes of attachment and separation, retain their potency throughout life. Individuals with loss and abandonment complexes are torn
between an overwhelming yearning to return to a symbiotic state of
existence and an equally strong urge to assert their separateness as
individuals. Symbiosis and separateness are equally threatening.
Symbiosis implies a dissolution of one's reality as a person whereas
separateness is associated with total isolation and abandonment.

Therapy with the handicapped persons described provided
them with the opportunity for a corrective emotional experience. In
the course of therapy, the analysands had to own and share the less
acceptable aspects of the self by facing and integrating their shadows. They also had to revise and renounce antiquated values and
restraints on their growth. In addition to working through personal

losses, they needed to deal with the losses that are part and parcel of the therapeutic relationship—for example, by accepting the imperfections of the analyst and the therapeutic relationship and the therapy. The reactions to those losses also had to be experienced.

The growth-promoting environment of therapy helped these analysands to differentiate inner from outer, self from nonself, and means from ends. Now they were more able to deal with intense personal experiences and affects relating to separation and loss. This facilitated a move toward higher levels of development in which a more differentiated psychic structure and new ways of relating became possible.

My task was to read the cues accurately and to respond to the symbolic communications at the cognitive and empathic levels. By being flexible at his or her own level, the analysand's own integration of cognitive and emotional components was fostered. Differentiation and orientation to reality occur when one's symbolic communications are read and responded to accurately. The more sensitive and selective my feedback, the more the patients could differentiate the various nuances of their communications.

In the transference/countertransference there was an acknowledgment of the early pain of the wounded infant. Often there is a direct correspondence between the primitiveness of the psychopathology and the intensity of transference/countertransference disruption. For persons whose unmet symbiotic needs are strong, the activation of these fantasies in therapy draws them closer to the therapist in the hope of obtaining gratification. Transformation takes place when the separation from the old way of being occurs and a new balance emerges. Weathering loss leads to new transformations, wherein a new, more integrated way of being emerges and a new equilibrium is achieved.

## References

Barton, K., and Cattell, R. B. 1972. Personality before and after a chronic illness. *Journal of Clinical Psychology* 28:464–67.

Bowlby, J. 1960. Separation anxiety: A critical review of the literature. *Journal of Child Psychology and Child Psychiatry* 1:251–69.

_____. 1961. Childhood mourning and its implications for psychiatry. *American Journal of Psychiatry*, 481–98.

_____. 1979. *The making and breaking of affectional bonds*. London: Tavistock Publications.

_____. 1980. *Attachment and loss*. New York: Basic Books.

Brewster, H. 1952. Separation reaction in psychosomatic disease and neurosis. *Psychosomatic Medicine* 14:154–60.

Burlingham, D. 1965. Ego development in the blind. *Psychoanalytic Study of the Child* XX:194–208. New York: International Universities Press.

Engel, G. 1961. Is grief a disease? *Psychosomatic Medicine* 23:18–22.

Fisher, S. 1972. *Body experience in fantasy and behavior.* New York: Appleton-Century Crofts.

_____, and Cleveland, S. 1968. *Body image and personality.* New York: Dover.

Fordham, M. 1957. *New developments in analytical psychology.* London: Routledge and Kegan Paul.

_____. 1976. *The self and autism.* London: Heinemann.

Fraiberg, S. 1979. *Insights from the blind.* New York: Meridian.

Jung, C. G. 1939. Conscious, unconscious and individuation. In *Collected works,* 9/i:275–89. Princeton: Princeton University Press, 1969.

_____. 1940. The psychology of the child archetype. In *Collected works,* 9/i:151–81. Princeton: Princeton University Press, 1969.

_____. 1960. General aspects of dream psychology. In *Collected works,* 8:237–80. Princeton: Princeton University Press.

_____, and Kerenyi, K. 1969. *Introduction to the science of mythology.* Princeton: Bollingen.

Mahler, M. 1961. On sadness and grief in infancy and childhood. *Psychoanalytic Study of the Child,* XVI:332–51. New York: International Universities Press.

_____. 1968. *On human symbiosis and the vicissitudes of individuation.* New York: International Universities Press.

Nagera, H. 1965. Aspects of the contribution of sight to ego and drive development. *Psychoanalytic study of the child,* XX:267–87. New York: International Universities Press.

Neumann, E. 1955. *The great mother.* London: Routledge and Kegan Paul.

Piaget, J. 1954. *The construction of reality in the child.* New York: Basic Books.

Strauss, R. 1962. The archetype of separation. In *The archetype,* A. Guggenbuhl-Craig, ed., pp. 104–12. Basel and New York: S. Karger.

Volkan, V. 1975. Re-grief therapy. In *Bereavement and its social aspects,* B. Schoenberg, ed., pp. 334–50. New York: Columbia University Press.

# Abandonment and Deintegration of the Primary Self

## Renaldo Maduro

This paper seeks to make a positive contribution to the theory of deintegration by selecting a nodal point along the life-cycle when abandonment could occur, and by asking how the clinical manifestations of mourning in the archetypal experience of separation/abandonment differ from person to person. How an abandonment is experienced depends on cultural mores because it is a social event, but also on the developmental tasks and ruling unconscious fantasies of a particular maturational phase because it is a psychological experience. Clinical material from an identical twin (Grace), prematurely born at six and a half months and placed in an incubator for eight weeks, is used to illustrate aspects of abandonment loss in the earliest phase of development.

The main objective of this paper is to operationalize the concept of deintegration of the primary self in an adult patient. Ford-

**Renaldo Maduro,** Ph.D., is Associate Clinical Professor of Medical Anthropology and Psychology, Department of Psychiatry, University of California Medical Center, San Francisco; faculty, C. G. Jung Institute of San Francisco; private practice in San Francisco. He is author of "Analytical Psychology" (with J. Wheelwright) in *Personality Theories, Research and Assessment* (1983) and of *Artistic Creativity in a Brahmin Painter Community* (1976).

ham's concept of *deintegration* is useful when applied to the ethological notion of *critical periods* of human development across the entire life-span, and when applied to the capacity for abandonment in the creative process. Deintegration is intrinsic to the broad process of individuation as Jung describes it, and is reflected in the dream images of the "swarming crowd" and the spiral.

In addition to the capacity to abandon oneself in creative process, clinical situations will highlight some pathogenic effects of abandonment occurring in the first year of life, touching on questions related to the oedipal phase and the midlife crisis (cf. Stein 1983), described by Jung (1930) as discrete archetypal rhythms (stages) of the life-cycle. In *Symbols of Transformation*, Jung (1956) provides a good account of pre-psychotic process involving deintegration during adolescence in the dreams, poems, and fantasies of Miss Miller.

### Archetypal Time and the Process of Deintegration

In my work it is critical to remember the distinction between maturation and individual development. In the light of this distinction, it has proven helpful to view abandonment as a particular kind of *loss complex* (Rochlin 1961) and constellation of internal objects. In the *abandonment loss complex*, the archetypes of separation and the *coniunctio* (primal scene) are activated for a variety of conscious and unconscious reasons (Hubback 1983; Samuels 1982; Strauss 1962). During and after abandonment, separation and union feature prominently, just as they do in early development when the universal task is to disentangle the masculine from the feminine. Differing amounts of love, hope, and union are mingled with hate, revenge, dread, pining, and separation. Pangs of persecutory and depressive anxieties can be penetrated by even more acute intrusive ideation related to a loss. All of these feelings of the abandonment loss complex affect the feeling quality of the inner *coniunctio* imago that each of us has as the basis of our close interpersonal relationships.

One may make a case for an archetype of abandonment, but I prefer to˜ see it as one of the many forms of the archetype of separation. It is, nevertheless, clinically useful to refer to states of *primary* (archetypal) *abandonment*, when the activated unconscious is intensely on the move and when the emergence of a hopeful new and as yet unknown unconscious content is possible. Does this occur with the first feeding after birth, or even before? Are there diurnal rhythms? At such moments during individuation, "archetypal time" seems to hold sway, to come unbidden. The individual then experiences inner and outer life as timeless, awesome, mythological, transpersonal, extreme, and absolute. It feels as if this event has never happened to anyone else before. One feels unique. When abandonment occurs in the analytic process, it can feel as if the ego were identified with the archetypal image of the abandoned child-hero mentioned by Jung in *The Psychology of the Child Archetype*:

> Abandonment, exposure, danger, etc. are all elaborations of the "child's" insignificant beginnings and of its mysterious and miraculous birth. This statement describes a certain psychic experience of a creative nature, whose object is the emergence of a new and as yet unknown content. (1940b, p. 167)

Abandonment can mean leaving behind old ego attitudes for something new. In the creation of mind, this is a typical or universal human experience. Therefore, because of its archetypal nature, it partakes of paradox, combining (as the image of the abandoned child does in myths and fairytales) feelings of both desolation (separation) and hopefulness (union).

When in development does the archetypal experience of abandonment first appear? The primary experience of abandonment is in infancy, and we are therefore all somewhat thin-skinned when we have to digest separation and loss. Although all experiences of abandonment touch on original early experiences, the integrated ego later in adult life has more resources to deal with inner and outer world loss than the relatively undifferentiated baby. The wider distribution of libido after object removal in adolescence also makes a loss, such as a parental bereavement, much less devastating later than to the child who invests so much more of his or her energy in only two parents. This makes it appear as if babies and children are closer to seeking communion than sophisticated mutual dialogue, although from the beginning they are individuals.

Nuclear life events are the building blocks of any individual's own individuation, or lack of it. The archetypal underpinnings of the process of individuation include critical periods of deintegration of the primary self. A sense of being caught in archetypal time is evident in analysis and in life during many unstable phases of deintegration (Fordham 1961, 1963, 1967, 1969a, 1969b, 1971, 1973, 1974, 1976, 1978, n.d.). Fordham's concept of the primary self, based on Jung's "unitary self," assumes a formative psychobiological wholeness present at birth. Out of this original wholeness the ego

complex and all other maturational potentials emerge, via deintegration, as self-differentiation proceeds. The self-objects of early life
are archetypal deintegrates in search of an environmental fit.

This paper links deintegration as a maturational (archetypal)
process to Jung's appreciation of innate potential for adult personality formation. To my knowledge Fordham's concept of deintegration has rarely been described, theoretically or clinically, in relation
to one of Jung's richest contributions to psychoanalysis, namely the
process of enhanced individuation throughout the life-cycle (Maduro 1974; Maduro and Wheelwright 1983).

The archetypes of separation, mother, father, child, and combined male-female figures (*coniunctio*) are seen frequently to accompany the process of deintegration ("unpacking the self" [Lam-
bert 1981]). They crystallize during critical periods of deintegration,
in one symbolic form or another, as spontaneous products from the
unconscious psyche if the capacity for symbol formation is achieved.
This implies an uncrippled capacity to engage in "as if" symbolic
process that utilizes the transcendent function. At these times the
ego must abandon the old in some form (i.e., leave the mother) and
embrace (synthesize) the new unknown unconscious content, much
as the abandoned child must be protected (contained) and then
*found*, so that new life and direction may grow up and take form in
the psyche. Because this always involves resistance, we analyze
resistance to facilitate emergence of the new contents.

In a healthy sense, the ego must surrender and abandon itself
to the wider needs or goals of the supraordinate self. This state can
feel perilous, depending on previous experiences. This is experienced as the need to let go, give up, and relinquish control over
natural unconscious forces, so that a playful sense of life-giving
abandonment can give way to the reconstruction and creation of
new inner structures.

### From Narcissistic Libido to Object Libido

From a quantitative point of view, a central question emerges:
What is the individual's capacity to transform narcissistic libido
(paranoid anxiety) into object libido (depressive anxiety)? In short,
at the time of abandonment, how mature is the quality of the object
relation that has to be given up, abandoned? What role did the lost
person play in the psychic economy of the individual, and what is

the impact of the circumstances around the loss? The role of surviving loved persons is also important. Just as in myth, the individual ego, in every abandonment scenario, is left feeling at the mercy of something or somebody else.

It is generally accepted by many analysts, especially Jungians and Kleinians, that the transformation of narcissistic libido (one-body relationship) into object libido (two-body relationship) occurs much earlier than Freud and classical psychoanalytic theory suggest. The capacity to transform libido is closely linked to the depressive position in the first year of life. It is possible that the capacity to use the transcendent function, a kind of reparation, grows out of a successful negotiation of an archetypal event of great importance: achievement of the depressive position, called by Abraham (1924) the "primal depression" (cf. Elkin 1972). From this event, the human capacity to symbolize and carry culture develops. The capacity to experience whole objects as *both* good and bad, not split up into all good or all bad, represents the integration of two archetypal opposites from which a third hidden "something" (the "child") has sprung. Although this content may be resisted in analysis, it is felt to be more important than the two opposites from which it came. It generally represents *the secret*, that which is as yet unknown to the conscious portion of the ego.

Klein (1935, 1957), Winnicott (1954, 1963), and many Jungians consider the resolution of the depressive position in infancy to be the first experience of mourning, setting the primary pattern for all later bereavement reactions. The depressive position is dated to the period roughly between six and twenty months of age (just before and after weaning). Abraham (1924) and most analysts recognize weaning as a severe narcissistic injury to the infant. Therefore in any abandonment another question is central: How has the lost tie been affected by negotiation or non-negotiation of the depressive position? It is here where a capacity to feel concern for another separate not-me person is first achieved in a two-body relationship with the mother.

The achievement of the depressive position is crucial to how an individual will react to abandonment in the clinical setting. We do not feel abandoned by someone about whom we do not care. We feel abandoned by somebody only when we are actively seeking a loving and positive connection and the other person disappears (in fact or fantasy). Although abandonment can take many forms, the central issue in clinical work rests on the psychological fact that one must have developed esteem for the object before we can speak about the separation experience of the *abandonment loss complex*.

After this point in development, we can also observe the role of the voice of conscience and the effect of culturally patterned ego ideals, which in the course of individuation may have to be forsaken or relinquished for wider perspectives. Culturally patterned separations may get resolved within the cultural construct, or they may be unanticipated and sudden. Abandonment in one culture may not be considered abandonment in another. In the psychoanalytic situation, we penetrate to a level of understanding of what any abandonment (inner or outer, life-giving or death-dealing) *means in psychic reality* to a unique individual, and it is always wise to take the cultural dimension of the patient seriously into account.

## Deintegration as Regression in the Service of the Self

Deintegration is an indispensable part of individuation. It is one of the natural or "nuclear processes" of transformation and symbolic rebirth requiring the psychological experience of abandonment (cf. Plaut 1966). We can say the ego is required to give up some of its executive functions. Deintegration facilitates or impedes both ego integration and self-realization throughout life (Gordon 1979). An active period of deintegration is a spontaneous and often healing event. As a symbolic expression of forces latent in the objective psyche, the process occurs on the side of life or on the side of death. Periods of deintegration are characterized by affectively charged states in which self objects predominate over real objects. It could also be said in relation to Bion's theories (1962, 1963, 1965) that deintegration is prior to alpha functioning and that it makes alpha functioning possible. During deintegration, alpha elements are being created out of beta elements by alpha function. Alpha elements give way to thoughts, dreams, and fantasies. Deintegration, as such, is reflected in the analytic process by dreams of crowds, swarming crowds of humans or non-humans. It is often depicted as a procession, or the active forming and breaking up of people organized and on the move. It occurs in archetypal images of festivals (Willeford 1981) ceremonies, parades, and religious rituals. My countertransference reaction to such dreams is often a flashback to some parade or crowd sequence in a Federico Fellini movie. Jung describes these intrapsychic phenomena at length in *Symbols of*

*Transformation.* Here he notes that Miss Miller's "dream-poem" anticipates a psychotic break:

> The vision that follows the birth of the hero is described by Miss Miller as a "swarm of people." We know that this image symbolizes a secret, or rather, the unconscious. . . . I have often noticed that the symbol of the crowd, and particularly of a streaming mass of people in motion, expresses violent motions of the unconscious. Such symbols always indicate an activation of the unconscious and an incipient dissociation between it and the ego.
>      The vision of the swarm of peopole undergoes further develop-ment . . . fundamentally, the idea of the swarming crowd is an expres-sion for the mass of thoughts now rushing in upon consciousness. (Jung 1956, pars. 300–302)

Following the Jungian interest in initial dreams and in the dream series, I have noticed in clinical work that crowds of people on the move are often anticipated by other dreams in which swarms of apes, birds (thoughts), snakes, symbiotic insects (often before a psychotic break), and other nonhuman creatures feature prominent-ly. When human crowd dreams are preceded by herds, flocks, mobs, and masses of other moving creatures, it seems to imply individua-tion and forward movement in the analytic process—at least the real potential for such movement. Archetypal potential in dreams is, of course, only impersonal when it first begins to deintegrate. Al-though analysis may not always feel human, our work is, hopefully, always humanizing; therefore, formal archetypal material is person-alized and individualized within the analytic container, most signif-icantly with the analysis of the transference and in the presence of an analyst who is also experienced as being reliable, alive, and real.

It would seem, however, that such newly activated archetypal contents in the psyche could remain in a relatively "low" or unde-veloped state. They may be split off from the integrative functions of the ego and any living interpersonal connection with the dreamer's process of individuation, if the transference remains unanalyzed, especially preverbal nuclear events in the earliest years of life before language and secondary process (directed thinking) develop. That is why I analyze persons, not dreams, in the analytic setting. For individuation in a personal sense to happen the analysis of infancy and childhood is important for the assimilation of the shadow.

In relation to alchemy, the crowd as a *massa confusa* could be explored in terms of personality development requiring successive abandonments of the old which is rooted in less individualized soil.

Moreover, it is possible to explore crowd figures in relation to sandplay therapy.

In following the synthetic work of the unconscious in a series of 59 dreams and visualizations, Jung (1936) looks at many themes in "Individual Dream Symbolism in Relation to Alchemy," especially the spontaneous appearance of mandalic images of the self. For my purposes, it is important to note that (1) the motif of the crowd in one form or another, such as a "swarm" of people, appears repeatedly (at least 27 times), and tells us a great deal in images about the individual's level of ego consciousness, and (2) these repetitions seem to appear in spiral-like patterns suggesting regression/progression—deintegration of the primary self. I was amazed to go through these dreams, dream by dream, only to see that the whole series can be said to reflect integration-deintegration-integration.

The most common settings for deintegrative activities in the dream are, in my experience, railway stations, audiences, churches, airports, hotels, resorts, hospitals, boats/arks—places where people potentially come and go. There is a clear alternation of these crowd/group dreams with symmetrical mandalic self imagery such as the square, the circle, the round (globe), etc., and many other containing environments. In my view these events in a dream series lend support to the theory of deintegration.

Healthy deintegration in the analytic situation depends on a good holding environment (*temenos*) which facilitates the ego's capacity to give up control and on the capacity to be alone in the presence of the trusted analyst. It also depends on the ability to relax, form symbols, and go with the flow of things. One must be able to let things happen in the psyche. Deintegration, like individuation, may also look and feel like a series of spirals: "two steps forward and one back." The spiral is a second dream-motif reflecting deintegration (Russack 1984).

In *Symbols of Transformation*, Jung (1956) underlined the positive value of regression of ego-consciousness, in contrast with then-current Freudian theory. Early in his career, Jung stressed the teleological function of symbolic interpretation *in addition* to causal-reductive analyses. "Living symbols" look forward in time, as well as backward. He felt that growth during analysis was possible only through regression of the ego to the very deepest levels of the unconscious psyche. Here powerful integrative forces urged not only compulsive repetition of previously experienced personal and archetypal conflicts, but future-oriented self-actualization as well. This was a major difference between the two greatest pioneers of psychoanalysis.

Jung's early stand in 1911 in *Symbols of Transformation* on the need for regression to archaic object relationships and to innate primordial modalities of the autonomous, unconscious psyche outside the comprehension of the ego relate directly to his emphasis on growth *and* repair (i.e., an analytic method which is both reductive-reconstructive and synthetic). The central issue raised above turns on Jung's definition of libido or psychic energy—a general force that invests mental processes and structures.

## Grace: Abandonment Loss in the Earliest Phase of Development

Grace, a very attractive, intelligent, and sensitive young woman of 37 began analysis three times a week nearly five years ago. She reported feeling "extra, like a clone, like I don't really fit anywhere or count for real in my family. I feel cut off from everybody. Lonely. They make me feel excluded and abandoned. I might look OK from the outside, but I feel like the living dead and all confused inside about just how I really am."

It is unfortunate for Grace that all fun and carefree abandon are equated automatically with early traumata and the fateful disappearance of a parental figure. Although there are many factors in development which help determine the formation of major inhibitions to let go and enjoy life, it is rooted in infancy when the achievement of basic trust and object constancy result in clear intrapsychic structural representations of self and others. For Grace things did not go well enough, and as a premature baby she was unable to found a strong belief in good-enough mothering which would allow her to trust and depend on anyone outside herself without tremendous anxiety. Nor did she learn early in life to trust in her own sense of goodness long enough to let go; as a result, she finds it hard to recognize her own ability to contribute positively to the analytic situation. Moreover, primitive early experiences in life are mediated through the body ego at a time when the somatic pole of the archetypes holds sway. Symbolic equations precede the capacity to form living symbols. For example, the eyes=breast=mother equation of part object psychology may be persecuting in paranoid psychosis, but life-giving in the tune "Drink to Me Only With Thine

Eyes." The mouth=anus equation and the geography of the body with its interchangeable zones is very important in infancy to the apperception of reality imagined to exist inside and outside oneself, especially the interest about what is going on inside mother's body. It was extremely difficult for Grace to "get into" me as a person, or "into" the analytic process. As one might predict, she did it by nibbling slowly—first starting with three hours a week, adding a fourth hour suddenly after a year. As development proceeds, the infant must develop the psychic equivalency of skin, become more and more "thick skinned" with boundaries between inside and outside. These are hard-won achievements, but with more inner and outer experiences of "good fit" the infant learns to trust and to let go of paralyzing anxieties and fears. The healthy infant can be observed to feed, pause, turn away playfully from the breast to babble, coo, gaze about refreshed, and finally relax or go off to sleep (cf. Henry 1984; Sidoli 1983, 1984).

Grace says she has "always" felt abandoned by her mother, feeling she had been left to die in the secure but emotionally arid substitute—an "incubator mother." Later in life she felt abandoned by her father, who got very close sexually and was personal but suddenly withdrew in a punishing way when she was eight years old. Today they almost never talk. In analysis painful dread of abandonment and the wish to live with more carefree abandon feature prominently. She has always felt abandoned because she is a prematurely born identical twin, but also because she and not her twin sister fell ill to the point of death soon after birth. Only Grace remained close to death day after day for weeks and was placed in an incubator alone for six to eight weeks. After we had done a great deal of reconstructive work ourselves in the analysis, Grace requested objective information about the events of her birth. Her mother confided in her cautiously and nervously that she went to the hospital at first, but after the separation, "It became too distressful for words—so I gave up hope for you." Grace's mother stopped visiting the hospital after only one visit, although she herself was a nurse.

For long stretches of her analysis, I have had to be content to do nothing else but hold and carry Grace's own potential hope for a good life: feeling herself to be not false, but truly alive and real in the world as an individual who counts. It was double jeopardy for Grace to be an identical twin; it complicated matters, as she could easily avoid the growing pains of developing her own individuality and live, as she reported, "in the shadow of my twin sister." She and her sister have almost exactly the same names; early in analysis she often referred to herself as "we."

For Grace it was not easy to be in touch with her own goodness because things got off to a slow and very painful start. Her mother reports recently that while Grace was in the incubator she saw "the shadow pass over" Grace. Under severe stress and despair the mother's fear of death changed into a conscious wish for Grace's death and indeed she gave up on her for dead and began to mourn and detach herself emotionally. It would appear that until this day Grace's very survival and continued existence activate intense persecutory guilt and anxiety in the mother who can barely look at her daughter's body without remembering that she once "gave up."

Grace is the first born of identical twins, the eldest child in a Roman Catholic family of 12 children where the father was chronically alcoholic, suffering "uncontrollable fits of rage." Grace refers to him as her "saving grace, like the incubator, but also bad for me in the end. He was my personal connection to the outside world, but he just went away." Her twin sister fared better at birth although she, too, was premature, and she continued to receive the benefits of better maternal feedback because of her mother's need to split in handling her anxiety: Grace became the "bad" daughter, "too emotional"—she could not express her deepest sadness ever to her mother, and when they had a few "heart to heart talks," Grace recalls that they took place in the bathroom alone with her. Whereas Grace had had tubes and needles poked into her and was force-fed, her sister was not so ill and came to be treated as if she were the mother's "good" preferred parts, the valued part of herself. Grace was, on the other hand, the depository for all the "bad" and devalued parts of the mother's intrapsychic life. Grace says she does not deserve love and she herself confuses feeling shitty with being shit.

Throughout her life Grace has been able to control her mother to get what little she can by mobilizing the mother's guilt. In analysis, too, her depressions contain a lot of attack. At times being oppositional tests to see that I am there for her, or she tries to point the wagging "If-it-weren't-for-you . . . " finger at me and to capitalize on any guilt I may feel (e.g., arriving late to a session). Her most common response is to become apathetic and to spare me any unpleasant confrontations. But of course these experiences of sparing me only make her feel more destructive and unable to depend on me. Attacking me with a depression to get what she wants is different from receiving love freely because one feels good and worth it. As a twin and as the only child in her family whose very existence seems curious and weird, painful, and because she has become associated with anxiety and guilt, she conveniently became the family scapegoat, feeling "cut-off," unwanted and "extra . . . like I'm not supposed to be alive with any real problems and pains." From the beginning Grace was a sparing child, polite and perfectionistic, and in analysis she is now at a point when she does not need to spare me negative feelings. Most important of all are the moments when she is feeling plunged into the "shadow" of death and can share her profound sadness with me. As she learns to tolerate her own sadness more consciously, the quality of her suffering has changed and she is becoming less apathetic about life and relationships, including sexual life. She has become more thick-skinned and less depressed. Fordham's work on infant observations shows clearly that a baby can be seen to develop patterns of sparing the vulnerable mother from a very early age (see baby N discussed by Fordham, above, in this volume). I have deeper insights and feel enriched by what Grace has had to learn—the more conscious suffering of psychic pain. In life the stages of suffering have to be endured as much as the highs.

In her second year of analysis Grace's father introduced her at a social gathering (a baptism) as "this thing." I could say in a nutshell that Grace's need to know that I wouldn't abandon her included knowing that I would not give up the work of her analytical life no matter how emotional she got or how rough the periods sometimes felt. At these awful down periods she is identified with the archetypal image of the abandoned child and needs to locate the hopeful part of herself in me for safekeeping. That part of herself in me which can see hope, "find" her goodness and acknowledge her positive contributions to the analytic process, is now more a part of herself in everyday life. It needs to be acknowledged as often as her internal rage and destructive parts. It is hard for her to "get into" me and her analytical life, just as it was so hard with her mother and her life after birth. She expects persecution and rejection from the outside world, which, when generalized, includes men, the "world of the fathers," and everything experienced as "not-mother." In childhood she felt very powerful but destructive, and her other solution was to opt for relationship situations where she could feel safe ("not make any waves") but unstimulated and dehumanized, like in the incubator. By means of idealization, splitting, and especially primitive denial, Grace can close her eyes to the reality of pain and displeasure; she will give up her freedom for security, although incubator=mother security implies lack of a human personal fit with me or somebody else by working through conflicts and knowing she loves and is loved. In her words, "The incubator= mother is always secure and always the same." The incubator= mother in her mind does not listen to Grace. She repeats blandly, while lying rigid on the couch time after time in the past, that she feels "cut off" or "tuned out" by life, and that her mind (psyche) feels disconnected from her body (soma).

During a period of intense deintegration, with crowd dreams in which separation from her twin sister and mother were represented, she said:

G: There's something wrong with my sense of myself. I'm real unhappy. I'm feeling real unhappy from deep inside. I don't want you to be mad at me for that. With this despair I feel so unloved. I know it has to do with not loving myself.

R: I think you're mixing me up with the mother in your mind who doesn't ever want to hear very sad things, but then you pay an awful price for sparing me because you go away feeling unheard, unloved—like you didn't get through to me "for real."

G: I guess I agree, and I am feeling very wounded today. I see the image of a sobbing child because there's so much unhappiness. I complain a lot to you because I don't want you to see how I really hurt—that part, my sad pain, the despair. When I feel the despair right now it feels so total, like complete loss, total abandonment. I just feel so unhappy at the very center of things. It affects everything else. (Grace moves only both hands upwards with a flick of her wrists and continues more self-assertedly.) Wait! There's a lot of things I want to say. Like its not being my own fault. I feel like I need to talk with you today but that I really shouldn't be here at all! I wonder if I'm getting through to you today. I know my part in it. I suppose I'm unhappy for not doing enough. I'm disappointed in myself. I don't want you to be disappointed in me for not allowing myself to be good enough to do something in my life.

R: Sounds like right now you're mixing yourself up with the disappointed mother who felt so sad when she had a sick

twin for a first child. She was an only child herself. Or do you
confuse me with your sister who wished you were somebody
else for her twin? Both hate your body, as you do, when you
think of hurting yourself with things.

G: I know that as I get through to you more and more and feel
better I also feel more upset and scared. I realize then—
when I feel closer and more personal with you—that I have
always felt so confused on a deep level. I know you're about
to say it's the end of the hour, and that it's Friday so I don't
want you to leave me. It's so sad. Over the weekend I've lost
you. I don't care about anything. I don't know. I just seem to
want to give up and die. I feel real close to death all the
time. I find it hard to win. I feel hopeless on Fridays and
think I'm going to die. Our work makes me so mad because
it makes me aware that I need other things. Oooops! There I
go again calling you a thing, as if you were the incubator=
mother and not a person. I still get confused about things
and people being different. I always felt I should have died,
but just now I remembered how you once said something to
me with hope and I felt more true and more definite to me.

After a period of working through material related to separation
from a mother who expected her to live as a disappointment to
herself, Grace began to take her body more seriously. There had
been a marked differentiation of the sensation and feeling functions,
as well as a sorting out of zonal confusions.

Last week a crowd dream announced the timely arrival of new
"foreign" potentials—alien, no doubt, to the ego, but potentially
enriching from afar. "A bunch of tourists have just come into town
to see the special events. I take an interest in seeing them." These
undifferentiated part personalities of Grace move from outside to
inside—a potential major advance for Grace, depending on how
further deintegration processes proceed. Of all the possibilities in
the universe, why did her unconscious choose the particular image
of tourists? For our work, the absence of paranoid anxiety in this
dream is most striking. The "outside" represents everything not-
mother in the "men's world." The masculine is no longer represented only as dangerous, murderous, and frightful. A movement from
dyadic object relations to triadic object relations raises the hopes
for further deintegration involving personal human relationships.
Triadic object relations open the possiblity for her to experience

Hades, as in the myth of Demeter-Persephone, as a seminal force in her everyday life.

## Analytic Interaction

I will turn to the experience of Grace's fourth and last hour of her analytic week with me before I left for a holiday. After three weeks of vacation we were to move to another office nearby. It was a Thursday when Grace walked with determination into my office, put her rather large pocketbook on a chair near the analytic couch, and lay down. She smacked her lips and moved her mouth, but otherwise her body remained still. She began by telling me how hungry she felt today:

G: I want you to speak a lot to me today. I feel abandoned by you when you are quiet. It's like I have to check it out, when you're silent. It's not even what you say. It's your tone of voice or something. Oh! It's because I miss it. . . . (Silence) When you are quiet it feels like you might be angry or that you disapprove of me. I feel upset and I find it real hard to contain it. Work on it and things like that. . . . (Grace cries softly) . . . I know it's like (Silence). . . . Ohh. . . . (Silence) Hmm. . . .

R: It seems hard for you to get something out right now. It feels like we're at a place again where you want to spare me.

G: No. . . . (Sighs deeply)

R: Please give words to that sigh.

G: (After a long silence) I think I'm upset about my body. I can't explain it. I sorta think you think I don't care about my body. It's not true.

R: What makes you say that to me right now?

G: I get that impression.

R: What gives you the impression that I think you don't care about your body?

G: Because I don't talk about it. I don't seem to move a lot on the couch.

R: Seems you brought up a good point yeaterday when you said you felt your body to be split off from your mind, probably since you were a baby.

G: It doesn't feel like it's *my* body. First there's the fact that I'm in pain and I don't really want to know it's mine. Then there is G. (Grace's identical twin), and how do I know it's even my own body? Then there's the fact that I thought it (*sic*) belonged to my body. When I get in touch with it and feel it's mine I get hysterical. I can't. It's real hard for me. Does that make sense to you?

R: Oh yes. That makes a lot of sense. (I am continuing the theme of active acknowledgment of her capacity to make a positive contribution to the analytical intercourse, based on her infancy, and begun in the earliest part of the hour, her having made a "good point." At the same time, I do not attempt to fling compliments at her or pick up on trivia.)

G: I was thinking of the way my body is so stiff. Almost catatonic I was thinking yesterday. . . . I don't know where it comes from. . . . I think it comes from feeling in pain and separate. It's like I don't want to remember my body. You know we talked about that split in one of my early dreams, and that split—oh, in the basement of the house—that split's between my mind and my body (long silence). It has to do with my always feeling I don't belong anywhere.

R: When I go off on vacation I leave you with that awful feeling, don't I? The feeling that you are *no body* and "don't belong anywhere with *any body*." I think it must be very scary to come back and start again in my new office—to change spaces.

G: Yes. Yeah.

R: I can see again that you're very sensitive about inside spaces. I am wondering how you feel about your space and how you belong to it, or not.

G: I don't feel I could define the space I have as outside. The space I have is inside. You know—I just—I mean there are spaces where I am . . . outside . . . but. . . .

R: "Outside spaces." (To go with the experience of dyadic feedback, separation, and the capacity to bear separation, anxiety, and pain, my interventions and interpretations are deliberately frequent but not devouring.)

G: Yeah. Where I live, and here. And where I work, but I don't know. It seems like our space here is important to me. But I don't know. I'm not sure. I'm not sure I create spaces for myself outside. I mean obviously I exist in different spaces, but . . . I'm probably least comfortable in spaces outside. I can say that outside myself in some way, not just in outside rooms. (Grace moves her feet and toes a little.)

R: Sounds like you're longing again for the comfort and security of the incubator=mother space during our separation. Union with me.

G: Exactly. Isn't that what I'm saying. It's a space that only involves me. But that's not the same either, because all of this I'm going through over your vacation is also missing you. So it's not the same (silence). I'm sure in some ways being in an incubator was good for me, like a saving grace (note that Grace talks only of her father and the earliest not-mother incubator experience as both being a "saving grace" in her life). Maybe I feel like I have that incubator space here. But I have also had you with all the feelings too. It's been here like it was there. I can remember things. But I can feel held by you. It feels quiet and self-contained here without a lot of noise and distractions. It seems ideal. It's probably why I feel reluctant. Because we're changing the space. But I wouldn't want to stay here without you. That would be very lonely. See what I mean?

R: Yes. That's an important point—that you'd miss me as a person.

G: It seems very mother-child, those times. You know (silence) . . . good mothering, I guess. . . .

R: What makes you say that?

G: That's how I feel about my time here. Like going back to trying to make it a little bit different from how it started for me. I don't know. It's not easy, is it?

R: Sounds like you are afraid you're being too hard on me again.

G: No. (Silence) What's different is that I'm not a baby. So I want to take a lot of things from you but I also want to give you things. I'm probably afraid I'll take too much. I don't want this to be one-sided.

R: I think you feel good right now because you hear me writing and that I value your words. It feels like you are making a positive contribution here, like giving good feedback to me. Then it can feel two-way, and not like in your family as a twin.

G: Yes. I mean why should I want it to be one-sided? Suppose I could but it's not my way. (Silence) I suppose—I don't know exactly what I'm trying to say today—suppose I'm trying to balance things a little bit more for myself. None of this changes my sad feelings—that I need you—but—I don't know. . . .

R: Yes, of course. Somehow I don't have a problem hearing that sadness.

G: Somehow it's not the end of the world. It's not going to destroy me. I suppose that's what I'm saying. I'm saying I could leave this space. I don't know. It's hard to leave and not know I can come back to this place. You take precedence over this place. It's not like you and this place are the same. If I leave this place it doesn't mean I leave you. But still I do feel I need the security of this place. I guess I'm saying it'll be all right.

R: I hear hopefulness and not just abandonment or sparing.

G: Um-hum.

Grace then talked without any comment from me about no "guarantees in life" and feeling "boxed in." In the remainder of the hour, she reported the following dream with associations to running and wishes for physical (including sexual) merger with me before a major separation:

Dream: *I'm running along this road. It was like years long. There was a male presence around, at the end. I cried toward the end which was about one-third of the way. I had this object in my hand and it was all wet from my crying so I had given it to this man.*

   Associations: I cried in the last part of it. Not my whole life, but it was a year long. I can't figure out what it was, the object I was carrying.

R: I think this week of analysis and analysis as a whole feel like a long run to you, and that I am present in the dream as the male figure who—like your Dad—can hold and handle your sad feelings and accept your tenderness.

G: I like to run down a country road by myself with no one else around. A big open space. Then it's all mine. There's no sense of loneliness when I run. I like the freedom of running by myself. I tend to be least aware of the outside when I run in an open space. . . . It's there but it's not separate. . . . One of the best feelings I have. Like body and mind working together. Just keep running. It's not pain-free, but your spirit needs to keep running and you don't want to stop. You finally stop because your body gets painful and exhausted, but you get above all that and feel good. I tend to get tired after about twenty minutes. It's the last ten to fifteen minutes I push to keep going. . . . I've done it for a long time. It's sort of like company for me to do it. It doesn't feel any different from when I began.

R: It feels the same.

G: I never feel alone when I run—even though I do. Not lonely. It's maybe like being in the incubator right after birth, by myself for six to eight weeks, but not alone in some way. Yes, running is like being in an incubator: no feedback, it all feels like one inside/outside. I do block out what's different. I keep running to stay alive, take another breath, I am left feeling totally alone with myself. I don't care about other people. I block them out.

## Consequences of Sparing in the Analytic Situation

I want to mention four consequences of sparing, with special reference to the beginning stages of an analysand's analytical life. The term "sparing" refers to an early life pattern developed in order to spare the mother. This pattern comes into the therapeutic relationship in many important ways. I will mention only four of them.

The major consequence of sparing is that the baby part of the analysand feels forced to fall back on his or her own resources. There is no opportunity to experience a "toilet breast=mother." The baby needs a toilet breast=mother so that he or she can flush out bad, shitty feelings. The patient needs to feel that dreadful anxieties are contained and valued. Anxieties are again and again "pushed into" the analyst to see what the analyst does with them. It is important that the analyst hold the anxieties firmly and empathically. Anxieties, fears, and associated archetypal imagery (introjected deintegrates of the patient's primary self) are metabolized by the analyst who responds, not always with words, and keeps the process feeling framed or contained. While sparing, the baby loses because it fails to get what it needs in terms of affirmation of creative aggressive impulses.

With massive projective identification and especially the withdrawal from active object relations, the baby loses everything. All the mother=analyst's good stuff is felt to be lost, along with fears of "losing it all." The baby loses weight, food, and feces. In extreme situations, by hallucinating a good breast, the thumb is used to "hold on."

Grace and I also refer to a specific aspect of the incubator= mother part of her mind as "the air breast mother." This is the mother who knows and understands everything by reading Dr. Spock a few times, but experiences nothing much at the gut level.

The air breast offers some kind of security, but like the incubator, it offers security without the guts, without the feeling, without the real milk. Individuals for whom the caregiving air breast experience is an important part of the mothering they received always look for what is real, and not for the air breast mother, in analysis. They are keenly sensitive to the analyst's moods and inauthentic gestures when they occur; they use the word "real" and "really" much more than others. They crave the "palpable" in their analytical lives, not air. The Bible also speaks of "the sincere milk of the Word."

Today there are many culturally patterned images of such an air breast mother, including the TV ("the boob tube") and also the automated express banking stops, where the illusion of an ever-bountiful breast is allowed to persist. By imposing limits on instant cash withdrawal, the air breast mother bank sets limits on greed. "Working" the machine requires complicated eye-hand coordination to get what one wants from the insides. Reflecting part object psychology, these bank stops are potentially addicting. Finally, like the incubator, the feedback from the express automated teller is not humanizing, even though everyone is given a "personal" number.

Grace needs to have "real" and embodied, mindless instinctual experiences in her analytical life. Like criticisms of the TV, analytical intercourse based on "air breasting it" is felt to lack "substance" or "the cream." Grace put it well, and remorsefully: "You know. My mother's not real for me. I can tell the difference right away between real and not real. It's like her heart is not in it for me. No heart."

A second consequence of the sparing pattern is that the mother=analyst begins to look worse and worse. With this perception of a depleted and impoverished source of life comes awful fears of completely emptying out the breast=mother. Nothing at all would be left. The loss of a living human connection would be death. In this state a patient might not use the analyst or expect much at all from the analytic breast.

A third consequence comes about because the father may have taken over in responding to the gentleness and tenderness of the baby. Patients report that "father is also mother." The father in this way can become the good breast. In infant observations, he gets the smiles.

Does the baby turn to the father out of resentment? If so, this can pose serious problems to the formation of a good therapeutic alliance, since every alliance in the patient's unconscious is equated with a hostile, murderous alliance against the mother. There are many other clinical manifestations of this attempted solution, especially later at the oedipal level.

Finally, continued sparing of the analyst leads to the feeling that the unused milk of the analysis has gone bad and soured. When a mother is drying out, the taste of her milk does change. It sours. Eventually the analyst's words feel "shitty" and contaminated, his interpretations are rejected as "poisonous," and the analyst incarnates the archetypal image of the bad breast.

In many analyses, the analysis of oral envy is central because it represents a self-destructive attack against the source of life itself. Moreover, oral envy seems to be activated and exacerbated by sparing. Because of the intense activation of oral envy, a sour grapes attitude toward analytical life develops, and this devaluation takes its toll. Of course, the unconscious wish to be totally unsparing toward the analyst's personality is the other side of sparing. Every analyst who has ever been "chewed out," "spit up," and attacked with a barrage of "biting" remarks knows what it feels like to be "gnawed down" and "cut up" like this in the delusional negative transference. The analytic breast is not taken in and digested. If left unanalyzed, the analytic breast will become so depreciated by destructive baby parts that the patient will want to turn away altogether in despair: "It's no good. So who needs you or analysis anyway?" It is not possible to enjoy life with such an attitude, and growth in analysis cannot proceed if the patient cannot use the symbolic *material* from the analytic breast. It is impossible at times to avoid a negative therapeutic reaction because envy has gained the upper hand.

## Typical Reactions to Separation-Abandonment

There are so many things one could say about Grace's life and analysis, her dreams, her progress, and especially her very difficult beginnings. To sum up the points which are most germane to our theme, I would include the following observations on Grace. To some extent they also relate in general to all abandonment losses in the earliest phases of human development.

When the care of another person is not forthcoming, Grace taught me how the baby part of her mind felt:

1. It would react with bodily feelings to mental pain. Even more than usual, analysis for this analysand must include archetypal experiences that feel *embodied* and down to earth so that her original splitting off of the hated body can be integrated and healed via mindless experiences.

2. It would substitute things for people, especially when they offer comfort, safety, order, and reliability. Personal intimacy could enrich her life, but still the attempts to escape from freedom prevail along with fantasies of finding bliss in mediocrity. The demands of life weigh on her. This is especially true since at such an early stage the mother or breast is felt to be so literal and concrete a need-satisfying object. The sorting out of zonal confusions in early life is similar to the same task in the beginning phase of analysis and connected intimately to sparing. When Grace withdraws and is "tight assed," she is also "tight lipped," lest anything shitty come out of her mouth=anus. The interchangeability of things with people for security partakes of part-object interchangeability of people to satisfy narcissistic needs. Moreover, things remain under one's control and are collectible, unlike people, who if allowed to be separate, can go away.

3. It would not depend on anyone else in a close way, because the "feeder" could go away or change suddenly. This includes the perfectionist need to do everything by herself without help from me and others. The "feeder" analyst giving feedback could in fantasy attack, counterattack, devour, or contaminate in some way. Or worse, the "feeder" analyst could become inconsistent. In addition to feeling abandoned and left at the mercy of the incubator=mother and all the emotional superficiality and sterile emptiness this implies, Grace is also left feeling at the mercy of frightening unconscious fantasies universally associated with infancy in the paranoid-schizoid and depressive positions: the fear of death, falling to bits and pieces, dismemberment. The fears are of somehow being destroyed and damaged, especially the paranoid fears of being devoured and absorbed by the mother=analyst, or of being poisoned and contaminated by the same. The other depressive side of the coin for Grace is feeling unlovable and fearing her own internal aggression. At these times, fears of closeness and mutuality (includ-

ing sex) are fears of destroying or damaging the loved object, by over-using or poisoning, or simply by feeling strong (in Grace's case simply "too emotional" with her parents). Grace had to gain insight into why she was so sparing and to see how self-defeating it was for her.

4. It would feel narcissistic depletion, emptiness inside with intense longing. This state leads to severe distress, and to harmful interference with a basic loving investment of one's own body image and the development of object relations. Before analysis Grace remained identified with the inner image of the dead (abolished) part object mother and incubator=mother, or with the damaged mother who was not only very vulnerable but disappointed with Grace's existence on earth. This is the nonplussed, depressed mother, who herself was fatherless in childhood with no siblings and had a conflictual relationship with her own mother. Grace's maternal grandmother had had twins who died before Grace's mother was born, and this psychological event undoubtedly contributed to Grace's mother's dread and reaction to Grace's birth and difficulties. It is the mother who could not or would not give her new baby hope in ongoing life, color, movement, and instinctual interchange. Grace is now less unconsciously identified with the mother who hates her twin body and with the reminders that she was "a bad mother" who gave up in disappointment, feeling inadequate as a woman while in unbearable pain. In psychic reality each of us must feel that goodness triumphs over badness, love over hate. The individual baby must accumulate enough good objects to outweigh the bad ones in order to feel alive and creative.

5. It would feel in touch always with a conscious deep sadness, but not necessarily depression, since in infancy the opportunity to consolidate the mother imago experiences did not occur. In a sense there will never be a replacement for the lost mothers of pre- and post-incubator times. Grace had needed support to fill up on while mourning the original losses: Despair, weepiness, and desperate crying are expected, and all feelings must be prized in the analytic setting.

6. It would be prone to utilize paranoid-schizoid mechanisms of defense because closeness is imagined to include mutual damage and destruction.

7. It would turn away from life with an attitude of sour grapes, derived from strong oral envy, or to detach and turn away in apathy. Grace resists archetypal deintegration with apathy, which is marked

by an absence of conscious suffering. We know that apathy can affect total body libido and lead to limited motoric discharge and even death (Spitz 1965). Grace's apathy and turning-away responses dulled her appetite for life, as well as the gradual loss of mobility, speech, and interest in the world at large. After protest came despair, and after despair came detachment. In this state of mind Grace fails to respond to me in analysis; she shows no sign of unhappiness or suffering and remains aloof, remote, and apathetic. At these times it is my job as the analyst to uncover in a most personal way the underlying affect (deep sadness) or ideational content, or both. To assist conscious recognition by interpretation is helpful, but not more than the frequent use of intuition and empathy to understand the preoedipal nature of her problems. It is also crucial in cases such as this to support the analysand's tasks of mourning, especially to feel and express great sadness.

8. It would use depression as an attack (can include pouting, sulking, etc.). There is a lot of attack in depression, and as Freud (1957) noted long ago (1917), there is often the wagging finger: "If it weren't for you . . . ." Since depression is a form of anger, it can be used skillfully to inspire guilt and control another, but at one's own expense in the end.

9. It would fear her own destructiveness and killing off the symbolic analytical baby, the pregnancy of analysis. Grace tends to accept the internal blame always for murdering the "baby" (potential for growth) in any process or relationship. This pattern was exacerbated by her mother's having 12 other children, along with several miscarriages that were denied totally within the family system. Grace also denied the unconscious significance of her mother's miscarriages because she felt intense blameworthiness. For this reason, she would stay masochistically in bad situations or relationships, unable to recognize that *things can go wrong naturally, with nobody to blame.*

10. It would cling for security to the omnipotent illusion that, based on her incubator=mother experiences, she could always manage a very difficult situation all on her own—without helpful feedback from other people. Grace automatically imagines that she must handle everything by heself. In attempting to do this, her life became constricted, neat and tightly packaged. To maintain this illusion she had to resort to extreme pathological introversion, again turning away from life. On the positive side, Grace has more perseverence than most people if she needs it, and she often can manage

very complicated situations on her own. In a work context she is a tremendous asset, because she also has a love of simplicity.

## References

Abraham, K. 1924. A short study of the development of the libido, viewed in the light of mental disorders. In *Selected papers on psychoanalysis*, pp. 418–80. London: Hogarth Press (originally published 1942).

Bion, W. R. 1962. *Learning from experience*. London: Heinemann.

_____. 1963. *Elements of psychoanalysis*. London: Heinemann Books.

_____. 1965. *Transformations*. London: Heinemann Books.

Elkin, H. 1972. On selfhood and the development of ego structures in infancy. *The Psychoanalytic Review* 59(3):389–416.

Fordham, M. 1961. Comment on the theory of the original self. *Journal of Analytical Psychology* 6(1):78–79.

_____. 1963. The empirical foundation and theories of the self in Jung's works. *Journal of Analytical Psychology* 8(1):1–24.

_____. 1967. Active imagination-deintegration or disintegration? *Journal of Analytical Psychology* 12(1):51–66.

_____. 1969a. *Children as individuals*. New York: G. P. Putnam's Sons.

_____. 1969b. Technique and countertransference. *Journal of Analytical Psychology* 14(2):95–118.

_____. 1971. Primary self, primary narcissism and related concepts. *Journal of Analytical Psychology* 16(2):168–87.

_____. 1973. Maturation of ego and self in infancy. In *Analytical Psychology*, vol. I, pp. 83–94. London: Heinemann Medical Books.

_____. 1974. Defenses of the self. *Journal of Analytical Psychology* 19(2):192–99.

_____. 1976. The self and autism. *Library of Analytical Psychology*, vol. 3. London: Heinemann Medical Books.

_____. 1978. *Jungian psychotherapy*. New York: Wiley.

_____. Some thoughts on deintegration. Unpublished.

Freud, S. 1957. Mourning and melancholia. *Standard edition*, vol. 14, pp. 237–59. London: Hogarth Press. (Originally published in 1917.)

Gordon, R. 1979. Reflections on curing and healing. *Journal of Analytical Psychology* 24(3):207–17.

Henry, G. 1984. Reflections on infant observation and its applications. *Journal of Analytical Psychology* 29(2):155–70.

Hubback, J. 1983 Depressed patients and the conjunctio. *Journal of Analytical Psychology* 28(4):313–28.

Jung, C. G. 1930. The stages of life. In *The structure and dynamics of the psyche*. *Collected works*, vol. 8, pp. 387–404. Princeton: Princeton University Press, 1960.

_____. 1936. *Individual dream symbolism in relation to alchemy*. In *Collected works*, vol. 12, pp. 39–223. Princeton: Princeton University Press, 1953.

_____. 1940a. Concerning rebirth. In *Collected works*, vol. 9/i, pp. 113–50. Princeton: Princeton University Press, 1959.

_____. 1940b. The psychology of the child archetype. In *Collected works*, vol. 9/i, pp. 151–81. Princeton: Princeton University Press, 1959.

_____. 1956. *Symbols of transformation*. In *Collected works*, vol. 5. Princeton: Princeton University Press.

Klein, M. 1935. A contribution to the psychogenesis of manic-depressive states. In *Contributions to psycho-analysis*. London: Hogarth Press.

_____. 1957. *Envy and gratitude*. London: Tavistock Publications.

Lambert, K. 1981. *Analysis, repair and individuation*. London: The Society of Analytical Psychology.

Maduro, R. 1974. Artistic creativity and aging in India. *International Journal of Aging and Human Development* 5(4):303–29.

———. 1976. *Artistic creativity in a Brahmin painter community.* Research Monograph No. 14. Berkeley: University of California Center for South and Southeast Asian Studies.

———. 1980. Symbolic equations in crative process: reflections on Hindu India. *The Journal of Analytical Psychology* 25(1), 59-90.

———, and Wheelwright, J. 1983. Analytical psychology. In *Personality theories, research and assessment,* R. Corsini and A. Marsella, eds. Itasca, Ill: F. Peacock, pp. 125–88.

Plaut, A. 1966. Reflections about not being able to imagine. *Journal of Analytical Psychology* 11(2):113–34.

Rochlin, G. 1961. The dread of abandonment. In *The psychoanalytic study of the child,* vol. 16, pp. 451–70.

Russack, N. 1984. Amplification: The Spiral. *Journal of Analytical Psychology* 29(2):125–34.

Samuels, A. 1982. The image of the parents in bed. *Journal of Analytical Psychology* 27(4):323–40.

Sidoli, M. 1983. De-integration and re-integration in the first two weeks of life. *Journal of Analytical Psychology* 28(3): 201–12.

———. 1984. Analysis: A space for separation. *Journal of Analytical Psychology* 29(2): 139–54.

Spitz, R. 1965. *The first year of life.* New York: International Universities Press, Inc.

Stein, M. 1983. *In Midlife.* Dallas: Spring Publications.

Strauss, R. 1962. The archetype of separation. In *The archetype,* Proceedings of the second international congress of analytical psychology, Zurich. Basel and New York: S. Karger, 1964, pp. 104–12.

Willeford, W. 1981. Festival, communion and mutuality. *Journal of Analytical Psychology* 26(4):345–55.

Winnicott, D. 1954. The depressive position in normal emotional development. In *Through paediatrics to psychoanalysis.* London: Hogarth Press, 1975.

———. 1963. The development of the capacity for concern. In *The maturational processes and the facilitating environment,* pp. 73–82. London: Hogarth Press, 1972.

# Birth's Cruel Secret/O I am my own Lost Mother/To my own Sad Child

## Gilda Frantz

### Introduction

The most difficult aspect in writing this paper had to do with the recollection of my own abandonment as an infant. I was abandoned by my father. In the loss of that relationship, the maternal archetype was also damaged and not able to be carried by my mother. This early abandonment has shaped my life and has colored almost everything I have done in terms of creativity, ambition, and a desire to find ways to nurture myself. Children like me possess an early awareness, a knowing, that they are born into a difficult situation, and this may make them more cautious and watchful. These qualities can be an enormous help in later life if they do not cause isolation.

The Great Goddess came into my life through active imagination and dreams in analysis. She watched over me and helped nourish me. My relationship with the positive mother archetype clearly came about through my contact with a woman analyst. But

**Gilda Frantz,** M.A., is an analyst in private practice in Santa Monica, California. She is chairman of the Board of the C. G. Jung Institute of Los Angeles and is recent past president of that Institute. A founding editor of *Psychological Perspectives,* she is the author of "On the Meaning of Loneliness" in *From Chaos to Eros* (R. Lockhart, ed., 1976).

the relationship to the "good father" came with my marriage, and the nurturing masculine was as much the "lost mother" as was the feminine. I hope it is understood that in speaking of this "lost mother" I am speaking of that which nurtures us spiritually. I submit the following material with deep gratitude for all that the gods have given to me, both good and bad.

I chose the title from a scrap of paper I found in my late husband's desk. Its cryptic meaning was numinous and touched me in the place of my own experience of abandonment; it seemed a poetic image of the suffering child.

"'Child' means something evolving towards independence. This it cannot do without detaching itself from its origins: abandonment is therefore a necessary condition, not just a concomitant symptom" (Jung 1959, par. 287). There are some for whom the necessary condition of abandonment comes before they can integrate its purpose or meaning. There are those whose experience begins *in utero*, children whose mothers are ill or depressed or die in childbirth or have been abandoned or whose birth was unwanted. There are those mothers who are unwed and offer the child for adoption with great suffering and reluctance. The result of these fateful births is that the lives of child and parents are deeply affected (cf. Woodman 1984, p. 2). This is akin to being born into the archetype of the abandoned one, and this child has the fate of having to integrate the inner nurturing mother as well as the inner abandoned child at some point in his or her life. Orphans are particularly prone to this path as are children of narcissistically wounded mothers (Schwartz-Salant 1982, p. 168).

What about the child who did not suffer any of the above circumstances? This child's abandonment comes through the lack of special nurturing by a mother who is not capable of such. The child can feel abandoned even though the outer circumstances of his or her life imply the opposite. Fate intensifies the already intense relationship between parent and child. While the fate of a child is restricted to the parents, the fate of an adult is not limited to the parents (Jung 1961b, p. 152). In the case material about Anne which follows, I will say more about this.

**Fate and Abandonment**

We make certain decisions in life and can avoid this or that, or decide when to marry and whom, but even those decisions send us in a direction that can seal our fate. "Humanity may possibly draw the conclusion that only one side of fate can be mastered with rational intentions" (Jung 1956, par. 165). But again, the use of rational will is only one-half of the picture. The other half is a hurtling toward a destination which we did not choose and which we cannot change. The Stoics called that "the compulsion of the stars," or Heimarmene (ibid., p. 67n).

A common thread I can observe in the people I see analytically is fate. Some have difficult lives, and not all the difficulty is earned. It is not always something they have or have not done that causes them to be abandoned. Often it is the so-called accident of birth that determines their fate. The challenge is to see what each one of us can do with the raw material of life. Life itself is an experiment and, as Emerson put it, the more experiments we make, the better.

Abandonment is a fateful experience in which we feel we have no choice. We feel alone, as if the gods are not present. If we feel the gods are present and supportive, then we are not abandoned. The word abandonment means literally "not to be called." It is etymologically connected with the word "fate." Fate means "the divine word" and is from *fari* and *fatum*, meaning "to speak" (Shipley).

Who is it that either summons us or does not? Let us discuss the Fates. They were divine beings who determined the course in human lives and were called Moerae (Moira) by the Greeks and Fata by the Romans, as well as Parcae. The Fates were the daughters of Nyx and their names were Klotho, Lachesis, and Atropos. Klotho means the one who weaves the thread; Lachesis, the one who spins the thread; and Atropos, the one who is unyielding and cuts the thread. Homer repeatedly referred to these three in writing about the destinies allotted to man by the gods. The sisters were always represented as spinning, measuring, and cutting the thread of life. The word shroud is from the root "to cut" (Skeat). Though there are many contradictions as to whether the Fates did the gods' will, it is evident that even Zeus was bound by their decisions.

The Fates and the Erinyes have a connection. The Erinyes were called the Furies by the Romans and were born from earth fertilized by drops of blood from the castrated Uranus. Aeschylus described them as hideous and frightening, but in sculpture and paintings they are not thus depicted. In their deeds the Erinyes were not regarded as unjust or even malign, even though they were said to inflict punishment. The retribution they meted out was considered a protection of those that human law failed to protect, such as those who were injured by members of their own families (Tripp 1970, p. 246).

The three Graces are associated with the Erinyes and the Fates as well. They were the Eumenides, the kindly ones. The combination of terrible and benign is frequently found in chthonic deities. Spirits, demons, deities, as well as heroes, were thought to live in or beneath the earth, and their concern was with the dead or with the fertility of the earth. Many of the chthonic divinities combined these two functions of punishing and kindness, fertilization and death. Those spirits who lived in the earth where the dead were buried and crops arose inevitably came to be associated with both events (Tripp 1970, p. 257).

During the process of thinking about abandonment, I had a dream. The word used for fate in my dream was *bashart*, a Yiddish word meaning "that which is meant is meant." As Dr. Clara Zilberstein interprets it, *bashart* means it *has* to happen at a certain moment in time. It is a semi-mystical concept that has to do with who has been promised to a person, one's intended. There is a genuine affection for the word among Jewish people, and it implies a true acceptance of what God gives us, good or bad. For me it implied that the unconscious accepted the presentation of this material—that it was "meant"—and that it focused me upon my fate as a Jewish woman, wife, and widow as well as on my having to deal with "what was intended by the fates."

"Without necessity nothing budges, the human personality least of all. It is tremendously conservative, not to say torpid. Only acute necessity is able to rouse it" (Jung 1954, p. 173). Suffering and abandonment awaken us. Through the awesome pain of not being called, we may find a way to change what needs changing in our lives. Alchemy says it this way:

> [*Liquefactio*] is one of the ways of first dissolving consciousness and getting closer to the unconscious which plays a great role in alchemy as well. One of the beginning stages of the alchemical work is very often the *liquefactio*, the turning into liquid in order to undo the *prima materia* which is often hardened or solidified in a wrong way and therefore cannot be used to make the philosopher's stone. The minerals must first be liquefied. Naturally, the underlying chemical image is the extraction of a metal from its ore through melting, but *liquefactio* often has the alchemical connotation of a dissolution of the personality in tears and despair. (von Franz 1972, p. 124)

A flame applied externally to melt the metals is alternately raised and lowered in intensity. The raising and lowering of the flame is the agony of abandonment. The flame is Fate.

## Tears and Abandonment

In the practice of analytical psychology, it is a common experience to have a patient enter analysis in the stage where there is death and mourning. The condensation of these vapors comes in the form of tears.

In an unpublished paper on depression, Kieffer Frantz (1966) did a survey of the literature, which included the then-current psychoanalytic position. He wrote the following:

> These characteristics would seem to be the most consistent observable evidence of the presence of depression. Yet, if we are not to accept a pathological evaluation as being the only point of view, how are we to appraise the observable phenomenon of depression?
>
> Let us begin with the dream of a woman who began therapy in a depression. The dream was that the dreamer was crying and tears were rolling down her cheeks. As the tears were rolling, they gradually turned into diamonds. The tears would certainly seem to substantiate the characteristics of hopelessness, helplessness, sadness and internal suffering described above. But what of the diamonds? A definite change has occurred. In *Two Essays on Analytical Psychology*, Jung states, "This transformation is the aim of the analysis of the unconscious. If there is no transformation it means that the determining influence of the unconscious is unabated and that it will, in some cases, persist in maintaining neurotic symptoms in spite of all our analysis and all our understanding. Alternatively, a compulsive transference will take hold, which is just as bad as a neurosis" (Jung 1953, par. 342).
>
> The dream points to a process that begins with tears and changes or is transformed to diamonds, the "pure water." The depression from this point of view may be conceived as the descent into the Unconscious for the purpose of beginning the journey. Between the beginning and the ending there are many different stages and perhaps many depressions.

My interest in tears as a *creative* expression of abandonment began with my reading of the paper, when an acquaintance asked me to find the aforementioned reference to tears and diamonds. The tears are the expression par excellence of abandonment. But what about the diamonds?

Diamond means "invincible." It is also called "adamantine," and from this we get our word "adamant." While adamant means "a very hard substance," it also means "to tame," "to conquer" (Skeat 1978, p. 6). Metaphorically, nature has to suffer in order to produce a diamond because of the enormous pressure and heat the earth has to sustain to turn carbon into diamonds. In the dream, diamonds evolve from tears. Through the operation of *liquefactio*, the washing away of an encrusted and improperly hardened *prima materia*, jewels are revealed. Thus, the dreamer is given some hope that something valuable may result from her intense suffering.

The diamond body is the Self that is within each of us (Blofeld 1978). Consciousness of the Self shapes and polishes this diamond, and upon our physical death the body drops away and this diamond is revealed in all its dazzling beauty (von Franz 1972, p. 237). In the example used, the diamond is revealed through the process of depression, or *nigredo*, and "conscious suffering."

In writing about her long relationship with Jung, Hilde Kirsch says: "The most important gift Jung has given me, and hopefully to mankind, is the acceptance of suffering as a necessity." In her paper she quoted a letter he wrote to a friend about suffering: "Try to apply seriously what I have told you, not that you might escape suffering— nobody can escape it—but that you may avoid the worst—blind suffering." Jung also wrote about himself,

> I think that God in turn has bestowed life upon me and has saved me from petrification. Thus I suffered and was miserable, but it seems that life was never wanting and even in the blackest night . . . by the grace of God I could see a great light. Somewhere there seems to be a great kindness in the abysmal darkness of the Deity. (Kirsch 1975, p. 11)

The dreamer above had the experience of conscious suffering, not of blind suffering. She was aware of her suffering and possibly knew the cause. I was once told by a victim of a disaster that "without this I would have been an ordinary housewife, but this loss forced me to change and now I have developed into a deeper person."

The symbolism of tears and abandonment is found in myths where creation is formed out of tears or by crying. Creation is also brought about by the loneliness of the gods. There is a Baluba myth in which the tears of the animals soften the earth and provide a place for the seeds to grow and become shelter for the animals (von Franz 1972, p. 122). In the Grimm's fairy tale "The Handless Maiden," the daughter is sold to the devil and is saved by her tears. When the devil asks to buy everything behind the mill, the father, unaware that his only daughter is there, sells the property to him. This abandonment of the daughter and subsequent betrayal is what provoked the tears that ultimately save her.

Cinderella is also abandoned by her father. After the death of her mother, the father remarries and she becomes part of what today would be known as a "blended family." Her stepsisters are treated as more important than Cinderella. When the father asks the sisters what they want from town, they ask for precious and costly gifts. As an afterthought, he asks Cinderella, and she only desires a branch from a tree that brushes his hat as he rides home. He forgets all about her after buying the stepdaughters their gifts, but his hat does brush the branch, causing him to remember. Cinderella plants the branch and waters it daily with her tears. The tears nurture the branch and a tree grows up. A bird comes to the tree and grants Cinderella three wishes. This bird is the spirit of her dead (lost) mother. The story of Cinderella is a beautiful example of the sad child redeeming the lost mother and the abandoning father through her relationship to the Prince.

What has been spoiled by the mother can only be healed by the mother, and what has been spoiled by the father can only be healed by the father (*I Ching* 1950, p. 81). Relationship itself can often be the healing "father" and can heal a wounded child and be a nurturing parent. We think we find a father in a man, but he may also be a good mother. In the Boddisattva of Compassion (Blofeld 1978), Kuan Yin was masculine and remained so until the twelfth century, when He became a Goddess and feminine. The masculine offers its own kind of nurturing (Foy 1983).

"The one who hears the cries" is how Kuan Yin is known. This myth is an ancient affirmation of the existence of abandonment and suffering and healing. In Tibetan Buddhism there is the concept of Duhkah, which loosely translated means "suffering," but which can also mean "unsatisfactoriness" (Dalai Lama 1966, p. 142). Suffering, in the Buddhist tradition, is understood to be "within one's 'own' mind and body and when it is understood one will know true happiness." Duhkuh may be physical pain or mental anguish and it refers to the facts of "birth, old age, disease and death" and to human conditions common to all, like "grief, lamentation (crying out), pain, anguish and despair" (pp. 142–43).

Weeping often accompanies the sowing of corn. It is the weeping and bewailing the death of the fertility god that ensures his return in the spring (de Vries 1974). When we cry out in despair, we cry tears and hope that someone hears our cries. Water is the living power of the psyche. When weeping and water symbolism occur during analysis, it calls for a sense of containment and at the same time is a purifying experience.

Lily was in her 50s when she came to see me. Her adult life had been spent in having babies, and she had a family of 12 sons and daughters. She found time only for her husband's and children's

needs. She felt she had betrayed something within herself in sacrificing her inner child by mothering all those children. Everything
made her cry—happiness, sadness, anger, frustration. There were
times when it seemed she used an entire box of tissues within an
hour. The tears robbed her of a chance to express her feelings;
instead of talking, she wept. Her sad child had emerged.

Lily was an abandoned child in that her mother was so self-
involved that she was unaware of her daughter's true nature. I sat
with Lily through many, many hours of crying, as container for her
tears. One day I asked her a question: "Where do all these tears go?"
She looked up in amazement and began to describe a deep and vast
natural pool or lake that had become filled by her tears. She began a
dialogue with her tears, and these dialogues brought old and buried
memories up from the depths. Often she recalled wrongs done to
her (usually of omission) by parental figures or siblings. She wrote:
"I hear the water running down the stream. I locate its sight and
watch the flow of water. Its movement is suddenly obstructed by an
unforeseen obstacle . . . of several rocks falling, disturbing its
current and redirecting it toward a new challenge."

These dialogues between Lily's ego and the unconscious, depicted as her tears, were truly healing. I am not reproducing the
entire dialogue out of respect for the organic and on-going quality
of the relationship, but it was active imagination, as opposed to
unconscious fantasy. Contact with the unconscious through written
dialogue, to use one example of the ways to make this connection,
occurs when the ego makes way for the unconscious by lowering its
hold (voluntarily), thus allowing archetypal energies a voice (Dallett 1982, p. 176). This is how Lily was able to come to a deeper
relationship to her tears, by encountering them within herself.

Lily's sad child was a child of the "earth and of starry heaven"
(Harrison 1903, p. 574), and was parched and dry and needed the
water of memory. She needed to remember, to take what had been
dismembered and lost. By drinking her fill of the cold water of
Osiris (ibid., p. 575), she could speak to the inner lost mother of
her sadness and mourning.

## Abandonment and the Creative Child

Etymologically, the word *mourning* means "to remember" and
stems from the same root as *memory*. In mourning we are held in
the memory of what has been lost or abandoned until we have found

a replacement for it. Mourning occurs whether we have ever experienced actual death or not. Most of us enter analysis in a state of deep grief and mourning. Mourning and depression are the other names of abandonment.

Anne came into analysis when *I* was still feeling abandoned and in mourning over the loss of my husband. It was a synchronistic moment. Being in that state myself I could see that she, too, was mourning a loss. Her presenting complaint had to do with many fears about so-called little things. She was reclusive and inclined not to answer her phone. As her story came out, it became apparent that some years before she had suffered the loss of a cherished goal. Perhaps what was lost was the illusion of this possibility in her life.

She had studied to be an actress from the age of seven or eight. At a crucial point in her studies, when she was around twenty, she felt she just didn't have what it took to be an actress and gave it up. A teacher had said you had to be "tough" to be an actress, and she didn't feel tough enough. She had planned to study in New York with a famous acting coach, and with almost no reflection she swiftly gave up her dream. This termination of her career deeply wounded the inner child.

Anne's mother was a strong, opinionated woman, and Anne was under the influence of a powerful negative mother archetype. She was used to having others determine her destiny, but she didn't count on what the loss of her dream would mean to her. In the 1970s she became interested in drugs and found some comfort in them, but this was no solution. Although she was now out of college and had another career in teaching, she often contemplated suicide because of the lack of meaning in her life. She was, in a spiritual sense, half alive. She didn't know she was grieving for her lost ambition, her abandoned career; she only knew she thought about death a great deal. The neurotic perpetually hesitates entering into life and is inclined to avoid the "dangerous struggle for existence." Refusing to really experience life forces him/her to deny life and thus they "commit partial suicide" (Jung 1956, par. 165).

My own loss experience had changed me. When I went back to work after my husband's death, I found that a gauzy veil that had formerly existed had disappeared. The veil could be called a "professional attitude." Through my bereavement, an almost egoless state, my psyche was more permeable, more open to the unconscious. I was less defended and more "there." It was almost as though there were trails of smoke, like those from a Bushman's fire, that circled between Anne and me. I became conscious of the presence of the healing power of the mother for the inner child.

Anne's dreams were frightening to her, yet they showed me that she had the ego strength for the journey, and that the journey would take time. Gradually she began to consider the idea that the acting she loved and had given up so many years ago might be in her life in another form. The idea to work in amateur theater was repugnant, but she did like studying, so she enrolled in some classes with local teachers and began to enjoy the contact with the world of acting. Instead of feeling helpless and identified with the sad child, she was beginning to find the lost mother. She was beginning to nurture herself.

Rather than being related to her inner sad child's needs, Anne had been *identified* with the child. Her destiny was tied to her parents. She feared what would happen to her if they died. She feared abandonment. If she could accept her abandoned goal, she might begin a new relationship to the Self. Recently, she has begun to grow up and enter the adult world, a world she had always identified with death and dying and abandonment. It is not to say that now she is without fears, or that her life is "perfect," but she is more in it and more alive to possibilities yet unknown to her.

## Abandonment and Loss

One instance of the "sad child/lost mother" abandonment is widowhood. Occasionally, we wounded children find in a mate the mother and/or father we have been deprived of in our early years. With the death of the spouse, we are plunged once again into the deepest mourning. Then the "child" is out, bewildered and in great pain. It is as though one connects with the mourning of Demeter and Persephone, or of Christ on the cross, asking why God has forsaken him.

Let me encapsulate widowhood so that something about the problem the widow faces in relation to the sad child can be understood.

> The position of widows in many cultures is one of the saddest in society. The simple fact that they were born women ensured their fate. The moment their husbands died, their own function in life was regarded as ended. Often they were destroyed to accompany and serve their dead spouses in the new life beyond death, as they had in his earthly life. (Taylor 1983, p. 48)

While we are too civilized today to allow widows to be put into the grave, the fact remains that many women live their lives through their husbands. Sylvia was a newly widowed woman. Her husband died quite unexpectedly and suddenly. She was a well paid journalist, in a profession she enjoyed. She was left with two children, her grief, and her anger. "How dare he do this to me?" she raged. What he "did" soon became clear. Her wounded, shy inner child had found a home within the breast of her husband. He was outgoing and aggressive. She was able to meet the outer world through his protection, and now she was abandoned.

When he died, she no longer felt able to meet the world and that part of her went into the grave. Her task, like Persephone's, would be to bring it back into consciousness or find another outgoing and aggressive partner. If she did not find such a replacement, then what was being lived unconsciously through him would have to be made conscious. This step requires an enormous change in attitude and consciousness and a new vessel for the sad child. This change is difficult: it is not desired; and it is not what one seeks willingly.

The experience of widowhood reconstitutes the abandoned child archetype. The feelings around the death of a significant other, especially a spouse, often are guilt, shame, anger, abandonment, depression, lack of libido, and hope. I think the *shame* and *guilt* directly connect to the tradition of widow murder, wherein the one closest to the deceased went with him or her into the land of the dead. By being alive, we feel guilty and ashamed that for us life goes on. This wilderness experience is one we all have, but the widowed need all the encouragement possible to leave the land of the dead and return to life. The pull away from life is very strong at such times.

In modern life one has the automobile, where one who feels abandoned may contemplate death or find a place to cry alone. The car is now the place of sanctuary, and as such it is the place that can allow for thoughts of death and dying. Not that this implies that the car is used to bring about death, but it is there that death is contemplated. Ask any newly widowed person if they use the car as a place to rage and cry and think of death, and the answer will often be affirmative.

Another thing to observe about widows has to do with money. Many newly widowed men and women obsess about money. Anxiety about money becomes a substitute for the fear of being on one's own. I have known wealthy individuals who become terrified that they are being cheated or robbed by the lawyers and accountants around them. This also applies to individuals without a great deal of money. They, too, find themselves obsessing about money when, in fact, they are grieving over their loss. While there *are* concerns, there is a special kind of concern the newly widowed express, and I think it is due to the feelings of abandonment and the "child." The newly bereaved feel so helpless and naked, so overwhelmed with the feelings of love, hate, loss, etc., that money anxiety becomes the container for all of the above.

> Widow murder was a natural consequence of the belief that the wife's life ended with the death of the spouse. And they were often killed with prescribed ritual. . . . As late as 1857 there was a law in Oyo, in Western Nigeria, ensuring that certain individuals in the king's retinue, including his official mother, various priestesses, as well as the king's favorite wife, all died when he died and by their own hand. (Taylor 1983, p. 49)

Today, widow murder is practiced in a much subtler form. We don't kill the widow: She is abandoned and becomes invisible. The more a woman is identified with her husband, the more prone she is to feelings of abandonment and desertion. In my own experience, I had a "life of my own," but the body blow of grief I was experiencing was that my marriage had been a safe container for my inner sad child. Alone I avoided this child, but with my husband it was safe to bring her out from time to time. I hated the idea that I would have to face her alone. But it was either that or, like one of the widows in the Melanesian New Hebrides, where a conical cap made of spider's web was used for smothering them, I would be smothered by being stuck in isolation and abandonment.

> When widows were permitted to stay alive, the problem of what to do with them had to be resolved by her own or her husband's relatives. Often she was regarded with suspicion and suspected of witchcraft, because of her contact with death, and the . . . fear that she might have caused her husband's death. In societies where a widow was allowed to remain alive she had to be ritually freed from contact with her dead partner before anyone could touch her or go near her, as death was believed to be very contagious. After a period of isolation she was permitted to re-enter her family in the unenviable new widow's role. The isolation of the widow continues to this day even in the Western world. (Taylor 1983, p. 51)

In Victorian times the term "widows' weeds" was used to describe the clothing the widows wore. This expression can be traced etymologically to the word *wadmal*, which is a strong, woven cloth. The word encompasses two meanings: *wad*, meaning "a tied bundle," and *mal*, meaning "time." Widows' weeds can imply a limit of time for the mourning period or the isolation, but to me the connotation of strong cloth indicates that the garment is made to last a lifetime.

It is not widely known outside of religious life that Catholic nuns took their habit from the garb widows wore. Sister Mary Patricia Sexton told me that, in and around the seventeenth century in France, nuns could go to rough waterfront dives to do the work of the Church knowing that no one would look at them or bother them if they dressed like widows. The symbolism of marriage to Christ in mourning clothes has other meanings, but from the standpoint of this paper, it is interesting to muse about what it was the widows and nuns had in common. Many early convents were started by widows. The clothes they wore were designed to be unchanging and to disguise their sexuality. This outfit, this attitude, was meant to last forever (Taylor 1983, pp. 48–60).

In certain tribes a ban was imposed on remarriage until the body of the dead husband had decomposed. The New Zealand Maori widow wore two special feather cloaks called "cloak of tears." The bones were eventually exhumed, wrapped in the feather cloaks, and reburied. Then the widow was free to remarry (Taylor 1983, p. 56).

In contemporary times words about death may be included in marriage vows. Yet, of all the widows and widowers I have asked, only one recalls actually hearing the words, "'til death do us part" at the wedding. "Attempts to expel death or not to take death into account are a deception committed by man on himself. No matter how hard man tries to shelve and hush up knowledge of the inevitable end of his earthly life, he never quite succeeds" (Feifel 1959, p. 124).

## Conclusion

Analytical psychology encourages individuals to give up attitudes that are too conventional or too collective and stifling. From the history of widow murder, it can be seen that within each of us there is a powerful, archaic pull to abandonment. I encourage analysands who are grieving to dare to be "different," that is, to be true to what the soul wants. A relationship to the fantasies and inner world is an appropriate counterbalance to the forces of collective consciousness that are inclined to isolate the abandoned one and are often destructive to his or her development. There is a journey to the underworld which the sad child makes. He or she becomes intimate with the dark, with fear, and with what can be the most decisive experience, that of being alone with our own self. Before we experience this, something we treasure is sacrificed and/or lost, abandoned. We have to become disidentified from the oneness of subject and object, from unconscious *participation mystique* (G. Frantz 1976).

Abandonment is to be in a state of constant connectedness to the lost object (G. Frantz 1980b). There is a time in the mourning process when there is a serenity in the bereaved, a time of grace. The journey to the underworld is a rite of passage and must be seen as such. One must cross the river and return again, alone. The danger is getting stuck halfway between one shore and the other. How many of us still mourn a childhood that was not what we wished for?

Next to the well of Mnemosyne stands the forbidden well of Lethe, forgetfulness. The notion of forgetfulness is that in death we can forget the sorrows of this world and forget the difficult journey to the next. This theme is elemental and human, and it belongs not just to the Greek and Orphic myths but occurs everywhere (Harrison 1955, p. 574).

Forgetfulness can be an obstacle on this journey. When childhood dreams or fantasies are recalled in the process of analysis, healing can occur. These memories have been hidden away to protect them. But if they are hidden forever, one can remain stuck in the sadness and mourning. A woman recalls a secret game played in childhood. She was an alchemist and invented the perfect food that would stamp out hunger in the world. This game was an attempt on the part of her unconscious to compensate for not getting the right food from her parents. I think that secret games from childhood are an attempt on the part of the psyche to protect what is healing and precious from the too close scrutiny of the negative parental image. This is also why children often stop drawing or coloring at an early age if the work is criticized by an authority figure. This protects further damage to the expression of the imaginal child's psyche until adulthood when, it is hoped, he or she can begin to allow it out once more (G. Frantz 1980a).

The archetypes of the sad child and the lost mother emerge

during times of intense loss and suffering and abandonment. Jung himself had such an experience after his break with Freud. A memory came to him with intense affect about himself as a young boy of 10 or 11. He remembered that as a child he liked to play with sand and stones and make castles and such. He realized that he had forgotten this young lad, but it was obvious to Jung that the child was still alive and wanted something from him. Jung proceeded to do whatever the inner child wished, carefully noting the images and fantasies that were activated by the contact. He called this activity "serious play" (1961, pp. 173–74). This occurred during the time that Jung was in despair over the loss of his relationship to Freud as well as over his own professional direction and life course.

Through this "serious play," Jung made contact with his forgotten and abandoned child and brought the child into his life. You might say that he became the lost mother to his own sad child. Through contact with this inner child came a burst of creativity. In the film, "Matter of Heart," von Franz said that whenever Jung was about to begin writing a book, he would go to the shore of the lake and dig in the sand and make passages for the water to flow (1983). He did not allow that inner child to be forgotten again.

What happens to many of us is that we allow the child to emerge within the vessel of relationship and often seek a relationship in which the child can come out into the open and play. When this container is broken by death or divorce or some separation of an abandoning nature, the child goes into hiding and suffers. Many have had this experience of bringing an abandoned, sad child into a relationship so that the other could nurture the child. When this occurs, the union can become a sacred vessel for the inner creative child or a substitute for a relationship to this child.

## References

Blofield, J. 1978. *Bodhisattva of compassion: The mystical tradition of Kuan Yin.* Boulder, Colo.: Shambhala Publications.
Dalai Lama, The XIVth. 1966. *The opening of the wisdom-eye.* Wheaton, Ill.: The Theosophical Publishing House (1981).
Dallett, J. 1982. Active imagination in practice. In *Jungian analysis*, M. Stein, ed., pp. 173–91. La Salle, Ill., and London: Open Court.
Feifel, H. 1959. *The meaning of death*, rev. ed., 1965. New York and London: McGraw Hill Book Co.
Foy, G. A. 1983. On feeling: The feeling function revisited. Paper presented at 13th Biennial Bruno Klopfer Workshop, Asilomar, California.
Frantz, G. 1976. On the meaning of loneliness. In *Chaos to Eros*, R. Lockhart, ed. Los Angeles: C. G. Jung Institute.

_____. 1980a. Images and imagination: Wounding and healing. Paper presented at the C. G. Jung Institute of San Francisco.

_____. 1980b. Are we all widows? Paper presented at "Knowing Woman" Conference for C. G. Jung Institute of Los Angeles.

Frantz, K. E. 1966. Depression. Unpublished paper.

Franz, M-L. von. 1972. *Creation myths*. New York: Spring Publications.

Grimm, J. and W. 1944. *The complete Grimm's fairy tales*. The girl without hands, pp. 160–66. New York: Pantheon Books.

_____. 1944. Cinderella, pp. 121–28. New York: Pantheon Books.

Harrison, J. 1903. *Prolegomena to the study of Greek religion*. New York: Meridian Books, 1955.

Jung, C. G. 1943. On ultimate things. In *Psychological reflections*, J. Jacobi, ed., p. 262. New York: Harper & Brothers.

_____. 1953. *Two essays on analytical psychology*. In *Collected works*, vol. 7. Princeton: Princeton University Press, 1966.

_____. 1954. *The development of personality*. In *Collected works*, 17:167–86. Princeton: Princeton University Press, 1964.

_____. 1956. *Symbols of transformation*. In *Collected works*, vol. 5. Princeton: Princeton University Press.

_____. 1959. The psychology of the child archetype. In *Collected works*, vol. 9/i. Princeton: Princeton University Press, 1969.

_____. 1961a. *Memories, dreams, reflections*. New York: Random House.

_____. 1961b. The theory of psychoanalysis. In *Collected works*, vol. 4. Princeton: Princeton University Press.

_____, and Kerenyi, K. 1949. *Essays on a science of mythology*. N.Y.: Princeton University Press, 1971.

Kirsch, H. 1975. Reveries on Jung. In *Professional reports* from Annual Conference of the Society of Jungian Analysts of Northern and Southern California. Printed by C. G. Jung Institute of San Francisco. Unpublished.

Leonard, L. 1982. *The wounded woman: Healing the father-daughter relationship*. Athens, Ohio, and Chicago: Swallow Press.

"Matter of Heart." 1983 Film, C. G. Jung Institute of Los Angeles.

Schwartz-Salant, N. 1982. *Narcissism and character transformation*. Toronto: Inner City Books.

Shipley, J. T. 1945. *Dictionary of word origins*. Totowa, N.J.: Littlefield, Adams & Co., 1967.

Skeat, ed. 1979. *Etymological dictionary of the English language*. Oxford: Clarendon Press, 1982.

Stein, J., and Urdang, L., eds. 1966. *Random house dictionary of English*.

Taylor, L. 1983. *Mourning dress: A costume and social history*. London: George Allen & Unwin.

Tripp, E. 1970. *The meridian handbook of classical mythology*. New York and Scarborough, Ont.: New American Library.

Vries, A. de 1974. *Dictionary of symbols and imagery*. Amsterdam and London: North-Holland Publishing Co.

Woodman, M. 1984. Psyche/soma awareness. Unpublished paper presented at Conference of Jungian Analysts in New York, May 3–6, 1984.

# Abandonment, Wish, and Hope in the Blues

## William Willeford

Often deeply moving, subtle, complex, and mysteriously condensed and ambiguous, the blues is a form of musical folk poetry originating around the turn of this century and developing through various phases and styles to the present. Geographically, it encompasses the Mississippi delta, the Texas panhandle, Georgia, the Carolinas, Tennessee, New Orleans, Memphis, and Chicago. A performance art, its notable singers have included Skip James, Mississippi John Hurt, Charley Patton, Blind Lemon Jefferson, Blind Willie McTell, Ida Cox, Ma Rainey, Bessie Smith, Leroy Carr, Memphis Minnie, Robert Johnson, Joe Turner, Jimmy Rushing, Robert Pete Williams, Lightning Hopkins, Muddy Waters, and John Lee Hooker, each of whom has an instantly recognizable musical and poetic voice. This individuality is manifest for the most part in variants of a simple musical form. The lyrics of a blues performance may be drawn from a vast stock of traditional "floating" verses, may be improvised to fit the occasion, or may take the form of set compositions, usually reworking traditional materials. Highly formulaic in

**William Willeford,** Ph.D., is a member of the Inter-Regional Society of Jungian Analysts and Associate Professor of English and Comparative Literature at the University of Washington. Also a practicing Jungian analyst in Seattle, he is the author of *The Fool and His Scepter.*

the manner of folk epics, the blues is itself a world patterned in accordance with characteristic themes, images, and symbols, a world familiar yet mysterious, public yet subjective and idiosyncratic, offering deep satisfactions to be had in no other way than through one's imaginative habitation of it.

In principle, blues lyrics can be about virtually any subject that strikes the interest of the blues singer or composer. Blues may celebrate good times, feeling good, partying, and sexual pleasure. But most blues are about "troubles"—hardships of lower-class black Americans—in the forms of thwarted love, abandonment, infidelity, death, murder, poverty, hard work for little pay, homelessness, natural disasters, drunkenness, drug-taking, gambling, prostitution, and jail. There are overtly joyous blues, often boasting or reveling in grandiose fantasy or in prospects of sexual pleasure. There are no blues about wildflowers or beautiful sunsets. And though a few blues artists (such as J. B. Lenoir) have dealt with such subjects as racial violence, social protest is rare in the blues, the many ironies of which have little to do with those of such "committed" writers as Bertolt Brecht.[1] Indeed, the most characteristic attitude of the blues is noncommittal, which is far from meaning simply "hopeless."[2] The broadest subject matter of the blues is *having* the blues, so that overtly joyous blues, too, usually refer at least indirectly to having the blues as a deplorable and probably inevitable condition.

Though noncommittal treatment of such themes as I have listed reflects a fatalism well justified by the real-life experience of many blues performers and much of the blues audience, I will focus on another reason for the inclination of the blues to leave problems unsolved or to temper any solution with at least the hint of further problems. Emotional life in general is predicated on the certainty of uncertainty, and feeling, as a special dimension of emotional life, is also so predicated. A mother must read and relate to the feeling-state of her infant, whom she must comfort even under adverse circumstances, and even in the certainty that circumstances now ameliorated will become adverse again. And the mother's feeling-relationship with her infant is the basis of further developments of feeling, which at the deepest level are concerned with survival. In

---

1. See especially Lenoir's albums, *Alabama Blues* (L + R, LR 4.2001) and *Down in Mississippi* (L + R, LR 42.42012).
2. D. Evans, *Big road blues* (Berkeley: University of California Press, 1982), pp. 19-22.

its exploration of such themes as what it is like to be on the "killing floor," the blues draws us back to this level of feeling.[3]

In its concern with knowing what to feel and with feeling what is proper to be felt, the blues is an extraordinary development in the education of the heart. The blues shows with special clarity things of importance about the relationship between individuality and community; the need for the whole person to remain open to the world with its contingency and pain; the emotional force and restraint necessary to differentiated feeling; and the ways in which the mother-infant dyad may be potently implicit in the artistic—or, more broadly, the spiritual—transcendence of real-life frustrations and conflicts. Further, despite the frequent bleakness of its subject matter, the blues is a comic art celebrating the triumph of both individuality and community. The blues shows with special clarity things of importance about the transformative workings of imagination—about imaginative transcendence—and about the interrelations between imagination and feeling.[4]

A blues performer does not need to have the blues at the moment in order to sing the blues well, though deep feeling is one of the valued qualities of a blues performance. Muddy Waters has been described as leaving the bandstand, after a strong performance, in a state of near-trance lasting about half an hour; another blues artist has been censured for "phoning in" his blues message as though it were an order to a business firm. And Texas barrel-house and saw-mill pianist Buster Pickens observes:

> The only way anyone can ever play the blues—he's got to have them . . .; nach'al blues come directly from a person's heart: what he's experienced in life. . . . Whether he's been troubled, whether he's ridden freight trains, where he's been put in jail; been beaten up by railroad dicks and everythin' else you understand—pushed around in life. . . . You have a tough way in life—that makes you blue. That's when you start to sing the blues—when you've got the blues.[5]

---

3. "Killing Floor," *Chester Burnett AKA Howlin' Wolf* (Chess 60016-2). The theme is explored by many other blues artists.

4. C. G. Jung, *The structure and dynamics of the psyche.* In *Collected works*, vol. 8 (Princeton: Princeton University Press, 1968), pp. 67–91. My use of the word "transcendence" here is meant to imply Jung's account of imagination as the "transcendent [or more properly, transcending] function" bridging consciousness and unconscious psychic regions in ways responsive to the Self.

5. Quoted in Paul Oliver, *Conversations with the blues* (New York: Horizon Press, 1965), p. 170.

Nor does the audience need to have the blues at the moment to appreciate a blues performance. But it is essential for performer and audience to know at least tacitly what it is to have the blues.

The relationship between having the blues and performing the blues is, however, more complex, subtle and—above all—indirect than Buster Pickens fully suggests. If blues performers and their audience were just sitting around having the blues, there would be no blues performance. This is because having the blues and not having the blues are essentially related to one another—most simply in that when one has the blues, one hopes that one will find the path to not having them, and that when one does not have them, one fears that one may already be on the path to having them. Having the blues and not having the blues exist, metaphorically speaking, at a distance from one another. And knowledge of both conditions is assumed and drawn upon in a blues performance. Basically, blues performers and their audience are not present at the performance because they now acutely have the blues. (Some may be present for this reason, but they do not supply the governing motive of the occasion.) Rather, they are present because they might come to have the blues, because the blues remains a potentiality to be faced now in the hope that it will not be actualized in an incapacitating way but will instead be converted to something else, to self-enhancing feelings and states, beginning with the vital, bodily good times of the performance. Thus, the blues performance assumes the present or available reality of not having the blues. This is as much the point of departure of the blues experience as is knowledge of having them.

Still, knowledge of having the blues is what could be called the emotional frame of reference of the blues experience. In calling it this, I am pointing to its character as existing at a distance from not now having the blues, though the two conditions are interrelated. I have in mind the semanticist Alfred Korzybski's oft-repeated summary statement that map is not territory, and am thinking of the emotional frame of reference as such a map. According to Korzybski, the word "cat," belonging to the figurative map, cannot scratch us, as it could if it were real as the territory mapped. Still, we must know something about the reality "cat" for the word "cat" to have meaning; some sort of knowledge of real cats provides a frame of reference for the word "cat." The condition of having the blues is the territory—the emotional frame of reference—that the blues performance attempts to map—attempts to bring to imaginative awareness. Some sort of prior knowledge of the condition is necessary for that awareness (though one need not have been beaten up by railroad dicks to know it).

A territory can be—and in a strong blues performance is—mapped by feeling. But as one might begin sketching without having the intention of representing anything specific, making a map can be—and in a strong blues performance is—inseparable from discovering what is to be mapped. One's prior knowledge of the condition of having the blues need not be specific; indeed, one function of the blues performance is to articulate the not-yet-articulated, even though what is thus expressed is in some sense already tacitly known. What is it to have the blues? how do we know what it is to have the blues? and what does having the blues have to do, even if indirectly, with performing the blues?

Though having the blues is in one sense the emotional frame of reference of a blues performance, having the blues is also an expression of emotional regions of the person that are inaccessible to consciousness. It can be only crudely translated by such words and phrases as "despondency" and "soul-loss." In a sense related to Spinoza's contention that by knowing the causes of our emotions we are freed from the passivity they entail, the blues as musical poetry is an ongoing process of trying to define what having the blues is.

Much of the blues is about "the blues," often, importantly, in such a way that it is not possible to draw a clear distinction in a blues text between the blues as having the blues and the blues as musical poetry. The lack of distinction is important; the ambiguity is calculated and deliberate. Thus Otis Spann, the splendid pianist with the Muddy Waters blues band for many years, sings: "When you in trouble, blues is a man's best friend. . . . Blues ain't goin' to ask you where you goin', and blues don't care where you been," and later: "We can't let the blues die, the blues don't mean you no harm. . . . I'm goin' back to the lowlands, that's where the blues came from."[6] The blues that we can't let die is probably (mostly) the consoling, soul-strengthening music; going back to the lowlands implies a return to the poverty of lower-class southern farmers that Spann and countless other blacks had moved to Chicago and other northern cities to escape; the blues of the lowlands is perhaps partly

---

6. Otis Spann, "The Blues Never Die," *The Blues Never Die!* (Prestige 7719).

the music but surely also the toil and pain out of which it was born. The line says ironically, "The blues as music and as an imaginative world-view makes having the blues harmless; so let us pay tribute to the music and the world-view by going back to the real misery, to the condition of having the blues, that made the music and the world-view necessary."

If we did not, at least tacitly, already know the unwilled condition of having the blues—if we did not already partly know the territory—the blues performance would not work in freeing us from the condition by offering us a provisional definition of it. Although map is not territory, in lived experience the ambiguity between them is as important as the distinction between them, and the blues exploits this ambiguity in ways that have rich implications for the psychology of feeling and imagination.

A child partly regards a doll as a real person; we partly forget that the people on a stage are actors representing characters in a play; we are usually unaware that we have performed a leap as we mentally pass from the word "cat" to an image-idea of the real animal that may scratch. Indeed, in emotional life we map the territory in order to gain the distance from it that we have lost or feel ourselves in danger of losing. Maps must be replaced by other maps, as new emotional situations in need of being read take form. Feeling is never final; feeling is process; feeling always begins again. Even habitual feeling-judgments must be continually enlivened by being experienced as part of feeling as process, if such judgments are to be validly binding and not lifeless things on a shelf. In its appreciation of the provisional nature of its products, feeling is essential to imagination, fraught as imagination is with ambiguities and tensions that link it to unconscious emotional regions of the person and that make any final map impossible. Spann knows much about this: If the best solution he can offer to the problem of having the blues is going back to where the blues was born, the problem is—subtly, indirectly—exposed as unsolved, and new imaginative maps will, as he knows, have to be devised to reveal the nature of the territory of having the blues. More blues will have to be played and sung; continuation and repetition are as necessary to the blues party as they are to solemn festivals.

By offering a specious solution to the problem, Spann is in a sense pushing his audience further in the direction of having the blues. But the nature of the emotional issue changes significantly in the process. The issue is no longer the direct danger of having the blues, though the audience is being vividly reminded of what it is to have them; rather, the issue is the disintegration of the defense against having the blues as the implications of the specious argument come to awareness.

Let us assume in Spann's audience—in ourselves insofar as we have firsthand prior knowledge of the territory he is mapping—an ongoing, "normal" defense against having the blues, this defense being related to the mental set that enables us to ignore distractions. Though useful, such a defense may, however, become too severe and thus result in an impoverishment of inner life and an increase in the danger that the defense will fail. In general in psychic life, letting in a defended-against force—any energy-charged psychic content—is a first step in arriving at a more adequate conscious attitude toward it. (For example, one must let oneself be depressed before one can find out what one is depressed about and then seek the most appropriate perspective in which to regard the object of one's depression.)

The letting in of such a force generates emotion which, if it is to remain ego-syntonic, demands a new distancing, in the form of a more alert and precise reading of the emotional situation—in our case, that described in the blues verses. Emotion thus motivates imaginative engagement in which distancing plays a necessary role. It is this distancing that allows the emotional situation to be read in the mode of feeling and allows the literal to open out to the metaphorical, the symbolic, the ironic. The distance thus achieved is, however, variable, and the process by which it is increased or decreased is subtle.

Indeed, though the blues is concerned with issues of pathos, blues verses and the blues performance as a whole are ironic, in the sense that what is said is always at some distance from what is meant. Occasionally the irony is clearcut, as when Howlin' Wolf ("three hundred pounds of comfort and joy") sings that he "ain't superstitious" and then lists his superstitions one by one.[7] Usually, though, the irony is more subtle, as in Spann's verses already considered, or in another piece in which he declares that he has a wonderful feeling everything is going to be all right, a feeling deep down in his soul, a feeling that he is going to love his woman every day and every night. The confidently loping melodic line and driving, charged

---

7. Howlin' Wolf, "I Ain't Superstitious," *Howlin' Wolf: His Greatest Sides*, vol. 1 (Chess CH-9107).

rhythm totally fit this joyous and hopeful sentiment. Still his declaration that she "done came back home" to him implies conflict and separation; and in admitting to being worried that she might leave him again, he hardly offers cause for feeling all that wonderful.[8]

Sometimes the clues to *how* ironic the tone is are unspecifiable. For example, if a blues performer sings about leaving his present woes and going somewhere else to begin anew, his message and manner may partly inspire our confidence. And yet we might have reason to wonder whether he really does have any new place to go, or if he will do anything other than find himself in a new version of his old situation if he does go, or if, indeed, flight is not also a form of defeat. Such ambiguity, forcing one to reach *through* the semantic text to the expressive features of the overall performance, is fundamental to what could be called the blues aesthetic.

Verses sung in 1983 by guitarist-singer Johnny Copeland offer a striking example of ironic distancing coupled with a breakdown between emotional map and territory. In high spirits he sings, at a brisk tempo:

> When the rain starts fallin',
> My feet start to itchin';
> I know that it's time to go.
> You know, I promised myself
> It ain't gonna rain in my life no mo'.
>
> When you all out of money,
> Things get funny;
> Look like everybody know.
> I'm gonna pack my bag, and down the road I go.
>
> Well, the rain keep a comin', and I keep a runnin';
> I'm movin' like the wind.
> You know, when the rain catch up,
> I'm on the move again.
>
> When you hear from me again,
> I'll be somewhere down the road.
> I'm gonna ride that train
> Just as far as my money goes.

8. Otis Spann, "I Got a Feeling," *The Blues Never Die!* (Prestige 7719).

> When the rain starts fallin',
> My feet start to itchin';
> You know, I promised myself
> It ain't gonna rain in my life no mo'.[9]

Having the blues is the rain the singer wants to escape. And his joyously imagined flight is predicated on certain defeat: If he is out of money, he cannot pay for a train ride. Moreover, as the clown Feste sings at the close of *Twelfth Night*, "For the rain it raineth every day," and as a once-popular song has it, "Into each life some rain must fall." Having the blues is ultimately no more controllable than the weather.

When a blues singer sings the traditional line, "The sun's going to shine in my back door someday," he is expressing hope that things will get better, and he knows, and we know, that he, like Feste, is speaking metaphorically when he sings with wistful resignation about the wind and the rain. Copeland's fantasy, in contrast, goes much further in the kind of concretization of metaphor we see when, in *A Midsummer Night's Dream*, the fairy Puck puts an ass's head on the fool Bottom and causes the fairy queen Titania foolishly to fall in love with him, or when in *King Lear* the distraught king exclaims, "Or ere I'll weep, O Fool, I shall go mad!" immediately after the sound of "*Storm and tempest*," symbolizing emotional turmoil and madness. The expressive features of Copeland's voice and music, with their soaring, charging energy, their brash exuberance, convince us that he takes his fantasy literally. He sounds utterly delighted to be actively not understanding the implications of what he is saying.

Our pleasure in the singer's self-confident delight is derived from our tacit awareness of the condition of having the blues. That awareness is affirmed even while its tacit character is insisted upon. We know what we are looking away from even while we are looking away from it. The artistic persona of the singer denies painful reality; the performance as a whole does not. Its irony serves the interrelated functions of detaching us from that reality while keeping us in touch with it. In the imaginative world-view of the blues, joy is born of pain; pain is not to be denied. Joy is not simply the denial of pain but represents an order of value in its own right. Irony assures that

---

9. Johnny Copeland, "When the Rain Starts Fallin'," *Texas Twister* (Rounder 2040).

pain is not denied, is taken into account, as the value of joy is affirmed.

In general, the blues is radically committed to what has been called the blues ideology, which holds that real-life problems are not soluble in real-life terms, or that if such a problem is solved in such terms, it will immediately lead to further problems. Nor does religion offer an alternative. (Blues people may go to church; some have been preachers; but religion does not acquire the force of conviction within the specifically blues context.) One must remain open to the reality of human misery. This openness is the price and the precondition of the artistic transcendence of misery offered by the blues.

The verses of Spann that we began by considering invite a process of reasoning that serves to maintain emotional distance. Some of the rawer and more intense blues of the impassioned, short-lived genius Robert Johnson illumine another aspect of the emotional engagement fundamental to the blues. Johnson begins "Preaching Blues" (recorded in 1936):

> I was up this morning, I got blues walking
>     like a man.
> I was up this morning, my blues walking
>     like a man.
> Well, the blues—give me your right hand.

It is the singer, not the blues, that proffers his hand. The singer reaches out to grasp the hand of the blues, thus to feel the blues, in a tactile sense, and thereby to learn something of its character, as from a handshake one learns something about a person. He hurls himself into the encounter, continuing:

> And the blues fell, Mammachild, and they tore me
>     all upside down.
> Blues fell, Mammachild, and they tore me all
>     upside down.
> Travel on, poor Bob, just can't turn you round.[10]

No longer "walking like a man," the blues have become a diffuse, shapeless power falling, perhaps like rain—often symbolically linked, as in the piece by Copeland, with having the blues—

---

10. *Robert Johnson: King of the Delta Blues Singers* (Columbia CL 1654).

their effects lacerating and bewildering. The last line (about travel-ing on) represents not flight, which would be futile, but rather the movement of someone who is under way because standing still is impossible but who is inexorably doomed, as Johnson proclaims himself to be in another blues in which he is pursued by a hell-hound on his trail.[11] So much is clear. But who or what is "Mam-machild," and what is his, and what is our, relation to the thing thus addressed?

"Mammachild" names the whole mother-infant relationship: the infant needing and receiving its mother's care, the mother caring for her infant. "Mammachild" is addressed as being on the singer's mind and relevant to the situation he is exploring, because abandon-ment in the sense of loss of contact with "Mammachild"—abandon-ment of the child—is tantamount to exposure to the blues. (The Texas streetsinger Blind Lemon Jefferson sang in 1926: "Blues jumped a rabbit, run him one solid mile. . . . That rabbit sat down, cried like a natural child.")[12]

We are in some sense *with* Johnson as he grasps the blues by the hand, with him as the blues fall on him, with him in having a relationship to "Mammachild." But the singer is not in any simple way drawing us into having the blues. He is singing *about* having the blues. He is at a remove from the blues he is singing about having, and we are at a remove from the dramatic episodes he is imagining. The term "identification" could be used to designate the process bringing the singer, us, the blues "walking like a man," the blues falling on him and tearing him "all upside down," and "Mammachild" into an imaginative relationship while keeping each separate. But it should be noted that to speak this way is to imply that identification has disidentification within it as a potentiality—for separation to be overcome, there must be separation—indeed, that identification and disidentification are complementary aspects of a complex process. That this is so can be seen frequently in psychotherapeutic practice.

I offer two brief vignettes based on observations made in psy-chotherapy, because the processes they illustrate—of identification and disidentification—are important in the blues.

For example, "Denise," who dislikes her businessman father

---

11. "Hellhound on My Trail," *Robert Johnson: King of the Delta Blues Singers* (Columbia CL 1654).

12. "Rabbit Foot Blues," *The Immortal Blind Lemon Jefferson* (Milestone 2004).

and who has shaped her life to honor values he does not appreciate, sometimes clearly exercises valuable traits she "has" from him when she is working at her best as the artistic director of a theatre. Moreover, from time to time, usually unbeknownst to herself, she overtly manifests in her behavior this or that of the traits for which she dislikes him, including his contentious willfulness. Or: "Charlotte," who had a dissolute, sadistic, neglectful mother, is an excellent psychotherapist in her work with disturbed children. The process by which she has become disidentified from her family background has given her a rich understanding of its psychodynamics, and this understanding enables her to identify with her young clients and to use that identification on their behalf. Occasionally however, the image of her mother possesses her as she bursts out in rage at her husband or a female co-worker.

Denise's moments of willfulness and Charlotte's of rage raise an important point: Just as for separation to be overcome there must be separation, so for identification—and, in turn, disidentification—to take place, there must be a prior knowledge of oneness. Identification and disidentification presuppose and work with vestiges of archaic identity.

In speaking of archaic identity, I am not assuming (as some have) that the original psychic state of the infant is one of nondifferentiation and nondiscrimination, and that this state is prominent in the psychic life of so-called primitive people. Rather, I find the phenomenological psychologist Stefan Strasser persuasive in remarking about interaction within the mother-infant dyad: "The most elementary of all human experience—we together in the surrounding world—is not at first perceived, thought, or sought after; it is primarily lived, through feeling."[13] We are first—and always, though we forget this—we together in the surrounding world.

Archaic identity is, then, the form of experience that prevails when the distinctions implicit in Strasser's phrase are annulled, for example, in sleep or in states of fusion. Though the capacity for union, in which boundaries are relaxed but preserved, is essential to psychic maturity and to mutuality, fusion, in which boundaries are negated, also plays an important role in psychic life.

Fusion is a process of dedifferentiation in which sameness is

---

13. S. Strasser, "Feeling as basis of knowing and recognizing the other as an ego." In M. B. Arnold, ed., *Feelings and emotions* (New York: Academic Press 1970), p. 306.

emphasized at the expense of difference, an emphasis that is basic to the identifications that make the human person a member of society, and to the workings of the imagination. The archaic identity resulting from this process is also a component of such feeling-toned complexes as those formed in Denise's relationship with her father and Charlotte's with her mother. And although *relationship* with emotional reality is possible—one can shake hands with the blues—the play of emotion, which can always assume unexpected and puzzling forms, is a constant reminder of unconscious regions of the psyche and of the subordination of the ego to the largely unknown self.

Denise may try, and may be right to try, not to be *like* her father, but map, in the larger whole of her life, inevitably gets lost for moments in territory: Though she has extensively qualified and differentiated, and partly discarded, her identification with her father, on the level of archaic identity drawn upon in the long life of that identification, and still drawn upon in her efforts at disidentification, Denise effectively *is* her father. On the same level, and in the same way, Charlotte effectively *is* her mother. These identifications, insofar as the archaic identity upon which they draw is indissoluble, are patterns of fate. (Both women have done much of value about, and with, these patterns. The women exemplify an important part of individuation as I understand it. But they have done so, necessarily, within limits implied by Jung's view that psychic problems are dealt with not by solving them directly but rather through an expansion of consciousness modifying their role, function, and value within the psyche as a whole.)

This is to say with another emphasis that feeling has emotion as a concomitant, that feeling is always partly *about* emotion, though it is about many other things as well, and that emotion, and consequently feeling, is rooted in the regions of the person that are ultimately autonomous with respect to conscious purposes and values.

To one's felt sense of who and what one is, emotional currents arising from these regions of the person sometimes do, and sometimes do not—like the hellhound on one's trail—seem to belong to oneself. Such currents display in this sense the ambiguity we have noted in the identifications of Denise and Charlotte—indeed, such currents are at work on those identifications. Especially owing to the bodily immediacy of such currents—as close to me as my body is to myself—they can largely overwhelm all sense of "me" and

"mine" as representing a secure center of appropriate and responsible action. Yet the ambiguity occasioned by this weakening of
ego-reference can bring with it a gain, since precisely in not knowing what I know in the way I usually know it, I may surmise the
activity of the Self, as it makes itself known in its own manner, like
the wind that bloweth where it listeth. This experience may revital-
ize and modify in a clarifying way the ego's capacity for appraising
value. And this brings us again to "Mammachild."

To speak of "secure" ego-functioning, as I did a moment ago,
is to recall that the first security is that of "Mammachild." The
archaic identity of "Mammachild" might well be thought to refer,
on the one hand, to the security the loss of which has delivered the
blues singer up to having the blues, and, on the other, to the
emotional frame of reference offering him the hope that he will be
able to maintain sufficient emotional distance to endure his present
state.

The emotional territory must be mapped and remapped. Losing
the map in the territory is an inevitably recurrent part of this
mapping and remapping. In this sense blues music is itself dangerous, though one may yield to the danger much as one may yield to
the bittersweetness of certain experiences of love. Thus, blues artist
John Lee Hooker speaks of "feelin' very normal, nothin' on your
mind, period," but then hearing a blues record that so threatens you
with "hurt" and "heartaches and things" that you take a walk or go
for a ride in your car:

> Because you'd rather *not* hear it than to hear it. Because there's some
> places in them records, there's somethin' sad in there that give you the
> blues; somethin' that reach back in your life or some friend's life of
> yours, or that make you think of what have happened today and it is so
> true, that if it didn't happen to you, you still got a strong idea—you
> know those things is goin' on. So this is very touchable, and that
> develops into the blues.[14]

Still, though blues music may cause the condition it is supposed
to relieve or cure, one can trust the blues—"The blues is man's best
friend," as Otis Spann sings; blues music will sooner or later do its
healing work.

In the blues as in life, feeling always begins again, regardless of
how forbidding the emotional territory to be mapped. And so in his

---

14. Quoted in P. Oliver, *Conversations with the blues* (New York: Horizon Press,
1965), p. 164.

charged encounter with man-like blues, Robert Johnson displays
and celebrates the courage to feel even the implications of a harrow-
ing emotional plight.

Johnson names "Mammachild" as the frame of reference within
which the individual contemplates the threat of annihilation and
the possibility of survival. But the mother-infant dyad also opens out
to community, of which it is the protoform. It is striking that in the
blues the mother-infant dyad remains the frame of reference for
further developments of relationship, especially those colored by
sexual love (and hate). This is evident in the fact that the most
common forms of address to a desirable woman are, interchangeably, "Mamma" and "Baby" (and for a man, interchangeably, "Pap-
pa" or "Daddy" and "Baby"). This is not that the blues denies the
triadic tensions touched upon earlier. On the contrary, in the blues
love is very often thwarted by a rival. Thus, the powerful pioneer
blues artist Charley Patton sang in 1929 about imagined instances of
the dreaded "back-door man":

> I'm gonna buy me a banty [rooster], put him in my
>   back door.
> I'm gonna buy me a banty, put him in my back door,
> 'Cause he see a stranger comin', he'll flop his
>   wings and crow.[15]

When Howlin' Wolf sings that "Evil is goin' on," he specifies
the evil by admonishing his hearers to guard against the back-door
man; yet in another blues, he moves from such warning to declaring,
"I am a back-door man," and detailing the advantages of that role.[16]
In 1938 the trombonist Jack Teagarden presented a compelling
blues statement consisting of two verses, "O Mammo, Mammo,
Mammo, where did you stay last night?" (two times), "The last time
I saw you your hat didn't look just right." Then: "I'm goin' to get
myself some brick, Lawd, and build my chimney high-o" (two
times), "To keep my neighbor's tomcat from puttin' out my fi-o
[fire]."[17] And New Orleans pianist Billie Pierce recalls the words to

---

15. "Banty Rooster Blues," *Charley Patton, Founder of the Delta Blues* (Yazoo L-
1020).

16. "Evil is Goin' On" and "Back Door Man," *Chester Burnett AKA Howlin' Wolf*
(Chess 60016-2).

17. Group led by George Wettling, "Serenade to a Shylock," *Jam Session at
Commodore* (Commodore [78 r.p.m.] CMS 1501), reissued in Time-Life *Giants of Jazz*
Series: *Jack Teagarden.*

the first blues she learned, at about the age of seven: "I never loved but one man in my life" (two times), "He was a married man an' I stole him from his wife."[18]

Tensions about rivalry are also exploited powerfully by the contemporary singer-guitarist-composer Jimmy Johnson, who, singing about his hopeless love for a woman who loves someone else, concludes by repeating three times, "I got nowhere to turn, so tired of being alone, I feel like breaking up somebody's home," making clear that the only way he can imagine getting out of the triangle he is in is to create a new triangle with someone else as a victim.[19]

Triangles in the blues can also take other forms than that of the singer, the loved one, and the rival. Floyd Jones, a Chicago blues performer, sang in "Stockyard Blues," early in the 1950s, about the triangular situation of needing money and facing a picket line blocking him from earning it.[20] And another Chicago blues artist, pianist Sunnyland Slim, sings (following Doctor Clayton): "Woman, I ain't goin' to drink no more whiskey, because you and liquor take advantage of me. . . . You keep me blue and disgusted as any man can live and be," thus describing a triangle in which the woman and whiskey are allies in opposition to him. He goes on: "I'm goin' stop drinkin' before you and liquor ruin my life," but then concludes ironically, "I done lost my money, I believe I lost my wife," making clear that he, on the one hand, and the Other-Woman-and-whiskey, on the other, have been two sides of a triangle including, further, his wife.[21] Rather than being resolved, the triangle is thus translated to a deeper level: Though some blues verses describe love as thwarted by death or abandonment, it is highly characteristic of the blues to find the cause of one's loss of love in a rival, and, for example, to contemplate the image of a stranger's muddy shoes next to the bed of one's woman.

In the community of which the mother-infant dyad is the protoform, individuality must be affirmed in a cooperation with others that withstands and resolves rivalries. Speech among individuals—

18. Quoted in P. Oliver, *Conversations with the blues* (New York: Horizon Press, 1965), p. 78.

19. Jimmy Johnson, "Breaking Up Somebody's Home," *Living Chicago Blues,* vol. 1 (Alligator AL 7701).

20. Snooky [Jones] & Moody [Prior, under whose names the record was issued], "Stockyard Blues," *Chicago Blues: The Early 1950's* (Blues Clasics 8, BC-8).

21. "Ain't Gonna Drink No More, *Sunny Land [sic] Slim Plays the Rag Time Blues* (BluesWay BLS-6068).

"talk"—facilitates such cooperation. "Talk," both as an activity and as a metaphor, is important in the experience of blues music. Various features of "talk" in blues performance provide a perspective on the ambiguities in the blues between twos and threes, and between the verbal and extraverbal, and on ways in which the mother-infant dyad is implicit in the transcendence the blues offers—also when the blues one has or might have as a soul-condition is caused by some form of triadic tension. Breaking down the distinction between twos and threes, the blues also breaks down the distinction between the verbal and the extraverbal. Ambiguities in the blues between twos and threes and between the verbal and the extraverbal are interrelated.

A recent study of blues in the Mississippi delta includes a chapter on "Blues Talk" transcribed from a blues party.[22] Such talk includes banter among members of the audience, between them and the performers, and among the performers. Rather than being extraneous to the performance, such talk is intrinsic to it, bringing the participants into a special form of relationship to one another— one very different from that which obtains in a classical concert hall, for example. Such talk gives the performers a means of gauging the mood of the audience and of influencing that mood if need be— interaction to these ends being especially important when whiskey, sometimes homemade, is helping the good times roll; and the performers can incorporate such talk in their performance in various ways, for example, by elaborating on a comment from the audience in appropriate verses.

Exclamations of blues performers to one another, and of the audience to the performers, might include "Talk to me!" and those of the performers to the audience might include "Hear me talking to you!" To say that a blues musician makes his instrument "talk" is to bestow praise. Guitarist-singer B. B. King "talks" to (that is, sings to as he plays on) his guitar "Lucille," and as the title of one of his blues numbers declares, "Lucille Talks Back." In the African background of the blues are the "talking drums" that function as an equivalent of speech.

A sub-genre of the blues is "talking blues," a blues monologue with musical accompaniment. And one blues scholar who conducted hundreds of interviews with blues performers was struck by how

---

22. W. Ferris, *Blues from the delta* (Garden City, N.Y.: Anchor Books 1979), pp. 107–13.

often the person interviewed would begin accompanying himself on an instrument such as guitar or piano, so that his verbal utterance was partly transformed into a blues performance.[23]

Generally, for talk (in the literal sense) to be possible, expressive sounds must have acquired semantic meaning within a framework of social conventions, thus becoming part of a field of discourse. This acquisition of meaning, making the difference between a sound and a word, is a form of transcendence. (My cat Lester would in important respects transcend his cat-condition if he could learn to talk.) But verbal meaning dies. (A month-old newspaper has lost much of its meaning. Sacred texts become mumbo-jumbo. As is easy to prove experimentally, simple repetition of a word may render it meaningless. When Macbeth says, "Tomorrow, and tomorrow, and tomorrow," he is actively realizing the meaninglessness of his future.) Moreover, verbal meaning has its limits: Painfully trapped within our words, we may find that music serves preciously to revive verbal meaning or to reach beyond it.

The verbal content of the blues is concerned with emotional situations implying stories that are usually not told explicitly; rather, the personal, subjective reactions of the singer or fictional persona are made the center of attention. That is, the blues, unlike the ballad, is non-narrative and often even anti-narrative in its suppression of the storyline. For example, Johnny Copeland, in another blues, sings about his daddy's telling him not to stop by the creek to swim on the way to school, advice which the singer had to ponder. The incident is treated in isolation from other incidents, and the significance that made the incident seem to the singer worth relating is left undeclared. One might imagine that the incident was fatal in the sense of initiating a process of dropping out of school, leading to other forms of dereliction that ended by shaping his life in a particular way. But no such story is told.[24]

Incidentally, the same blues by Copeland suggests something of the way in which the non-narrative or even anti-narrative tendency of the blues is sometimes clearly related to the nonspecifiable

---

23. Quoted in P. Oliver, *Conversations with the blues* (New York: Horizon Press, 1965), p. 9. A fascinating example of such an improvised interview-monologue is that of Buster Pickens, "Santa Fe Train," on a Flyright album under his name (FLY-LP 536), transcribed in P. Oliver, *Conversations with the Blues* (New York: Horizon Press, 1965), pp. 73–74.

24. Johhny Copeland, "Don't Stop by the Creek, Son," *Texas Twister* (Rounder 2040).

irony common in it. After singing, "Don't stop by the creek, Son, that's what my daddy said," the singer remarks that he "almost didn't obey"; but after elaborating on his daddy's advice, he admits that that was where he "went astray," only to fall back thereafter to claiming that he "almost didn't obey." The interest of the account centers in the fictional persona's wavering between maintaining and dismantling an edifice of lies about the course of his life and about the extent of his responsibility for it. Since it is essential in the blues, as an art of survival, not to sentimentalize and to see to it that false hopes are treated ironically, bravado and other forms of apparent wish-fulfillment are to be heard in a double perspective. Bravado in the blues often asks to be heard as: "This grandiose posture is fun and an ego-strengthening exercise in courage and in demanding what I want; it is nonetheless make-believe, a form of 'lying' (or tall-tale-telling)."

The anti-narrative tendency of the blues is related to its tendency to develop its materials more in an associative than in a linear or logical fashion. Indeed, the verbal content of the blues and its development sometimes seem dreamlike. Thus, Howlin' Wolf sings, "Smokestack lightnin', shining just like gold," which is for Sam Chatmon "Smokestack lightnin', bell what shine like gold," and for Lightning Hopkins, "Smokes like lightnin', velvet shines like gold."[25]

As one writer about blues lyrics comments, perhaps consoling himself for fruitless efforts at comprehension, "It's not that what [blues singers] sing is trivial exactly. It's just that it does not entirely reflect what they are singing about."[26] Indeed, often in the blues performance only snatches of the verbal content are intelligible. (Son House, a blues-artist contemporary of Charley Patton, confessed that he often could not understand the words of Patton's blues.) Often fragmented in our comprehension of them, blues verses give glimpses and clues inciting associative processes in the listener—much as one may make up a meaning for what one is hearing in an unknown language. Though it is a relief when one comes to understand blues verses that had baffled one, it is in keeping with many other elements of the blues aesthetic that a

---

25. Howlin' Wolf, "Smokestack Lightnin'," *Chester Burnett AKA Howlin' Wolf* (Chess 60016-2). Chatmon: quoted in Evans, *Big road blues* (Berkeley: University of Calif. Press, 1982), p. 288. Lightning Hopkins, "The Hearse is Backed Up to the Door," *The Legacy of the Blues*, vol. 12 (GNP Crescendo GNPS 10022).

26. P. Guralnick, *Feel like going home* (New York: Vintage 1981), p. 41.

blues performance does not necessarily stand or fall on the basis of the intelligibility of the words. Just as the blues tends away from the linear, rational, explicit, toward the diffusely global, irrational, suggestive, so it tends to press through the semantic altogether toward extraverbal expressiveness.

In the blues, everyday speech is expressively altered in various ways. A syllable might be prolonged or divided, or be given a stress it would not have in conversation, or be rendered falsetto or as melisma (the ornamental elaboration of a syllable as a succession of notes). In the singing of blues verses, words may be replaced by expressive but nonsemantic sounds, such as moans, humming, and musical figures played by guitar or piano or harmonica. A special case is presented by such blues artists as Mississippi John Hurt and Fred McDowell when they sing only part of a verse line, or do not sing it at all when the singing of it is expected, so that the listener must "hear" the words in the guitar part—in a way related to B. B. King's making Lucille "talk." In this case it would not be quite true to say that words are being replaced by nonsemantic but expressive and communicative sounds, since the listener does, in a subliminal way, "hear" the expected but unsung words. By such devices the blues performer blurs the distinction between the verbal and extraverbal or creates and explores ambiguities between them. Just as making expressive sounds into words is transcendence, so the decomposition of words into expressive sound may be transcendence of another kind.

In this extraverbal transcendence, words are reabsorbed into gestural, postural, proprioceptive, sensory, emotional currents of the body. These currents are basic to one's experience of oneself as having a personal vital core. And attending to these currents is a means both of acknowledging (from the side of the ego) the value of that core (as the self) and of making its vitality manifest.

Magical and religious ritual may, by drawing attention to such currents and to that core, revivify one's sense of self through procedures intended to help assure such boons as the vitality of cattle and crops. As I have said, the blues in its basic spirit, unlike such ritual, refuses to declare commitment to a belief that life will get better. (Many blues verses assert that life will get better, but they do so as a partly ironic strategy for fending off the danger of having the blues, and such utterances are no more to be taken at face value than are verses in which a rejected lover boasts of his irresistible charms.) Still, the blues generate vitality in the way that ritual does, and it is more than casual analogy to describe a blues performance as a ritual.[27] In its engagement of these deep bodily currents, blues ritual and blues "talk" activate the dyadic level of the psyche, in which residuals of the early mother-infant relationship constructively live on.

I have been suggesting that for activation of the dyadic level in later life to have salutary effects, feeling—in its concern with gradations, transitions, continuities, and coherence—must take up into itself, and must contain, potentialities for disruptive emotion. (For there to be such salutary effects, neither mother nor infant of this inner dyad can be falling apart, like an exasperated or exhausted real-life mother, or a real-life infant crying itself blue in the face.) The blues is especially knowledgeable about the matters I have been discussing and demonstrates its knowledge of them in its interrelating of verbal and extraverbal expressiveness.

Though the real-life problems described in the blues are often triadic, dyadic elements juxtaposed with the triadic are essential to the larger artistic effect of the blues. As we have seen on the level of verbal content, the mother-infant relationship is suggested by the frequent epithets of "mamma" and "baby" as expressions of yearning for security and warmth, though the epithets are heard as highly metaphorical—and though the yearning is expressed in such a way as strongly to imply that it will not find concrete fulfillment. The double elements—the instance of "two"—do not themselves directly refer to the mother-infant relationship, but they do suggest the mirroring and the active mutuality characterizing that relationship, which is basic to the individuality and community, which are a major concern in the blues.

Basic to the musical structure of the blues is the African call-and-response pattern characteristic of field- and work-songs sung by black Americans on southern plantations and also characteristic of religious singing and preaching in black southern churches. In this pattern a lead singer sings a line to be followed by a choral response, or one group sings a line to be followed by the response of another group.

The most usual blues form consists of stanzas, each consisting of twelve measures (bars) of 4/4 time, based on a characteristic blues scale—most often thought to correspond to the Western

---

27. This aspect of the blues is emphasized by C. Keill in *Urban blues* (Chicago: University of Chicago Press, 1966).

diatonic scale, with the difference that the third, seventh, and sometimes the fifth intervals are treated with considerable—and important—expressive ambiguity, so that it has been proposed that these intervals be called not tones but tonal areas.[28] Each stanza repeats variants of a simple harmonic progression (I-IV-V-IV-I), and is divided into three sections, the first verbal line of which (A) is repeated, sometimes with a slight variation, the stanza closing with a different line (B) usually assonant or rhyming with the first. Thus the AAB structure itself suggests the subsuming of the triple (the three lines of the stanza) to the double AB, with the B line being, in effect, the "response" to the "call" of the A line. Further, the words of each line fill slightly more than two bars and are followed by an instrumental response to the voice. Indeed, this instrumental answering to the voice is so important as a structural principle that it may override the convention of twelve bars, so that some performers may produce stanzas of thirteen or thirteen and a half bars. The instrumental line, too, amounts more to a second voice than to a musical accompaniment subservient to the verses; and some performers succeed by various devices in keeping multiple melodic lines going, either successively or simultaneously.

Thus, though realistic problem-solving is foreign to the aesthetic and ideology of the blues, in the blues performance as a whole there is a great deal of answering. In the blues, complaints are stated and heard, and what is said is taken up in a deeply related response; whether accepting or rejecting, compassionate or mocking, the response interacts or even unites with the statement in a way that often suggests implications of which the fictional persona embodied by the singer was not aware at the outset. This answering, which is of more significance than any solution the blues verses propose or might propose to the problems as stated, is the transformation of energy effected by the blues performance. In the blues, as in life, problems are in important respects phenomena in the movement of energy. Just as there must *be* life in order for life to be impeded or endangered, so in these respects what is happening in the larger movement of energy is more important than the idiosyncratic features of one's problems.

The effect of personal problems on the movement of energy may be readily seen in such psychopathological symptoms as de-

---

28. Evans, *Big road blues* (Berkeley: University of Calif. Press, 1982), p. 24.

pression, emotional ability, and motoric excitement. In psychotherapy, energy in the form of conscious attention and concern may be
brought directly to bear on one's personal problems to the end of
releasing energy from them. But they may also be affected by energy
brought to bear upon them more indirectly by such means as music,
bodily movement, and modeling with clay. Whenever energy moves,
no matter what makes it do so, the energy invested in one's personal
problems has a different value in the psyche as a whole than when
energy is dormant.

The name of the blind bluesman Sleepy John Estes, a highly
distinctive rural singer-guitarist from Brownsville, Tennessee, is
derived from his habit of unexpectedly falling asleep, presumably
as a primitive reaction to stress. (One of his record albums is
entitled, alarmingly, *Electric Sleep*—perhaps because on it his singing and old-fashioned acoustic-guitar playing is accompanied by a
more modern amplified guitar; still, the phrase "electric sleep"
aptly and graphically suggests charged stasis, a need for transforming outward expression and gaining access to community.) In Estes's
case, singing the blues with the words inflected by his characteristic
sob is an answer to listlessness and the condition of being a helpless
victim. In general, the blues, employing a vast array of expressive
means, activates emotional currents of the deep body, and guides
them to be taken up by feeling; in this way it generates energy. In
generating it, the blues performance answers in the broadest terms
the having of the blues, while the content of the verses, concerned
with problems, is placed in an embracing and liberating context.

In blues verses, personal problems are treated both pathetically
and ironically in ways that neither deny the reality of such problems
nor strive for realistic solutions to them: the verses raise no false
hopes, though they may treat false hopes ironically. (In the final
stanzas of his "Wee Baby Blues," the Kansas City blues shouter Big
Joe Turner buoyantly claims that his disaffected woman can't get
away now, that all his troubles are gone, and that she will spend the
night "rolling" in his arms, as the instrumental accompaniment
concludes with a figure that can be heard as shrugging off the fantasy
as dismal foolishness leading to an even worse state of having the
blues.)[29] But in the blues performance as a whole, the verses play
an important role in maintaining an awareness of personal problems

---

29. *The Boss of the Blues* (Atlantic 1234).

as the very stuff of life, but one nonetheless subordinate to the more fundamental aim of generating the energy, which having the blues depressively saps. Recovering it, the blues performance awakens the sense that, in William Blake's words, "Energy is Eternal Delight."

I have observed that the AAB verse structure most common in the blues creates an ambiguity between two and three, related to the ambiguity between the three verse units in the twelve-bar stanza and the vocal part and instrumental answering within each unit. Further, though I described the blues as basically in 4/4 time, owing to syncopation and the use of triplets, musicologists have often been puzzled as to when a blues performance should be notated as some version of modified 4/4 time, and when as some version of a triple rhythm. These ambiguities between two and three are related to those in the blues treatment of its verbal content. Often, as we have seen, conflicts described in the blues are triadic in character (the stranger's muddy shoes next to one's woman's bed). But the resolution of a conflict in this noncommittal art is through an opening to feeling, which tacitly draws on its model in the mother-infant relationship. This amounts to an affirmation of individuality, including the ability to be alone with oneself, and to commune with oneself. Thus, when the contemporary bluesman Albert King sings of the visit of Queen Elizabeth II to San Francisco, he treats in a jocular way a public, formal occasion (albeit to his imagination an aborted one). Yet in the course of the piece, his interacting guitar lines and moans, like a conversation of a person with himself, seem to celebrate his own robust personal joy in being alive.[30] The opening to feeling, even in solitude, implies an affirmation of community. (Thus, an album of another contemporary bluesman, Albert Collins, is entitled, ironically, *Love Can Be Found Anywhere [Even in a Guitar]*.) Many a blues performer has used the interaction between voice and instrument as the means of re-creating a world with others, at the verge of isolation and defeat.

The triadic world of mother, father, and child generates tensions that, both in themselves and in the strategies used to master them, have been actively present as motives in some of the highest human achievements. But the mother-infant relationship remains in

---

30. "They Made the Queen Welcome," *Albert King San Francisco '83* (Fantasy F-9627).

a special way implicit in differentiated feeling, and in this sense that relationship may return in force on a level more embracing than the triadic.

There are certainly grounds for favoring another view of the dyadic and triadic elements in the blues than the one I am proposing. In this alternative view, the blues could be regarded as the artistic product of a social group that is mother-centered and—in a certain construction of this fact—pre-patriarchal, a group having a psychology that is, in psychoanalytic terms, pre-oedipal. And the dyadic elements of which I have spoken could be understood as offering regressive consolation for rigors attendant upon the incipient patriarchal, or oedipal, stage. So, too, the triadic elements concerned with betrayal and envy could be regarded as fascinated glimpses of issues belonging to a developmental level not yet securely attained—glimpses related to what psychoanalysts call the primal scene. Such a view would call attention to anxieties that arise when the time comes for the mother-infant relationship to be transformed through a more realistic recognition of the reality of other persons. The regrettable price of this partly valid but too specialized focus is the neglect of the intricate differentiation of feeling achieved by mother and infant in their interaction—and in the blues as it reflects and builds on that interaction. The differentiation of feeling in the blues is precisely an important means of maintaining and restoring coherence despite envy and thwarted desire.

In sum, whatever St. Paul means by seeing face to face, it has its protoform in the mirroring of mother and infant that I have been discussing—in the mother who can see and feel as her infant does but who can also respond to the infant in a reasoned way. In the world of disorder and trouble represented in the blues, proper modes of feeling are necessary to survival, and the art of the blues celebrates them. When the blues performer calls his "mamma" "Baby," or calls his "baby" "Mamma," he is acknowledging where proper modes of feeling begin.

After describing the poverty and hardship of his life, one black Mississippian remarked:

> . . . and you get to thinkin' about where can you go, or what can you do for to change. And there is no change. That's when the blues gets you. When there's nothin' else *to* do but what you doin' . . . and sing the blues:

I know . . . I know . . . I know . . .
I hope one day my luck will change.

I done had to work so hard,
Nothin' still won't go right,
I don't have no girl friend,
The onliest one I had, she lef' me las' night.

That can be bad, and the truth it's sad,
Oh so sad, when you lose the best girl you ever had.[31]

The most potent image of having the blues is that of being abandoned by one's woman or man; the cause of the condition is imagined as for now unchanging, and the single most dominant sentiment in the art of the blues is, "My luck is bad right now, but I hope one day it will change." What is the blues form of hope?

Let us begin with what the blues form of hope importantly is not: It is not wish. Wish makes up much of the content of the blues presentation. But it does not follow that the expression of wish in the blues amounts in any simple sense to wish fulfillment. Indeed, reflecting upon hope and wish in the blues must lead one to question the adequacy of Freud's understanding of the role of wish in imaginative products more generally.

It is useful to think of wish as the product of fantasy as a relatively passive process, expressing the feeling-toned complexes described by Jung in a way that is compatible with ego-defenses and other impedimenta to a more genuinely imaginative life. Thus, a certain man has what he calls his "pornography complex." What he means by this is that when his conscious energy becomes depleted, certain sexual preoccupations emerge in a way that he pictures as an object exposed owing to the lowering of the level of sinking water. These preoccupations then get played out in stereotyped fantasies vivid enough to be distracting or pleasantly diverting but not forceful enough and not of such a character as to engage him in a way that challenges or alters his workaday asssumptions about what his life is about. Much popular fiction serves purposes related to this kind of private fantasy, and it may be fair enough to call this wish fulfillment, provided that one does not assume too readily that one knows what constitutes this "fulfillment" and what it means to call the urge to this fulfillment "wish." Importantly, this kind of

---

31. Quoted in Oliver, *Conversations with the blues*, p. 2.

fantasy is partly continuous with, but also partly of another order than, imagination of a kind that does challenge ego-assumptions and is transformative in a deeper way.

As an art of survival, the blues cannot afford the idle luxury of wish divorced from a deeper transformative process. In the context of the blues, a good name for wish so divorced would be "false hope." Denying that the blues-inducing circumstances can be changed at least now, never proposing what are meant to be taken as realistic and adequate solutions to real-life problems, and always allowing that a problem solved may soon be replaced by a problem of at least the same magnitude, the blues plays with wish in a rich variety of ways, implicitly exposing it as false hope. The result is not hope as a plan of action, but it is hope as affirming and enhancing both the vital core of the individual and the community of the blues performance, and of the larger blues world of shared idiom and attitude. In the blues performance, hopelessness is sacrificed to such affirmation and enhancement.

Taking being abandoned by one's woman or man as the basic image of having the blues, one might say, with an oddness that may prove illuminating, that the blues detaches one from one's abandonment. My purpose in speaking in this odd way is to contrast the sort of detachment I have in mind with behavior to which John Bowlby applies the same term in his study *Attachment and Loss* (1969). By this term Bowlby means the kind of affectional distancing to be seen in children who react to their mother's prolonged absence by adapting dully to having a succession of caretakers and by listlessly turning away from their mothers when they do return.[32] This affectional limbo is related to the pornography complex discussed earlier. In contrast, the blues would say, *"Feel* your pain; *want* to reconnect." This pain and this want are hope and life, which must be served by various kinds of distancing, framing, and detachment that allow wish to be seen as false hope, and abandonment to be protested against. The pathos of the blues is characteristically treated ironically.

Let us take a simple example of blues wish. A familiar line has the singer boast: "Never had one gal at a time, always had six, seven, eight or nine." In one sense, this sounds like an insurance policy against both abandonment and the complications that come with

---

32. J. Bowlby, *Attachment and loss*, vol. 1: *Attachment* (New York: Basic Books, 1969), p. 28.

trying to deal with a single woman. Of course, this is also sexual boasting, but how is it to be heard? In the culture reflected in the blues, women are for men a value, albeit often a problematic one. But only the right amount of a good thing adequately makes up for the lack of that thing, and in this line the right amount is lost in a wishful vision of plenty. Considering the misery of triangles, we are able to appreciate the jealousy, spite, confusion, and mayhem that would be unloosed by a man's attempts to deal with nine women at once: Having nine women would surely leave a man worse off than having none.

Similarly, the ironic perspective of Fred McDowell's "Good Morning Little School Girl" is apparent at the outset, as a clearly adult male presents himself as a schoolboy proposing that he walk a girl home. After talking about buying her a diamond ring, there is an enigmatic hint at an altercation; then she is gone, apparently without a trace, and he is looking for her. He says that he will buy an airplane and fly from town to town, and that if he does not find her, he will not let his airplane down. Can a schoolboy or a black Mississippi farmer buy an airplane? Of what use is an airplane if one has no particular destination? What kind of looking for a woman can one do from an airplane? Presumably this perpetual-motion airplane is fueled by the same kind of magical power that operates the ever-ready sexual apparatus of the man with six, seven, eight, or nine women. Moreover, after describing the airplane trip, he again speaks of buying his woman a diamond ring, thus denying that she left him, and dealing with his sense of loss and injured self-esteem by reminding himself of his imagined wealth and, hence, power.[33]

Johnny Copeland assumes a similarly heroic and foredoomed stance when he pictures himself on an airplane to North Carolina, where he is sure that his woman is "somewhere." Airlines do not sell tickets to "North Carolina," though they do to Raleigh-Durham, Fayetteville, High Point, and Charlotte: Practically, arriving in North Carolina will have him no closer to the elusive woman than he was in New York City, where his imaginary trip started.[34]

In other ways, too, the ironic stance may offer means of making the best of a bad lot. Thus, Muddy Waters, abandoned, hears what "sounds like" his "little honey bee," who has been all around the

---

33. Mississippi Fred McDowell, *"I do not play no rock'n'roll"* (Capitol 0898 SM-409).

34. Johnny Copeland, "North Carolina," *Texas Twister* (Rounder 2040).

world making honey and is now coming home to him: He expresses pleasure in the return, ending his abandonment, of a woman he shares with countless other men. Then again, the "lot of buzzin'" he hears is pretty indefinite; perhaps it is not his little honey bee after all.[35]

Small children do not understand irony; the irony of the blues is pervasive, complex, and often highly ambiguous. Blues pathos draws upon experiences of attachment and separation within the mother-infant relationship. While insisting that we know the painful reality of abandonment, deprivation, and constriction, the blues ironically plays with wish, for the delight of play, and to the end of mocking the delusions to which wish may lead. By its beauty and generation of energy, the blues reawakens the joy in survival that is the basic form of hope—and draws one into the blues community of survivors.

---

35. Muddy Waters, "Honey Bee," *More Real Folk Blues* (Chess VG 405 515020).

# Symbol and Ritual in Melancholia: The Archetype of the Divine Victim

## Tristan O. Cornes

> *There was the god Baal, with a cruel mouth like*
> *a slit (a wrinkle in the side of a bed), waiting*
> *to devour me as a living sacrifice. There was*
> *Hecate, who used generally to appear in pillows,*
> *her shape was, I think, the most horrible of all.*
>
> John Custance, "Wisdom, Madness
> and Folly," 1952

### Introduction

Psychoanalysts who have followed the maps of the unconscious drawn by Freud and Jung have not been richly rewarded in their efforts to mine the darksome lodes of melancholia. Many have tunneled to seeming dead ends, while others, making minor find-

---

**Tristan O. Cornes,** Ph.D., is a psychotherapist in private practice in Melbourne, Australia. A graduate of the University of Auckland and California School of Professional Psychology, Berkeley, he completed doctoral internships at Diabasis and the Clinic of the C. G. Jung Institute of San Francisco. This article forms part of a work in progress on melancholia and is based on his dissertation entitled, *The Ego-Self Relationship in Psychotic Depression: The Archetype of the Divine Victim, Examined with Reference to the Symbolism and Ritual Process in Ancient Near Eastern and Israelite Psalms of Lamentation.* He is the author of "Yahweh and the Great Goddess in the Freud/Jung Conflict" (forthcoming, *American Imago*).

ings before tiring of the painstaking work, set off in search of new and more accessible treasures.

The most promising discoveries were made during the early years of psychoanalysis. Abraham (1911, 1924) explicated the crucial role of the ambivalent, oral relationship with the mother, while Freud (1917) described how one part of the ego (later to be called the "superego") sets itself over and against the other which it then dominates, judges, and punishes. Freud found that whereas in the mourning process the world has become poor and empty, in melancholia it is the ego itself which has become impoverished: "The patient represents his ego to us as worthless, incapable of any achievement and morally despicable; he reproaches himself, vilifies himself and expects to be cast out and punished" (p. 246). Soon Rado (1928) made a major—but much neglected—breakthrough by conceptualizing melancholia as a process of *penitence, self-punishment, and expiation* evolving from the ego's relationship to its isolated objects (or "instinct representations") of love and hate: the "good mother" and the "bad mother" (p. 431). When the adult melancholiac gives play alternately to the "exaggerated ambivalence" of this instinctual disposition and "thus succeeds in completely withdrawing his consciousness from the light or dark side of the object" (p. 434), an internal dynamic is set up where the ego introjects the bad object. The ego then becomes the "whipping boy . . . and victim of the sadistic tendency now emanating from the super-ego" (p. 435) in a process of anticipatory self-punishment and expiation aimed at atoning with and winning back the lost, "only good" object. Rado continues:

> It is as if the ego of the melancholiac were to say to his super-ego: "I will take all the guilt upon myself and submit myself to any punishment; I will even, by ceasing to care for my bodily welfare, offer myself as an expiatory sacrifice, if you will only interest yourself in me and be kind to me." (P. 424)

The first manifestation of a penitential process of guilt→punishment→atonement unfolds when the baby's experiences of hunger, frustration, and rage at the absent breast are followed by a primitive guilt. There dawns the realization that just as hunger is the "deserved punishment" for the angry outburst, satiation is the reward for a penitential atonement process. Rado stated:

> The torments of hunger are the mental precursors of later "punishments" and, by way of the discipline of punishment, they come to be

the primal mechanism of self-punishment, which in melancholia assumes such a fatal significance. At the bottom of the melancholiac's profound dread of impoverishment there is really simply the dread of starvation (that is, of impoverishment in physical possessions), with which the vitality of such part of his ego as remains normal reacts to the expiatory acts which threaten the life of the patient in this disease. But drinking at the mother's breast remains the radiant image of unremitting, forgiving love. It is certainly no mere chance that the Madonna nursing the Child has become the emblem of a mighty religion and thereby the emblem of a whole epoch of our Western civilization. I think if we trace the chain of ideas, *guilt—atonement— forgiveness*, back to the sequence of experiences of early infancy: *rage, hunger, drinking at the mother's breast*, we have the explanation of the problem why the hope of absolution and love is perhaps the most powerful conception which we meet with in the higher strata of the mental life of mankind. (1928, p. 427)

Rado concluded that melancholia's "synthetic function" (p. 430) or intrapsychic penitential process thus "represents an attempt at reparation (cure) on a grand scale" (p. 435).

Readers who are conversant with Kleinian psychoanalysis may find that Rado's theory sounds familiar! Indeed, the striking similarity between Rado's explication and Klein's almost simultaneous (1935) discovery of the *depressive position* is all the more significant given that Klein's views have found considerable favor with many analytical psycologists. For example, Klein used the term "imago" to denote "a phantastically distorted picture of the real objects upon which they are based" (1935, p. 262), and in 1912 it had been Jung who introduced the term *imago* into psychoanalysis (Laplanche and Pontalis 1973, p. 211) to denote an autonomous psychological factor "which has a living independence in the psychic hierarchy" (Jung 1912, par. 62, n.4). This distinguishes between an object and "an image of the subjective relation to the object" (Jung 1921, par. 812), and Jung explained that in his later work "I use the term 'archetype' instead, in order to bring out the fact that we are dealing with impersonal, collective forces" (Jung 1912, par. 62, n.4). The primacy of imagoes as inner fantasy figures lies at the very heart of Klein's psychoanalysis. Klein recognized that the operation of imagoes, "with phantastically good and phantastically bad characteristics, is a general mechanism in adults as well as children" (1929, p. 203), and Fordham has noted that Klein's close collaborators, Isaacs and Heimann, both define unconscious fantasy "in terms almost identical with a definition of the archetype used by Jung" (1976, p. 7).

Kleinian object-relations theory can, therefore be adequately translated into the structural language of ego-Self processes; part and whole objects may then be seen as part and whole Self-objects.

Klein (1935) proposes that the roots of melancholia lie deep within the depressive position, a developmental task where crucial ego integration is achieved if the ego reconciles its ambivalent relationships to loved and hated parts of the object (i.e., the "good" and "bad" breasts) into a relationship with one whole object (the mother) who is both good and bad. The successful working through of depressive position conflicts between the "good" (satiation, warmth, togetherness, love) and the "bad" (hunger, discomfort, abandonment, hatred) leads to the recognition that alongside states of mourning, hatred, anger, and sadness there is guilt and an urge to make reparation, restoring the lost and injured loved object. When the ego does not achieve this capacity to contain the conflict between the life and death instincts, the ego either falls victim to the death instinct's devouring maw or leaps into a manic triumph over death, hatred, and loss by "feasting" upon the object world.

This conception of the depressive position is central to Kleinian theory and practice, and has also been highly valued by Winnicott (1948, 1954) and members of the London School of analytical psychology (Fordham 1970, 1973: Lambert 1981; Redfearn 1980). However, while many of the *patterns* described by Klein are accepted as valid, analysts with a Jungian background doubt Klein's dating of the processes and her emphasis upon understanding all of these processes as due to ego functioning (Fordham 1976). Her critics from within Freudian psychoanalysis consider that the complex processes which she believes to take place are not possible due to the rudimentary state of the ego during the early months of infancy, yet a theory of a primary or original Self—out of which the ego evolves—partly mitigates this criticism by transferring the plane of intrapsychic events from the developing ego to the original Self and its archetypal unconscious. Fordham proposes that:

> The processes Klein defined, or which have been elaborated by her followers, may be correctly described but wrongly understood; in short, she is trying to describe in terms of the ego processes that are the result of deintegrations of the self, not essentially attributable to the ego but to the way in which the opposites in the archetypal unconscious interact. (1976, p. 60)

In order to deepen these earlier psychoanalytic understandings of severe depression, our inquiry must, therefore, be transposed into the framework of the ego-Self relationship. This is where the study of religious and mythological symbolism sheds light upon the vicissitudes of melancholia's intrapsychic relationship between an "I" and its "Thou."

## Shadow Adumbrations

Jung's demarcation of the *personal shadow* from that experience of "absolute evil" which signifies the appearance of the *shadow as an archetype* (1959, par. 19) has provided a new conceptual tool to further the quest for melancholia's mother lode. For it is precisely this archetypal dimension of evil which is a dominant force in the infant's original Self, and at whose mercy is the weak and vulnerable ego. Fordham describes how Jung's distinction between the personal and the archetypal shadow applies to the infant's psychological processes at the time of the paranoid-schizoid and depressive positions:

> In *Aion* [Jung] . . . is particularly clear that there are two aspects of the shadow: first, its personal elements that can be assimilated into the ego; second, there is absolute evil, which cannot. It is evident that in maturation the first can be developed only when there is sufficient ego formed and when the child's psyche is structured enough for there to be a repressed unconscious. Without being dogmatic, it would seem that this takes place during and after the oedipal conflicts and their resolution. Absolute evil, however, must refer to a much earlier phase; then infantile affects have indeed characteristics that are most suggestive. They are known to be total in feeling; there is either total and blissful love or else total cataclysmic destruction. (1976, p. 29)

The archetypal shadow can be seen as the *shadow side of the Self* or the *negative Self.* The "death instinct," for example, may be understood as a valence of the Self (Gordon 1960) whose archetypal imagery is most dramatically evoked by the Wrathful Deity and the Terrible Mother. Indeed, Jung's extensive discourses on the archetypal ground of such (psychoanalytic) images as the "good mother" and "bad mother"—besides "stressing the inevitability of the dual mother fantasy so important in Klein's work" (Fordham 1970, p. 20)—are the theoretical root of that death instinct which Klein views as dominating the psyche in melancholia. It was Jung's influence, especially his formulation of the Terrible Mother "who devours and destroys, and thus symbolizes death itself" (Jung 1912, par. 504) that led his pupil Dr. Sabina Spielrein to develop the idea of a death instinct, which was eventually taken up by Freud.[1] In other words, the death instinct derives from the Wrathful Deity/ Terrible Mother[2] dimension of the negative Self or archetypal shadow, and it is this destructive Thanatos aspect of the Self which, at the seeming "invitation" of the ego, debases, tyrannizes, and may even murder the negatively inflated ego-as-victim in melancholia. The "death threat" to the ego typically arises from the overwhelming activity of the Self (Fordham 1976, p. 10), and it is during severe depression that the Self is especially "constellated predominantly in negative and destructive images" (Wilke 1978, p. 111).

Both the *negative Self* and the *positive Self* can be further differentiated into bi-polar components. The destructive aspect of the negative Self is symbolized by *Divine Wrath*, an affect-image whose "inseparable companion and opposite" is the *Divine Victim* (Edinger 1960, p. 7). The Divine Victim takes on "an excessive, unbounded sense of guilt and suffering. We see this in cases of melancholia which express the feeling that 'no one in the world is as guilty as I am.' There is just too much guilt" (Edinger 1972, p. 15). This mythological archetype of the Victim or Outcast stands opposite to that of the *Chosen One* (Baynes 1940, p. 718). Within

---

1. A brief exposition of Spielrein's paper on "Destruction as the Cause of Coming into Being" is found in a recent book dealing with her important role in the early years of psychoanalysis (Carotenuto 1982, pp. 141–42, 191–92). A synopsis of a partial presentation of the paper to the Vienna Psychoanalytic Society on November 29, 1911, together with the subsequent discussion by the group members, is recorded in Nunberg and Federn (1974, pp. 329–35).

2. We must recognize that this aspect of the Self may well be sexually undifferentiated. In a fascinating paper which bridges Freudian, Kleinian, and Jungian psychoanalysis, Elkin describes how a primordial anxiety of holy terror in the face of a cruel or indifferent Other is followed by a stage of impotent primordial despair, and then salvation arrives with the intervention of the merciful Other. He writes:

> These polar images, which give effective coherence to the infant's now blissful, now terrifying experiences in the newly revealed physical world, are developments of the primordial conceptions, or *archetypes*, that reflect the dual aspect of the primordial Other, best denoted by the terms God and Devil, from an intermediate, preculminating phase of primordial consciousness. Hence the infant's images can be termed more realistically (in the sense of more closely reflecting his immediate experience) *Divine Mother* and *Diabolic Mother*, if we bear in mind, however, that these images, like that of Freud's *Father* . . . are sexually undifferentiated. The Divine Mother revives feeling-memories of communion with the primordial Other as mercifully omniscient and omnipotent Loving-Cognition, whereas the Diabolic Mother revives those of panic terror at the sight of the primordial Other's satanic aspect, wrathful, mocking, inscrutable, or cruelly indifferent. (1972, p. 401)

the schema outlined in Figure 1, the Divine Victim and the Wrathful Deity are bi-polar archetypes contained within the negative Self, whereas the Chosen One and the Benevolent Deity are bi-polar archetypes contained within the positive Self. The Divine Victim and the Chosen One form the nucleii or mythic centers of melancholia and mania: In melancholia there is a state of *negative infla-tion* where the ego identifies with the negative Self's archetype of the Divine Victim—"the individual takes upon himself a degree of guilt and responsibility that is transpersonal and collective, not properly belonging to the finite ego" (Edinger 1960, p. 7)—while mania represents a state of *positive inflation* where the ego identifies with the positive Self's archetype of the Chosen One.

This structural understanding adequately accommodates Klein's and Rado's theories that the central dynamic in melancholia and mania is a radical disruption in the ego's integration of good and

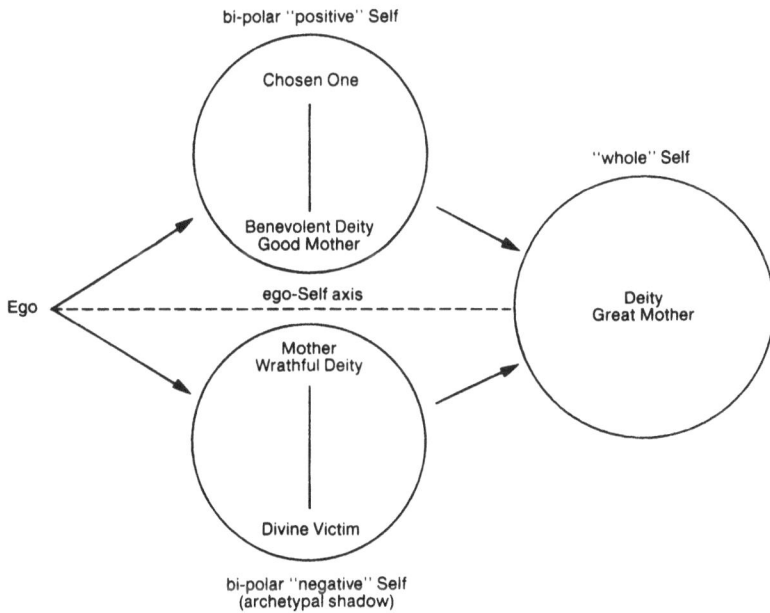

**Figure 1. The Task of the Depressive Position.**
The ego synthesizes part-Self object relationships into a relationship with a whole-Self object.

bad part-object relationships into a whole-object relation.[3] Both Klein and Rado are essentially describing melancholia's state of negative inflation where the ego, identifying with the Divine Victim aspect of the archetypal shadow, submits to a "deserved punishment" by the Wrathful Deity/Terrible Mother pole of the archetypal shadow in an expiational quest for atonement with the Benevolent Deity/Good Mother pole of the positive Self.

A simplified schema of intra-psychic structure, shown in Figure 2, illustrates how the personal shadow draws from, but is not to be identified with, the archetypal shadow or negative Self, whereas the "superego" draws from both the positive (Benevolent Deity) and negative (Wrathful Deity) aspects of the Self. Again we see a meeting ground of Freudian and Jungian psychoanalysis, for this conceptualization of superego structure is compatible with Freud's explication of melancholia's harsh superego punishing a "worthless" ego. The superego does, in fact, have many characteristics which Jung ascribes to the Self. For example, there are points of juncture between Jung's idea of the Self as the central archetype of order and Jacobson's thesis that "the centralized, regulating power of the superego . . . becomes a governing force for all our moods . . . [and] may properly be called an indicator and regulator of the entire ego state" (1964, p. 133). Jung viewed the superego as Freudian theory's closest approximation to the Self, but the superego is really only "a

---

3. Envisioning melancholia as a state of negative ego inflation due to identification with the Divine Victim also elucidates Freudian psychoanalytic observations that in melancholia there is "an impoverishment of the ego on a grand scale" (Freud 1917, p. 246) where the criticising and punishing agency "negatively invests the nucleus of the ego" (Alexander 1931, p. 79), with the consequence that the melancholiac accepts a suffering which "expands more and more, relentlessly and endlessly into a psyche that seems endless in its capacity to experience sorrow" (Arieti 1978, p. 242). Jungians have described a similar intra-psychic state as a loss of binding energy and an excess of repulsive energy in the ego, where the archetypal imagery "reflects the primal loss of unity" (Hobson 1955, p. 46); a "primal complex" where an aggressor and a victim are locked into a dark containing enclosure (Moody 1961); a harsh animus victimizing "a deprived, weakened, and at times structurally deficient ego" (Alex 1968, p. 66), a negative constellation of the primal relationship which inundates the ego nucleus, creating a "negativized ego" or "distress ego" whose archetypal imagery of hell is attended by hunger, loneliness, pain, and the void (Neumann 1973, pp. 74–81); a "Shadow drama" which possesses ego (Curry 1975); a weakened and infantile ego tyrannized by a demonic superego, destructive shadow, and negative Great Mother figure of the Self (Blomeyer et al. 1975); an ego which is negatively related to the Self (Newton and Redfearn 1977); and an "unbearable concentration of energy in the ego . . . [with an] unbearable sense of guilt, unworthiness and remorse which finds suicide as the only way out to bring expiation" (Vitale 1980, p. 220).

bi-polar "positive" Self

Chosen One

Benevolent Deity,
Good Mother

"whole" Self

Superego

ego-Self axis

Deity
Great Mother

Ego

Terrible Mother
Wrathful Deity

Personal Victim

Divine Victim

Personal Shadow

Archetypal Shadow
(bi-polar "negative" Self)

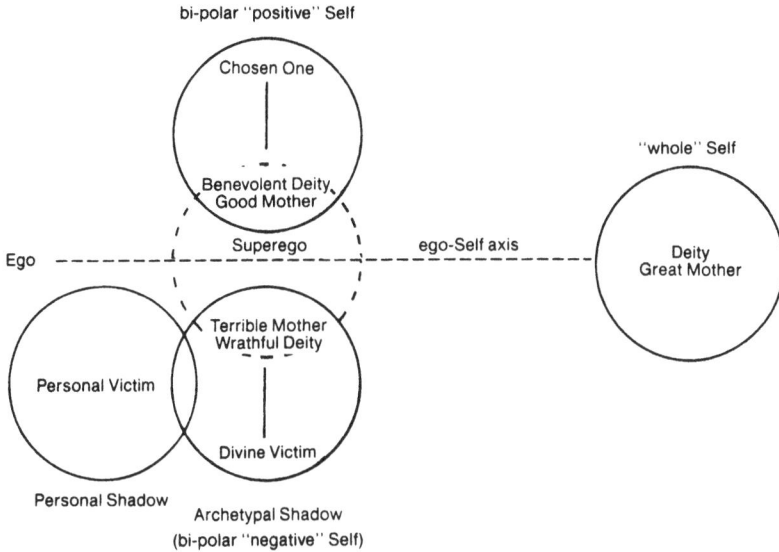

**Figure 2. Intra-psychic Structure.** The personal shadow draws from the archetypal shadow, and the superego (in its role as an unavoidable substitute for the Self) draws from the split apart aspects of the "positive" Self and "negative" Self.

necessary and unavoidable substitute" for the Self (1942, par. 394). If the Self is withdrawn from projection as a general moral principle or collective ethos, one's inner conflicts will be resolved through dialogue with the Self. Jung wrote:

So long as the self is unconscious, it corresponds to Freud's superego and is a source of perpetual moral conflict. If, however, it is withdrawn from projection and is no longer identical with public opinion, then one is truly one's own yea and nay. The self then functions as a *union of opposites* and thus constitutes the most *immediate experience of the Divine* which it is psychologically possible to imagine. (1942, par. 396; italics added)

It is precisely the ego's relationship with the "whole" Self (i.e., with the "Divine within") which is seriously disturbed in severe depression. Rado's characterization of melancholia as a process of expiation, sacrifice, and atonement is, therefore, particularly evocative for two reasons. First, it lies close to the manifest phenomenology of melancholia's many "religiously" colored images and rituals such as lamentations over the aloofness of God; confession of sins; weeping, wailing, and moaning; fasting; sleeplessness; sitting in stupor; and self-mutilation. Second, Rado is accurately (albeit intuitively!) describing "religious" parameters of an intrapsychic dynamic which concerns the ego and the Self, an "I–Thou" relationship whose meaning can best be understood by referring to the symbolism of the *covenant* in ancient Near Eastern religion. The Divine Victim enacting a process of expiation, sacrifice, and atonement is just as dramatic a protagonist in melancholia as the Divine Victim whose utterances and petitions are found in ancient religious *psalms of lamentation* dating from 2000 B.C. The striking difference is that melancholia's atonement process is intra-psychic: Its symbols and rituals are dimensions of a subjective relationship between the ego and the Self, whereas the ancient lamentations are renditions of a more literally and objectively perceived relationship between human and Deity.

### Religious Symbolism in Melancholia

The symptoms of severe depression have been described consistently throughout successive eras of history. If we compare modern accounts of symptomatology against our earliest written records from the Egyptians, Greeks, Hebrews, and Chinese, it is clear that the syndrome has remained essentially the same for well over 25 centuries (Arieti and Bemporad 1978; Lewis 1934). The vivid description of melancholia given by Aretaeus of Cappadocia in the first or second century A.D. portrays a clinical syndrome surprisingly similar to that found in a modern-day textbook of psychiatry: Aretaeus "described very well the *religious, guilt-ridden,* and *self-sacrificing* attitudes of the melancholiac and the gay and overactive behavior of the manic" (Arieti 1974, p. 452; italics added).

The melancholiac's preoccupation with guilt, sin, and sacrificial punishment was also described in Plutarch's amazingly accurate accounts written about 100 A.D. (Grinker et al. 1961). Particularly significant is Plutarch's idea that as a man approaches the gods he is likely to develop a depression. When the human-Deity relationship is interpreted at the subjective level, the image of a man developing melancholia as he approaches the gods aptly symbolizes how the depressive process is determined by the ego's encounter with aspects of the Self. The following passage by Plutarch thus deserves our careful attention:

> When a man is depressed, every little evil is magnified by the frighten-ing spectres of his anxiety. He looks on himself as a man whom the gods hate and pursue with their anger. A far worse lot is before him. He dares not employ any means of averting or remedying the evil lest he be found fighting against the gods. The physician, the consoling friend, are driven away. "Leave me," says the wretched man, "me the impious, the accursed, hated of the gods, to suffer my punishment." He sits out of doors wrapped in sackcloth or in filthy rags. Ever anon he rolls himself naked in the dirt, confessing about this and that sin. He has written, eaten, drunk something wrong. He has gone some way or other which the Divine Being did not approve of. The festivals in honor of the gods give no pleasure to him but fill him rather with fear. He proves in his own case that the saying of Pythagoras is false that we are happiest when we approach the gods, for it is just then that he is most wretched. Temples and altars are places of refuge for the perse-cuted, but where all others find deliverance from their fears, there this wretched man must most fear and tremble. Asleep or awake, he is haunted alike by the spectre of his anxiety. Awake he makes no use of his reason, and asleep he enjoys no respite from his alarms. His use of his reason slumbers; his fears are always awake. Nowhere can he find an escape from his imaginary terrors. (Plutarch, quoted in Grinker et al. 1961, p. 33)

The religious content of severe depression was also recognized by Kraepelin (1904). Describing a case of melancholia where a 59-year-old farmer began confessing the sins of his youth by complain-ing "I am so apprehensive, so wretched; I cannot lie still for anxiety. O God, if I had only not transgressed so grievously," Kraepelin realized that the most common delusions are ideas of sin which generally have a religious coloring: "Such are the ideas," wrote Kraepelin, "of having fallen away from God and being forsaken, or of being possessed by the devil" (p. 66). For example, this patient insisted that he had fallen away from God, and that the Evil One was in the room and would carry him off; "He also has a strong feeling that some great change has come over him, and that 'he is not the same as before' " (ibid).

The accounts in Kraepelin's case vignettes are not significantly different from the lamentations of today's patients. Arieti's picture of "self-blaming melancholia" is just as stark as the ancient (and earlier twentieth century) portraits. Arieti writes:

> These patients do not appear shallow or superficial as do the patients suffering from claiming depression. It is true that they are also very

conventional but their conventionality finds sources in the traditions of the culture to which the patient belongs. It is true that they are poor in verbal symbols or in imagery, but their symbols often retain an augustinian or medieval flavor, with duty, sin, guilt, punishment, as the recurring themes. *God often becomes the dominant other.* In these cases the message the patient conveys is not, "Help me," but "I do not deserve any help, any pity." When suicidal ideas exist the message is not, "You should prevent my death," but "I deserve to die; I should do to myself what you should do to me, but you are too good to do it." (1978, p. 223; italics added)

Although there often appears to be a poverty of verbalization in melancholia, upon listening closely we find that many decidedly religious images are evoked. When the ancient religious psalms of lamentation are interpreted as symbolic accounts of the ego's encounter with the shadow side of the Self, we are close to the archetypal substrata of melancholia's penitential process of guilt, self-punishment, expiation, and atonement. Jacobsohn (1968) recognized the parallel themes in an ancient Egyptian lamentation (recorded on papyrus around 2000 B.C.) and the lamentations of today's depressed patients. Although this Egyptian lament is strictly classed as a Wisdom text rather than a psalm of lamentation (Pritchard 1969) it portrays a similar, intensely personal, inner process of transformation which has been heralded by a feeling of being separated from God. This tragic process of suffering the despair and terror of godlessness has many affinities to the penitential process described in Mesopotamian and Hebrew psalms of lamentation, religious texts which portray the symbolism and rituals involved when a supplicant is gripped by absolute evil. The experience is seen as a consequence of some sin or rebellion against a deity. Suffering divine wrath and vengeance, abandoned to be cast alone into the wilderness, the supplicant confesses to all manner of defilement and sin, and through a ritual process of penitence and sacrificial expiation seeks to make atonement with the benevolent deity.

### The Ritual Process in Melancholia

Not only are the melancholiac's verbalized themes of sinfulness, alienation, poverty, and deserved punishment more symbolically meaningful than is commonly recognized, but the entire depressive syndrome is characterized by dramatic and stereotypical modes of behavior which have close affinities to religious lamentation rituals. Once we raise the possibility that the melancholiac is unconsciously enacting some kind of penitence, expiation, sacrifice, and atonement, the patient's ritualistic behaviors may be seen to comprise a rich—but often overlooked—dimension of both the depressive *content* and the depressive *process.*[4]

Just as the schizophrenic process is dominated by the symbolism of *renewal,* melancholia embraces the symbolism of *repair.* In contrast with the schizophrenic's ritual process of renewal where the ego-Self relationship is torn asunder as the ego is overwhelmed in a regression to an original Self state which paves the way for a major reforging of the ego-Self axis (Perry 1962, 1976), melancholia presents a ritual process of lamentation, expiation, and atonement aimed at repairing a profound state of alienation and imbalance within the ego-Self relationship. Structurally, melancholia and mania do not share schizophrenia's drastic level of ego disintegration; rather, considerable ego cohesiveness and an alarming energic "ego intensity"—the negatively inflated Divine Victim in melancholia, and the positively inflated Chosen One in mania—wounds the ego-Self axis by disrupting the ego's potential to "dialogue" with the whole Self. Whereas the schizophrenic's drama of intra-psychic renewal involves a "return to beginnings" which resembles and parallels the image-sequences of the ancient Near Eastern ritual pattern of divine kingship—"an annual seasonal ceremony for the renewal of the year, of the world, of the kingdom, and of the kingship, on the days of the New Year" (Perry 1962, p. 859)—the melancholiac's drama of penitence, aimed at repairing the ego-Self relationship, resembles and parallels the image sequences in the ancient Near Eastern ritual process of lamentation, expiation, and restoration of a breach in the covenantal and dialogical human-Deity relationship.

When digging through the sub-strata of mythology, religion, alchemy, and literature in search of melancholia's archetypal center, I struck upon the ancient lamentation texts and was overcome with awe. The very archeologists who unearthed these cuneiform tablets from the desert sands must have been as excited as this! How had

---

4. Other than brief passages where Alexander (1931) and Roheim (1955) draw attention to the similarities between ascetic rituals—which function to propitiate the superego—and the behavior of the severely depressed patient, the significance of melancholia's decidedly archaic and "religious" rituals does not appear to have been developed within psychoanalysis.

the images and actions of my severely depressed patients been
documented thousands of years ago? I read, for example, the following descriptions of depressive suffering:

> I heard and therefore cried Woe!,
> > and tore asunder my princely garment
> > and uttered lamentation.
> Like a lion I roared, and my spirit was stirred,
> > (Widengren 1936, p. 229)

> [Priest]
> In sorrow there he sits
> With cries of affliction, in trouble of heart.
> With bitter tears, in bitter sorrow,
> Like the dove he moans grievously,
> > night and day.
> Unto his merciful god, like a wild cow,
> > he cries,
> He makes a grievous sighing.
> > (King 1899, pp. 211–12)

Was this not the elderly woman who regularly stirred from her
wide-eyed depressive stupor to moan like a wild cow and roar like a
lion, her laments resonating mournfully along the hospital corri-
dors? Similarly, only months after observing a young man whose
melancholia was a darkness truly "black, blacker than black"—
convinced that the devil was coming for him, this patient had
stripped naked and was sitting on the floor of his security room,
eating his excrement—I came upon the following passages:

> For food I eat filth and weeping.
> For wine I drink water of the limbs and penis.
> For the wine of life I drink bitter waters.
> > (Langdon 1923, p. 13)

> I spend the night in my dung like an ox,
> And wallow in my excrement like a sheep.
> > (Lambert 1960, p. 45)

The deeper I delved into these ancient religious texts and their
modern interpreters, a slow dawn began to rise over melancholia's
*nigredo.* Not only are the psalms, at the subjective level, a "theological" container for the images and rituals of melancholia's ego-Self

relationship, but two closely related schools of psalm exegesis have provided a structural analysis of lamentation as a process of penitence, expiation, and atonement. The psalms of lamentation can, therefore, illuminate melancholia's lamentation process where a negatively inflated Divine Victim ego complex seeks to make atonement with the Benevolent Deity/Good Mother aspect of the Self.

While Gunkel's (1930) "form-historical" or "type-critical" approach to psalm research was later to be developed into a deeper analysis of the psalm's ritual significance by Mowinckel's (1955, 1962) "cult-functional" or "cult-historical" school, it was Gunkel who first described a formal structure of "principal components" in the lamentation psalm. These components can be outlined in the following schedule:

The Address: (a) Invocation of God, with descriptive attributes; (b) praise of God

The Lament: (a) Aloofness of the God; (b) penitence formulas; (c) complaints of various evils; (d) transition formulas

The Prayer: (a) Atonement; (b) forgiveness of sins; (c) removal of various evils; (d) life and prosperity

The Thanksgiving: Formulas of gratitude and blessing. (Widengren 1936, p. 37)

Keeping in mind that this schedule is an ideal reconstruction and that the order and occurrence of any formula may vary considerably within a psalm text (Dalglish 1962, p. 3), each formula can be further differentiated into image themes and accompanying ritual actions. For example, in both religious lamentation and melancholia the "Aloofness of God" evokes images of abandonment, alienation, divine wrath as punishment for sin, rejection, and hunger, whereas the "Complaints of various evils" include images and rituals concerning weakness, confusion, and wandering; weeping and tears; fasting; sleeplessness; somatic distress; silence and stupor; binding and imprisonment; sinking into morass or the abyss; being cast into a pit, grave, underworld, or desert; impotence; poverty; being attacked by enemies or wild beasts; and being judged guilty in lawsuits.

While a more detailed explication of melancholia's intra-psychic structure and its process of lamentation and attempted repair of the ego-Self relationship will be presented in a later paper, an overview can be seen in Figures 3 and 4.

Figure 3 illustrates the initial stages of severe depression. As with the approach to schizophrenia at Diabasis (Perry 1976), the

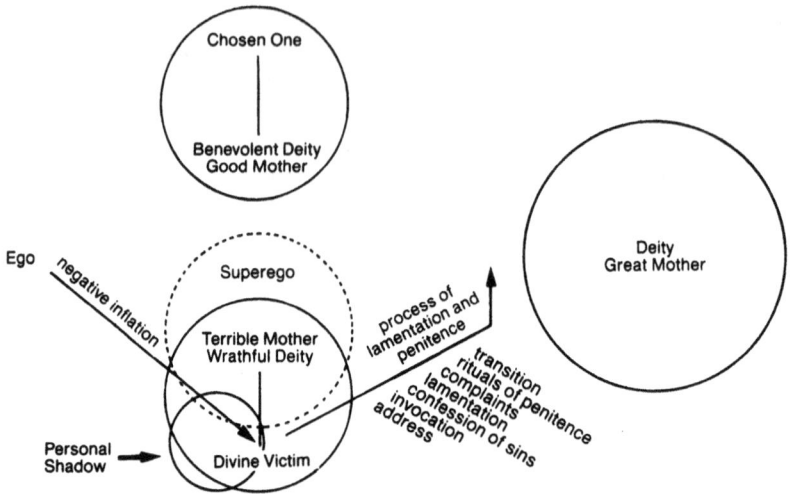

**Figure 3. Melancholia: Initial Stages.** The ego identifies with the Divine Victim, and the superego becomes a harsh, terrible, and condemning persecutor.

verbal utterances and ritual actions must be given a chance to unfold in a safe and supportive atmosphere. In these early "complaint" and "confession" phases of the lamentation process the psychotherapist, like the priest in religious lamentation, is essentially an empathic listener who is fully present and is participating as a mediator to the dramatic, "covenantal" exchange between ego and Self. Freud recognized this similarity in the roles of the psychoanalyst and priest when, having proposed that the rituals of psychopathology are as "perfectly significant in every detail" as those minutae of religious ceremonial which "are full of significance and have a symbolic meaning" (pp. 119–20), he wrote:

> It is one of the conditions of the illness that the person who is obeying a compulsion carries it out without understanding its meaning—or at any rate its chief meaning. . . . we must remember that as a rule the ordinary pious individual, too, performs a ceremonial without concerning himself with its significance, although priests and scientific investigators may be familiar with the—mostly symbolic—meaning of the ritual. In all believers, however, the motives which impel them to religious practices are unknown to them or are represented in consciousness by others which are advanced in their place. (1907, pp. 122–23)

It is later in the transition from "complaint" to "petition" and "atonement" that the psychotherapist may play a more actively interpretive role. In her work with severely depressed patients Jacobson found that, contrary to the belief that analysis proper is restricted to a "free interval" between mania or melancholia, analysis may proceed during severely retarded depressive phases "provided that the analyst has sufficient patience to adjust to the slowed-up emotional and thought patterns of such patients" (1954, p. 604), and from Chestnut Lodge Pao writes that:

> Inasmuch as the patient's ability for analytic work is greatly curtailed during the manic and incapacitating depressive phases, I have noted . . . that the verbal and nonverbal products of the patient during these periods are rich in content and meaning, and that it may prove useful for the therapist to stay with the patient during such severely psychotic moments. (1980, p. 125, n.10)

The "transition" phase, replete with imagery of sacrifice and rituals such as self-mutilation, is a critical juncture in the lamentation process. Here melancholia may follow various routes. One is

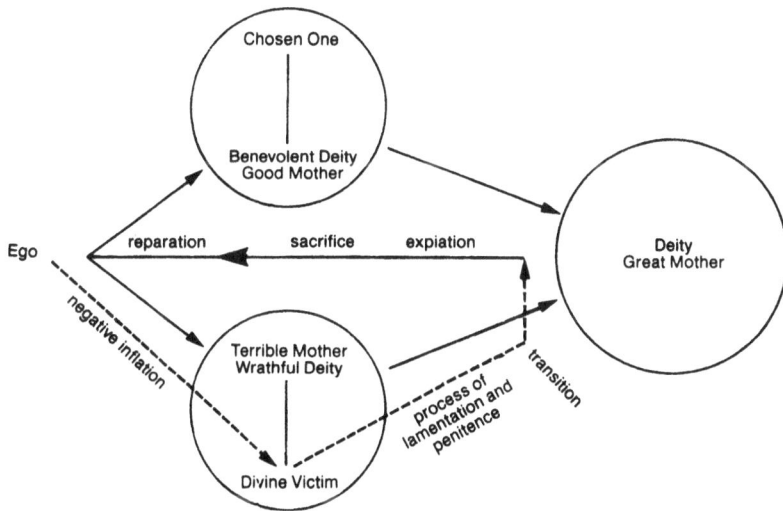

**Figure 4. Melancholia: Resolution.** Sacrificing its quest for (false) atonement with an "only good"-Self object, the ego finds a capacity to repair the covenantal ego-Self relationship by reworking the depressive position.

the tunnel towards final darkness, where the Divine Victim, the need for punishment and expiation, and the death instinct assume their most literal and tragic form: The full fury of the Wrathful Deity/Terrible Mother is unleashed into suicide and homicide. Alternatively, there may be a leap into mania, an identification with the archetype of the Chosen One and a "positive" relationship with the Benevolent Deity which is as one-sided—and hence as alienated from the "whole" Self—as the melancholiac's "negative" relationship to the Wrathful Deity.

If melancholia is to follow the pathway to reconciliation and at-one-ment with the Self, the ego will be led to an acceptance of the "sad truth" (Rado 1928) that the "good" and the "bad" are necessary attributes of a whole (Fig. 4). The quest for an "only good" mother must be sacrificed if the ego is to rework a relationship which can accomodate the tension between the light and dark sides of the Self. With the help of dreams, transference analysis, and imaginative activities such as free association, art work, and sand play—the rituals of psychoanalysis—the atonement process becomes a working through of the depressive position. Disidentifying from the Divine Victim archetype, the ego finds instead its individual capacity to be a *personal victim* who can feel sadness and guilt but who will know that damage or loss can be repaired.

## References

Abraham, K. 1911. Notes on the psycho-analytical investigation and treatment of manic-depressive insanity and allied conditions. In *Selected papers on psychoanalysis*, E. Jones, ed., pp. 137–56. New York: Brunner/Mazel.
_____. 1924. A short study of the development of the libido, viewed in the light of mental disorders. In *Selected papers on psycho-analysis*, E. Jones, ed., pp. 418–501. New York: Brunner/Mazel.
Alex, W. 1968. Depression in women. Paper presented at the meeting of the northern and Southern California Societies of Jungian Analysts, Carmel, California.
Alexander, F. 1931. Buddhistic training as artificial catatonia. In *The scope of psychoanalysis 1921–1961: Selected papers of Franz Alexander.* pp. 74–89. New York: Basic Books.
Arieti, S. 1974. Manic-depressive psychosis. In *American Handbook of psychiatry,*. vol 1., pp. 449–90. New York: Basic Books.
_____. 1978. *On schizophrenia, phobias, depression, psychotherapy, and the farther shores of psychiatry.* New York: Brunner/Mazel.
_____, and Bemporad, J. 1978. *Severe and mild depression: The psychotherapeutic approach.* New York: Basic Books.
Baynes, H. G. 1940. *Mythology of the soul.* London: Rider & Company.
Blomeyer, R. 1975. Some theses on depressive patients and their typology. Unpublished manuscript.
Carotenuto, A. 1982. *A secret symmetry: Sabina Spielrein between Jung and Freud.* New York: Pantheon Books.
Curry, A. 1975. Shadow quaternity: A geography. Unpublished manuscript.

Dalglish, E. R. 1961. *Psalm fifty-one in the light of ancient Near Eastern patternism.* Leiden: Brill.

Edinger, E. F. 1960. The ego-self paradox. *Journal of Analytical Psychology* 5:3–18.

_____. 1972. *Ego and archetype.* New York: G. P. Putnam's Sons.

Elkin, H. 1972. On selfhood and the developmental structures in infancy. *Psychoanalytic Review* 59:339–416.

Fordham, M. 1970. *Children as individuals,* rev. ed. New York: G. P. Putnam's Sons.

_____. 1973. Maturation of ego and self in infancy. In *Analytical psychology: A modern science* (The library of analytical psychology, vol. 1), pp. 83–94. London: Heinemann.

_____. 1976. *The self and autism* (The library of analytical psychology, vol. 3). London: Heinemann.

Freud, S. 1907. Obsessive actions and religious practices. In *Standard Edition* 9:116–27. London: Hogarth Press and The Institute for Psycho-analysis.

_____. 1917. Mourning and melancholia. In *Standard Edition* 14:243–58. London: Hogarth Press and The Institute for Psycho-analysis.

Gordon, R. 1960. The death instinct and its relation to the self. *Journal of Analytical Psychology* 6:119–35.

Grinker, R. R.; Miller, J.; Sabshin, M.; Nunn, R.; and Nunnally, J. C. 1961. *The phenomena of depressions.* New York: Hoeber.

Gunkel, H. 1930. *The Psalms: A form-critical introduction.* Philadelphia: Fortress Press.

Hobson, R. F. 1955. Archetypal themes in depression. *Journal of Analytical Psychology* 1:33–47.

Jacobsohn, H. 1968. The dialogue of a world-weary man with his Ba. In *Timeless documents of the soul,* J. Hillman, ed., pp. 1–54. Evanston: Northwestern University Press.

Jacobson, E. 1954. Transference problems in the psychoanalytic treatment of severely depressed patients. *Journal of the American Psychoanalytic Association* 2:595–606.

_____. 1964. *The self and the object world.* New York: International Universities Press.

Jung, C. G. 1912. *Symbols of transformation.* In *Collected works,* vol. 5. Princeton: Princeton University Press, 1956.

_____. 1921. *Psychological types.* In *Collected works,* vol. 6. Princeton: Princeton University Press, 1971.

_____. 1942. Transformation symbolism in the mass. In *Collected works,* 11:201–96. Princeton: Princeton University Press, 1958.

_____. 1959. *Aion: Researches into the phenomenology of the self.* In *Collected works,* vol. 9, pt. ii. Princeton: Princeton University Press.

King, L. W. 1899. *Babylonian religion and mythology.* London: Kegan Paul, Trench, Traubner and Co.

Klein, M. 1929. Personification in the play of children. In *Love, guilt and reparation & other works 1921–1945,* R. E. Money-Kyrle, ed., pp. 199–209. New York: Dell Publishing Co.

_____. 1935. A contribution to the psychogenesis of manic-depressive states. In *Love, guilt and reparation & other works 1921–1945,* pp. 262–89. New York: Dell Publishing Co.

Kraepelin, E. 1904. *Lectures on clinical psychiatry.* New York: William Wood & Co.

Lambert, K. 1981. Emerging consciousness. *Journal of Analytical Psychology* 26:1–17.

Lambert, W. G. 1960. *Babylonian wisdom literature.* Oxford; Oxford University Press.

Langdon, S. H. 1923. *Babylonian wisdom.* London: Luzac & Co.

Laplanche, J., and Pontalis, J.-B. 1973. *The language of psycho-analysis.* New York: W. W. Norton & Co..

Lewis, A. J. 1934. Melancholia: A historical review. *The Journal of Mental Science* 80:1–42.

Moody, R. 1961. A contribution to the psychology of the mother-child relationship. In *Current trends in analytical psychology*, G. Adler, ed., Proceedings of the First International Congress of Analytical Psychology, pp. 128–37. London: Tavistock.

Mowinckel, S. P1955. Psalm criticism between 1900 and 1935. *Vetus Testamentum* 5:13–33.

————. 1962. *The psalms in Israel's worship.* Oxford: Basil Blackwell.

Neumann, E. 1973. *The child.* New York: G. P. Putnam's Sons.

Newton, K., and Redfearn, J. 1977. The real mother, ego-self relations and personal identity. *Journal of Analytical Psychology* 22:295–315.

Nunberg, H., and Federn, E., eds. 1974. *Minutes of the Vienna Psychoanalytic Society*, vol. 3 (1910–1911). New York: International Universities Press.

Pao, P n. 1980. The dream in manic-depressive psychosis. In *The dream in clinical practice*, J. Natterson, ed., pp. 111–30. New York: Jason Aronson.

Perry, J. W. 1962. Reconstitutive process in the psychopathology of the self. *Annals of the New York Academy of Sciences* 96:853–76.

————. 1976. *Roots of renewal in myth and madness: The meaning of psychotic episodes.* San Francisco: Jossey-Bass.

Pritchard, J. B., ed. 1969. *Ancient Near Eastern texts relating to the Old Testament*, rev. ed. Princeton: Princeton University Press.

Rado, S. 1928. The problem of melancholia. *The International Journal of Psycho-Analysis* 9:420–38.

Redfearn, J. W. T. 1980. The energy of warring and combining opposites: Problems for the psychotic patient and the therapist in achieving the symbolic situation. In *Methods of treatment in analytical psychology*, I. F. Baker, ed., Proceedings of the Seventh International Congress for Analytical Psychology, pp. 206–18. Fellbach-Oeffingen, West Germany: Bonz.

Roheim, G. 1955. *Magic and schizophrenia.* Bloomington: Indiana University Press.

Vitale, A. 1980. Psychotherapy in depressive psychotic states. In *Methods of treatment in analytical psychology*, I. G. Baker, ed., Proceedings of the Seventh International Congress for Analytical Psychology, pp. 219–21. Fellbach-Oeffingen, West Germany: Bonz.

Widengren, G. 1936. *The Accadian and the Hebrew psalms of lamentation as religious documents.* Uppsala: Almqvist & Wiksells Boktryckeri-A.-B.

Wilke, H. J. 1978. On depressive delusion. *Spring*, pp. 105–14.

Winnicott, D. W. 1948. Reparation in respect of mother's organized defense against depression. In *Collected papers: Through paediatrics to psycho-analysis*, pp. 91–96. London: Hogarth.

————. 1954. The depressive position in normal emotional development. In *Collected papers: Through paediatrics to psycho-analysis*, pp. 262–77. London: Hogarth.

# Book Reviews

**Dream Analysis: Notes of the Seminar Given in 1928–1930 by C. G. Jung**
Edited by William McGuire. Bollingen Series XCIX. Princeton: Princeton University Press, 1984. 758 pp. $35.00

Reviewed by Joseph L. Henderson

William McGuire is to be congratulated on producing this version of Jung's second English seminar series and the Princeton University Press for putting it in such a handsome volume. I never imagined this material could be offered publicly, though it has been available in rough mimeographed editions for members of the seminar and students of analytical psychology for many years. I was a member of this seminar for its second year, and I recall that several of us painfully wrote down in long hand what we heard or thought we heard, following which we put our scratchy offerings together for the editor, Mary Foote, to print for us to read as an *aide-memoire*. Toward the end of my stay in Zurich, she prevailed upon Jung to allow a trained stenotypist to attend the seminars and record them in shorthand. Much later Jung agreed to read the final version but I think he made very few changes. He recognized the value of letting the spoken words carry their own meaning however unfinished or, at times, outrageous they might look in cold print. He sometimes said to us, "Don't put down all the nonsense I speak."

**Joseph L. Henderson,** M.D., is founding member and training analyst of the C. G. Jung Institute of San Francisco and former vice-president, International Association for Analytical Psychology.

I have read the whole series through in the new edition and, far from its being nonsense, I believe it reads well and contains a timely record of the basic concepts and methods of treatment for that time. Not being intended for scholarly inspection, it maintains the freshness of spontaneous communication. Jung was really enjoying himself, and in colloquial English he was free from those academic scruples to produce the kind of reasoning so admired in the Swiss and German lecture halls. Though he had due respect for that kind of intellectual display, he never failed to escape from its bondage whenever he could, and his seminars, consisting mainly of his own analysands, offered a special freedom of expression for his native genius.

(A previous English seminar, held in 1925, allowed Jung to present his basic concepts for the first time to a sympathetic audience following his break with Freud. That series also exists in mimeographed form but would not stand exposure to a larger public today because it omits his later developments in theory so necessary to understand his work as a whole. At that time he still spoke of the archetype entirely as an image and had not yet formulated its connection with the pattern of behavior. His introverted nature was happier and his expression clearer in relation to the inner images. However, what he was to conceptualize later appears in this series, so to speak, in *statu nascendi*, in the ferment of creation, and this is what makes the new volume so interesting in spite of its archaisms.)

I found it intriguing to ask myself what are some revisions we might think advisable to make today. One is Jung's habitual denigration of persona as being only a mask or a thin paste to obscure the real human being, or shall we say to obscure the existence of the *shadow*. There is a confusion here that is further confused by a diagram (Nov. 28, 1928, p. 51) that shows the persona as the opposite, not of the shadow, but of the anima or animus. Here the "individual" occupies an uncomfortable position in the center between the dark shadow side of a circle in the light side of which the ego seems to reign in sun-like splendor. On this same page his discussion of the persona limits it to a form of defensive narcissism and neglects to accord it any true psychological function, namely, the function of mediating differentiated social interactions. However, as we read on we find that Jung's one-sided statements open the door to a discussion of the nature of the shadow and the anima which throws light on these obscure regions in a way that might not have been possible starting from more soberly correct formulations.

The modern reader may also be somewhat baffled by Jung's statement that the man who has produced this dream series is not at all neurotic. Considering how many deep-seated problems come to light in the course of his analysis, one may wonder how much psychopathology Jung himself accepted as part of a normal life situation at that time. Although it is true that no gross abnormality comes to light in these pages, we cannot but notice how much of the shadow side of life remained unconscious in the post-Victorian culture of that time so that Jung, like Freud before him, had to step carefully lest his patients bolt at the suggestion that certain counter-cultural traits might have to be acknowledged as their own. Some of this comes out in a particularly amusing form in the interchange between Jung and Linda Fierz-David over the interpretation of a dream about a mouse (Dream 24, p. 531). Jung had asked the women of the seminar to interpret the symbolism of the mouse because it seemed to have to do with sex as eros and he said women know more about this than do men. But no woman dared speak up. At the next seminar there lay a communication on Jung's desk, signed "A Mouse." This was Linda's reply to Jung on behalf of the women who did not, she said, speak up because the cat, implying the critical presence of Jung's anima, might be lying in wait to pounce upon them with his superior male "knowledge," which would of course disparage the validity of their feminine eros. Jung took this criticism like a man, but he did not like it very much. The official charge of male chauvinism for such failures to honor the feminine point of view was something he never lived to encounter in its modern form.

If some of the interpretations in this volume seem dated, there are others that are still new and vitally interesting for anyone concerned with cultural history as a form of amplification. Certain dreams do not come from personal associations, nor yet from the collective unconscious, but from the culture-patterns of the Western world. I think Jung was often in error by calling these patterns aspects of the personal unconscious. For a long time I have been convinced they should be called aspects of a cultural unconscious. In support of this view the pages of this volume are filled with meaningful references to what we might call the unwritten history of our culture. Other members of the seminar felt as I did that we were specially fortunate to be taken on a journey through certain areas of this cultural unconscious with Jung as our guide. He had found his way into the early Christian era and from there into Greco-Roman culture and back still further into the Mycenaen culture with unerring instinct, and, thanks to his friendship with Richard Wilhelm, he was newly alive to ancient Chinese culture for another kind of insight into the Eastern world to which we may have access in the West if we can relate it individually to our cultural situation. Or so he seemed to say.

There are to be found here a number of subjects that Jung was in the process of developing, for example, the theory of synchronicity, and there is a lively discussion of the relevance of astrology in modern psychology. His conception of the *puer aeternus* appears here in its original form before it became a synonym for arrested development. He first saw it as the archetypal image of youthfulness, pure and simple. He uses it in the interpretation of his patient's dream of a divine youth and amplifies it with reference to Goethe's *Faust*, where it appears in three forms: the boy charioteer, Homunculus, and Euphorion. Jung's discussion of this is found at the end of the seminar of March 13, 1929 (pp. 174–75).

This brings me to a suggestion for the reader who may not have time or interest to wade through this whole book but would like to get the flavor of Jung's style. Frequently, as exemplified in the passage I have just mentioned, we find statements that are really inspired utterances that he let fall without needing to elaborate them further, and they frequently come at the end, or toward the end, of each seminar. This is even more marked in later seminars. Another example in line with the previous one is to be found at the end of the seminar notes of June 26, 1929 (pp. 293–95), with a remarkable interpretation of Meyrink's *Der Golem*. A still more remarkable passage in the December 11, 1929, seminar of the text and interpretation of Dream 21 (pp. 432–35) expresses a clear and very satisfying imagery of the Self as it pertains to individuation. I would also advise the reader to refer first of all to the synopsis of the dreams from the beginning by Dr. Mary Howells (p. 567), since early synopses are inadequate, including Jung's own history of the case.

When the case is reviewed as a whole, it can be seen that the true novelty of this series clearly lies in its exposure of Jung's method of working with the personal material of his patient in a way that is not apparent in his later case studies, such as the *Visions* seminar series or in *Psychology and Alchemy*, where personal material is ignored or repressed in favor of archetypal content. He had a good reason for this, since he was a single pioneer in his field, but reading those cases (and this was also true of the case of Miss Miller in *Symbols of Transformation*) we simply have no idea what kind of people they were in their families or in the world. The man in this series is real flesh and blood. He was a Swiss businessman, recently retired, and we have a clear picture of his origins, way of life, tastes, and the very human problems he had with his business associates or with his wife and children. Above all, he is an average patient, not a specially gifted professional or artist nor an interesting borderline person with a highly developed intuitive function, as we so commonly find in Jungian case reports.

This allows us to observe Jung in a role much closer to our own position as psychotherapists, and we can see how careful he was to assess the individual potential of his patient and how far to go in helping him develop it. In these seminar notes there shines forth a kind of therapeutic philosophy that I have always found very sustaining in my own work: It may be stated as Jung's honesty with his patient and with himself in limiting the goal of the work to what can be realized and not to be carried away by the love of teleology for its own sake. At the same time, he was ready to respond enthusiastically to those occasional miracles of healing or transcendent experiences that take place in any full analysis. The true Jungian "method" comes out most clearly in his interpretive skill in relation to the transference of his patient. It begins in his discussion of Dream 22 (pp. 444–62), which comes rather late in the series. I will let him describe this:

> This really was the first dream in which I got a glimmer of hope that this man would tackle his own problem, that he would develop perhaps such a love of fate that he would pull his courage together and take the wheel into his own hands. . . . He must follow his individual choice, his individual fate, and that cannot be foreseen. (Feb. 5, 1930, p. 461)

Up to that time this man's dreams had shown him all sorts of possible goals for therapy, but also many evasions. What held him to the main task of self-realization was, of course, the transference to Jung, and this is beautifully displayed in Jung's interpretation of the intricate symbolism of Dream 27 (p. 624), where a *compte-jointe* (joint account) is established between two business acquaintances, Michel and Jalobout, concerning the exportation of coffee from a certain plantation. By disentangling the threads of the patient's associations together with his awareness of his own countertransference, Jung shows how a patient feels and how we should treat him or her when it is time to honor the analysis as a kind of joint account where both partners must learn how to withdraw what they have put into it without depriving the other of his own rightful share.

Besides the dream analysis, this volume contains reference to some research carried out by members of the seminar at Jung's instigation. One was a method of making a pictorial graph of the dream motifs to assess the degree of progression or regression. Since the individual diagrams were not available for publication, the account of them is rather thin. But there was another research project that is fully displayed. Lecture V, November 6, 1929 (p. 340) was given by Dr. William Barrett on the cross as a symbol, while Lecture VI on November 13, 1929 (p. 367) was given by Dr. Esther Harding on the crescent as a symbol. We had all been divided into two groups to explore the symbolism of the cross and the crescent, because they had appeared as artifacts thrown together in a pot in one of the patient's dreams. Dr. Barrett and Dr. Harding had been chosen to gather our material and write a report, since they were the most experienced analyst members of the seminar.

Unfortunately, they were not equally experienced at conducting their research projects. Although Dr. Barrett was able to use this opportunity to learn something of the method of amplification, he was limited as to its psychological applicability. Dr. Harding, with her wider experience, found in the crescent, as a symbol of the moon with its cyclical character, a springboard for her exploration of the feminine psyche, which appeared two years later in her best-selling *The Way of All Women* and later when the main content of this research was included in *Women's Mysteries*. Both reports are well illustrated, and we have a glimpse of Jung's talent as teacher in drawing out the various individuals to talk bout their contributions to the project.

All in all, the *Seminars on Dream Analysis* afford the reader with an opportunity to turn the prism of C. G. Jung's personality so as to show the analyst, the scholar, the teacher, and the man. The book is a valued complement to the formality of the *Collected Works.*

**Energies of Love: Sexuality Re-Visioned**
June Singer. Garden City, N. Y.: Anchor Press/Doubleday, 1983. 314 pp.
$16.95.

Reviewed by Ann Mankowitz

Eros, which binds together the masculine and the feminine in the act of love, is also the power that unites the human with the divine. The energies of love underlie both sexuality and religion. In Michelangelo's fresco on the Sistine Chapel's ceiling the great figures of God and Adam are joined by the finger tips. June Singer writes: "This passing of the spark from God to man may be seen as an act of love. In the most subtle sense it may contain the essence of sexuality as well, for the fire that passes from the one to the other is fully generative; it brings humanity into being" (p. 275).

The subjective experiences of mystic union and sexual union have frequently been described in strikingly similar terms, and we see in the graphic representations of saints and mystics expressions that mirror the heights of sexual ecstasy. From an archetypal perspective religion is based on man's awe-struck response from his own human nature to the totality of the natural universe around him, at the center of which is the conjunction of masculine and feminine in the mysterious act of creation. How is it, then, that acts in the name of *religion* are often cruel and destructive, and acts of *sexuality* unloving and divisive? It is the long black shadow that divides the two and their potential for re-integration through expanded consciousness that Singer is examining in her latest book.

She places her new vision within the historical context of changing world-views in western society, starting from the Middle Ages, a time when religion was lived in everyday life, and proceeding through the Renaissance and the beginnings of natural science and philosophical humanism toward the dualistic philosophy of Descartes in which matter was separated from spirit and the sacred from the profane, each having its sphere of influence. As religion became more personal and subjective, so natural science characterized by Newtonian physics came increasingly to be the only objectivity. The progressive separation of natural science from philosophy, of the body from the soul, of reason from emotion, characterized the world-view Singer calls the "paradigm of modernity" (p. 25).

Sexual mores were, inevitably, changing with the vast movements of social history. By the end of the nineteenth century the roles and functions of men and women were clearly differentiated from each other in daily life and work; and with the advent of specialization in all fields of industrial and increasingly technological society, the sexes were more and more segregated, and sexuality became a furtive and private activity to be engaged in

**Ann Mankowitz,** Ph.D., is a member of the Inter-Regional Society of Jungian Analysts and has a private analytical practice in Santa Fe, New Mexico.

behind closed doors. Established religion sanctioned only married sexuality and mainly the procreative aspects. "Sexual repression's shadow side expressed itself furtively through pornography, obscenity, and prostitution (mostly for men); for women a vast passionate romantic literature, where love and violence jostled with each other in one breathless situation after another" (p. 29). The image of the feminine was sharply divided into the wife and the whore, and the double standard for men and women dominated sexual mores. Freud discovered that the most prevalent illness of the mind from which his middle-class female patients suffered at the end of the nineteenth century was conversion hysteria, in which the suppressed energies of love burst out in bizarre *bodily* symptoms.

By the beginning of the twentieth century, just when it seemed that modern society was prospering, it was undermined, like Freud's patients, by the eruptions of the unconscious, and the "paradigm of modernity" began to break down. Its dualistic influence, however, continued up to World War II (and still exerts itself), but it was in the 1950s and 1960s that the big changes began to happen, and the "sexual revolution" was at hand. "Sexual revolution" is a shorthand phrase for a whole complexity of ideas, movements, discoveries, and awakenings that came together in the 1960s in a surge of vital energy and heightened consciousness: the new sciences and the eastern philosophies, the women's liberation movement, the birth control pill, the drug culture, ongoing wars, the presence and threat of the bomb, and new psychotherapies emerging from the human potential movement all played their part in the new era.

Singer selects four men to represent the breaking of "the boundaries of Western intellectual tradition": Carl Jung, Abraham Maslow, Alan Watts, and Huston Smith (p. 96). If her choices seem eccentric, her reason is that all four had backgrounds in one of the traditional religions of the west while at the same time having a strong interest in Eastern religion, particularly in Taoistic philosophy, which was beginning to influence the counter-culture movements.

Jung was almost alone among psychologists and psychiatrists in focusing on the numinous dimension of the psyche. He believed that psychic energy fueled all aspects of human creativity, including sexual relationships, and his conviction that sexuality is spiritual and archetypal as well as biological and personal gave rise to his concept of the contra-sexual aspect of the psyche, anima and animus, and a possibility of the union of the masculine and feminine within one psyche.

A striking aspect of the emerging paradigm as seen by Singer was in the changing direction and expansion of the scientific disciplines. The distance between the science of the west (hitherto dependent on evidence of the senses) and the philosophies of the east (approached through inward meditation and intuition) began to close. Singer finds a fascinating analogy between Chuang Tzu's Great Knowledge/Small Knowledge concept and physicist David Bohm's idea of implicate and explicate order. Implicate order is like the Great Knowledge of Chuang Tzu, but also it is analogous to Jung's concept of the archetypes and the collective unconscious. The archetypes only become conscious when they manifest in archetypal images, i.e., become explicate.

Of the four men who "broke the boundaries," Alan Watts was the one who really addressed the subjective experience of sexuality. He believed that too much emphasis is placed on sexual technique to enhance pleasure, and that it is important to return to a sacred dimension of sexuality.

> For pleasure is a grace and is not obedient to the commands of the will. . . . There is obviously nothing degrading in sensuous pleasure which comes "of itself" without craving. . . . Pleasure cannot be given unless the senses are in a state of accepting rather than taking, and . . . they must not be . . . paralysed and rigidified by the anxiety to get something out of the object. (Pp. 111–12)

Singer is an able synthesizer. She has selected and focused on a wealth of data pertaining to the personal and collective, the inner and outer developments of western society, over a period of time up to the present day. For both her wide sweep and her particular and original points of selection and focus, her book is fascinating reading.

Yet somehow in the plethora of data, the new vision of sexuality gets blurred. It emerges best in the experiential statements and personal imagery of the author and of her mentors. Also I feel that she dismisses the Women's Liberation movement too lightly in her assessment of important influences; and although this feminist force itself has no doubt emerged in the wake of other upheavals, its effects on the balance of power between the sexes, and on social and family life, are too significant and ongoing to be seen merely as a "separatist force [that] has been in decline for some time now" (p. 143).

As I understand it, Singer's new vision of sexuality does not include an endless battle between the sexes, with the power gravitating from male to female and back again. Her re-visioning is a unifying one, containing not only a hope of healing age-old schisms of the psyche, but also a trust in the imminent possibility of collective progress toward this state. This trust seems to come from the stage she has arrived at in her own life, which she describes as the "transpersonal stage" at which one is able to "see life whole" (p. 275) and love in a transpersonal way that goes beyond ego, and unites the personal ego with the larger Self.

While believing in and respecting Singer's advanced stage in her own individuation process, I find the claims of Transpersonal Psychology, which go beyond Jung's concept of personal individuation, unrealistic, even inflated. For Jung the goal of complete individuation, whatever that may be, is never attained, and as far as we can see, the process begins when life begins and ends when life ends. Jung is Singer's "mentor," but she also has embraced Transpersonal Psychology at the point at which it leaves the real ground of Jungian thought and takes flight into the ideal. Thus, the holistic vision of the totality of Self, the unity of masculine and feminine, ego and Self, human and divine, is seen to be attainable, not only for some individuals, but also for society, the collective. This credo, not in its essence, but because it goes too far, effects her re-visioning of sexuality in the way that idealization always blurs reality and confuses the essential message, which is worth communicating. The touching of finger tips between God and Adam is a beautiful and telling image of the procreativity between the human and the divine, yet we cannot fail to notice that nowadays Adam and Eve are hardly making contact at all, or else making war. Is it that their common humanity and perfect biological fit are displaced by narcissistic needs to explore their gender identities before union can take place? Or perhaps they are too young and unevolved to have reached the stage where ego may give way to Self in transpersonal love.

In *Memories, Dreams, Reflections* Jung wrote of transpersonal love:

> Eros is a *kosmogonos*, a creator and father-mother of all higher consciousness. . . . We are in the deepest sense the victims and the instruments of cosmogonic "love." I put the word in quotation marks to indicate that I do not use it in its connotations of desiring, preferring, favoring, wishing, and similar feelings, but as something superior to the individual, a unified and undivided whole. *Being a part, man cannot grasp the whole.* (Jung 1961, pp. 353–54; emphasis added)

## Reference

C. G. Jung. *Memories, Dreams, Reflections.* New York: Random House, 1961.

## Image Formation and Psychotherapy

Mardi Jon Horowitz. New York and London: Jason Aronson, Inc., 1983. 319 pp. $27.50

Reviewed by James A. Hall

*Image Formation and Psychotherapy* is both an exciting book and a disappointing book. Had I read it during psychiatric training, it would have been exciting, for it clearly documents the usefulness of imagery, a neglected aspect in the training and practice of psychotherapy. There also are several categorical analyses (such as neurobiological influences on image formation) that are clarifying and helpful in conceptualizing some confusing images found in clinical practice. One woman, for example, reported seeing a red hue that she called "the blood of Christ," which appeared after a "shower of sparks"—certainly a pregnant psychodynamic remark! It was found on medical examination, however, that she had suffered a retinal hemorrhage, which initiated the altered imagery she had interpreted in religious language.

---

**James A. Hall,** M.D., is clinical associate professor of psychiatry, University of Texas Health Science Center, Dallas, and a founding member of the Inter-Regional Society of Jungian Analysts.

Having read the book after my Jungian training (and after considerable experience with hypnotherapy), I must say that it is disappointing in a certain lack of depth in regard to imagery. Dr. Horowitz frequently refers to "transformation and disguise" in relation to image formation; he frequently seems to be writing from a classical Freudian position without wide awareness of the rich Jungian and hypnotic literature on the nature of images in the process of psychotherapy. He does cite Jungians Gerhard Adler, Christopher Whitmont, John Perry, and Jung himself, as well as Martin Orne and Paul Sarcedote, major figures in hypnosis research. Horowitz even shows some acquaintance with the psychical research literature, something frequently overlooked in academic writings. His scholarship is excellent.

An exciting, but not fully explicit, model in this book is the suggestion (p. 71) that consciousness may *sample* thought, so that thought processes are continually present, though unconscious, and may be sampled at various points by ego-consciousness. A similar concept, that of "schematic images . . . considered as role-relationship models or the two-person dyads" (p. 87) suggests an underlying pattern of what I have called *identity structures* or *object-relation patterns*, actually various patternings of complexes with which the central ego can identify or *dis*-identify, as most readily seen in the structure of serial dreams. Horowitz, however, places emphasis on the defensive nature of shifts of identity within such dyadic patterns rather than upon the (Jungian) tendency of the mind to represent such patterns in dreams and elsewhere for the purpose of furthering individuation through a relativization of such patterns of complexes within the wider coherence of the ego-Self axis.

Horowitz suggests an important aspect of image representation of object relationships is to maintain a defensive ambiguity of reference, since the ego-identity can be assigned to either pole of the object-relation dyad: "In other words, the persons may experience the image without awareness as to who is hurt, who is hurting." Representation in images is contrasted to *lexical representation* "with its primarily sequential organization" which is less capable of serving a defensive function since lexical thought "identifies persons more clearly because word names are used" (p. 88).

This model allows Horowitz (p. 88) to present an interesting discussion of varieties of regression: (1) a return to earlier systems of representation, as from words to images or enactions; (2) a regression *within* a system, as to an earlier rather than a contemporary body image; (3) a return within one system to earlier controls, as a decrease in inhibition. The structure of thought is presented in three different systems, of which images are but one, the other modes being enactive and lexical. With this triform model of thought, plus allowance for translation from one system into another, Horowitz avoids many problems of placing enactive (body) thought as more primary to lexical thought (as in the proliferating schools of body therapy). He also avoids the position of Lacan in considering lexical arrangements more primary than other modes in the unconscious. "The goal of psychotherapy, when the condition is not one of severe organic impairment, is to reestablish continuity between ideas and attitudes in various modes of representation" (p. 94).

In a discussion of visualizing techniques, a quite useful table of defensive inhibitions and related clinical interventions is presented (p. 291), with examples of both interpretive interventions and more directive interventions. If images are not associated with word meanings, the therapist might say, "Describe your images to me in words." If enactive (body) representations are not translated into images, an interpretative intervention might be, "Perhaps you are afraid to picture your present weight because the self-image would embarrass you." A number of visualizing techniques are reviewed, including Jung's active imagination (p. 286), which is fairly, though briefly, described. Consistent with the general stance of the book, Horowitz agrees with "the prevalence of archetypes in fantasy images" but reduces the archetypal image to "basic patterns of the human life situation" (p. 287) rather than to the structure of the objective psyche. "Perhaps, if we substitute childhood or unconscious fantasy for prehistoric, archetype, and ages past, this mystic theory is not as incompatible with psychologic theories as it might seem" (p. 242). Similarly, the concept of symbol is used in a typically non-Jungian fashion as "a process by which one object, feeling, or situation may be chosen to signify another"—precisely the meaning of *sign* or *semiotic sign* in Jungian thought.

Horowitz has presented a provoking and competent exposition of the history, form, and utility of incorporating imagery techniques in psychotherapy as one part of a balanced approach to the patient. "Image techniques should be related to a larger, well-formulated plan for how a patient may change. This should include attention to how the therapist's intervention influences the patient's immediate train of thought and views of the relationship with the therapist" (p. 305).

There are three major values to this volume. For Jungians it provides a non-Jungian conceptual framework that causes us to think through again some of our assumptions; mandala images, for example are reported as one of the "redundant elements of form" seen in some mystical visionary experiences and may be produced by some of the anatomic structure of the eye, possibly the optic disc, the central scotoma or natural blind spot in the eye. For non-Jungian psychotherapists, the book is a bold call for the use of images in psychotherapy.

The third an perhaps most important value of the book is as a conceptual bridge, one end resting on the rich clinical material of analytical psychology (and fields such as hypnotherapy) and the other on the experimental sciences. During the current era, while academic psychiatry seems committed to a neurobiological model of mental disorder, an emphasis on the psychodynamic meaning of mental images, even if cast in a problematic Freudian mode, can only be a helpful corrective. Also during this time, there is danger of Jungian psychology becoming too self-absorbed, unconcerned with the difficult questions with which Jung himself struggled—the experimental investigation of psychic structure (as in the word association experiment and the objective interpretation of dreams), the profound mind/body connection of psychosomatic illnesses, and the deep underlying unity of the mind and the world revealed by synchronicity. Jung was concerned with more than psychotherapeutic method. His most abiding concern seemed to be for a clearer vision of the underlying unity of the mind and the world as reflected in both science and religion. A more complete unfolding of Jung's vision requires that Jungians pay more attention to the questions raised by such books as *Image Formation in Psychotherapy* and that such investigators as Horowitz more fully understand and apply the rich insights of analytical psychology, which offer a needed corrective to the implicit reductionism of both neurophysiological models of mental disorder and the classic Freudian model of the mind.

**Object Relations in Psychoanalytic Theory**
Jay R. Greenberg and Stephen A. Mitchell. Cambridge, Mass.: Harvard University Press, 1983. 437 pp. $25.00

Reviewed by Alfred Collins

In this excellent and timely book, Greenberg and Mitchell argue that the history of psychoanalysis can be viewed as a series of efforts to resolve a problematic relationship between the drive theory enunciated by Freud and "object relatedness," i.e., the fundamental importance of relationships with other people.

Why is this a problem? It seems obvious, after all, that our relationships with others are not free of drive-like motivations (needs for sexual satisfaction and dependency, perverse aims such as masochism, etc.), and the very concept of drive has always implied some sort of object through which it could be satisfied. The precise nature of the connection between the relational and drive-like elements has been debated, particularly the issue of which is primary. Greenberg and Mitchell go further and make a compelling, but I believe finally unacceptable, case for the thesis that two fundamentally irreconcilable viewpoints underlie all object relations theorizing from Freud to the present.

The first, called the "drive/structure" model, argues for the primacy of drives and their derivatives, leaving the object only a subsidiary place in theory; analytic work is internal to the psyche of the analysand and results in structural reorganization of the mind. The second, the "relational/structure" model, claims that the effort to establish certain kinds of relationships with others is more basic than drives, which typically operate only in the service of these relationships or as breakdown products when the relationships are disrupted. Analysis is a process of removing obstacles to healthy, mature forms of relatedness to others. (Some relational/structure

---

**Alfred Collins**, Ph.D., is a clinical psychologist in private practice in Anchorage, Alaska. He is a candidate-in-training in the C.G. Jung Institute of Chicago.

models involve *internal* objects and relationships to these; hence success-ful analytic work operates essentially on both inner and outer object relat-edness, both of which are theoretically primary.) Clearly within the drive/ structure model are Freud himself, Hartmann, Jacobson, Mahler, and Melan-ie Klein (who is transitional); within the relational/structure model are Sullivan, Fairbairn, Winnicott, most of Kohut, and Kernberg (who mistak-enly believes that he belongs to the first category).

While Greenberg and Mitchell claim to provide no more than a value-neutral "reader's guide through major dimensions of the history of psycho-analytic ideas" (p. 380), their book continually betrays the underlying thesis that the relational/structure model is superior, and that psychoanalysis as a whole is evolving in the direction of increasingly relational models. Both authors are members of the Sullivanian William Alanson White Institute in New York, so their relational bias is not surprising, but it could have been made more explicit. The "political" aspect of theory-building (the forma-tion of sects and denominations within psychoanalysis, with the associated phenomena of excommunication, inquisitions, and loyalty tests) is themat-ically considered throughout the book, and one may speculate that the downplaying of their Sullivanian loyalties is a political move by Greenberg and Mitchell aimed at making their book more acceptable to old-line drive theorists. The hypersensitivity to dissenters shown by medical psychoanal-ysis in America suggests that this aim is unlikely to be achieved.

What exactly *is* the "relational/structure" model, and how is it irrec-oncilable with the Freudian drive model, even as modified by later psy-choanalysts? In a superb chapter on Sullivan, the authors outline a number of points of divergence, of which the most important seem to be three:

1. The basic unit in relational theories is the interpersonal field, not the individual psyche. For instance, the mother-child bond for Sullivan consists of a field within which both are suspended: a field of need for nurturance (child) and need to nurture (mother). Neither side makes sense or can exist without the other; hence it cannot be merely a case of the baby's "oral libido" alone. The need is reciprocal and involves an "integrating tendency."

2. Experience is inherently bipolar for relational theories. Thus the self for Sullivan "is composed of a collection of prominent 'me-you' patterns loosely held together by a set of rationalizations" (p. 98). An example would be the "me-you" pattern of the mother and child just described: need to be responded to tenderly (me)—need to respond tenderly (you). Many of these bipolar patterns are more or less pathological, being motivat-ed by a need to protect good self feelings from anxiety. Examples include: "the self as victimized/the other as . . . tyrannical; the self as special/the other as admiring" (p. 98). These habitual patterns superimposed on interpersonal reality obscure actual relatedness in the present.

3. The environment is not separate from the self. When the world responds appropriately to the needs of the person, a balanced sense of self-world wholeness can exist which contrasts sharply with the satisfaction of a drive. For Freud, drive satisfaction brings about a *loss* of interest in the environment. On the other hand, failures of the environment, especially the early human environment, to respond appropriately to the self brings

about a constriction of experience, limitation of awareness to selected aspects of the self and world, and especially a compensatory inflation or grandiosity of the self image. Classical drive theory accounts for environ-mental influence by the "reality principle," but drives are at best *controlled* by psychological structures representing reality; they are not intrinsically *comprised* of environmental factors interacting with inner ones.

Greenberg and Mitchell seem to be covertly addressing an imbalance personified by the classical psychoanalysts, and Jungians could also benefit from the corrective of the interpersonal/relational model. The concepts of archetype and complex share with drives a tendency to minimize the influence of the environment, to ignore the existence of interpersonal fields, and to neglect the bipolar quality of experience. On the other hand, there are theorists within the Jungian community working to redress these omis-sions. Hillman and the archetypalists have worked extensively on the bipolar quality of archetypes (senex/puer, anima/hero, etc.); Goodheart has brought the interpersonal field into Jungian work; and Fordham and the British group around him have emphasized the environment and its effects on the developing psyche. The difficulties these thinkers have had in being heard by Jungian orthodoxy parallel the outcast status of interpersonal theories within classical psychoanalysis.

But the problem is not simply political. There is, as Greenberg and Mitchell argue in the final section of their book, a basic antinomy in Western thought which makes it hard to integrate individual-centered and socially-centered views of man. The latter claim that "the individual by himself cannot create a fully human life. . . . Individual man is, by himself, incom-plete." Conversely, individual-centered theories argue that the individual person is the primary datum of social life, and that his or her social relations exist only in the service of private aims.

Individuation, for drive theories, is ultimately good, while for relation-al theories it smacks of grandiosity that devalues the significance of the environmental context. Conversely, for relational theories the bipolar field of person and world, adjusted in balance and mutual appropriateness, is the highest good, while for drive theories it smells of ego weakness, merger, oceanic feelings, and the "black mud tide" of regression.

Like most antinomies, the drive/structure—relational/structure oppo-sition serves an important heuristic purpose; it organizes the theories neatly and shines a bright light into many dark corners. For this reason the book deserves, and will repay, close reading and rereading. But the sword of discrimination that the antinomy provides cuts perhaps too well, rendering asunder things that cannot really be separated. I believe a closer reading of *each* of the theories Greenberg and Mitchell discuss would reveal that each theorist *believes* he or she has resolved the antinomy, and to a greater or lesser extent, they are right.

To suggest briefly how a theorist *not* discussed by Greenberg and Mitchell, namely C. G. Jung, tries to resolve the paradox, consider the nature of an archetype, for instance, the mother archetype. A newborn child is preprogrammed to need and seek nourishment; this need is guided intrinsically toward the mother image derived from the archetype and represented by some actual person (not necessarily his mother, or even a female) in the environment. For Jung, the *instinct* of needing nourishment intrinsically contains an *image* expressing both the instinct itself and its satisfaction. The image guides the instinct toward satisfaction but also elevates it to developmentally higher levels where it becomes part of a larger structure, the Self.

But the archetypal image associated with the instinct is a sort of *object*; it represents both the immediate goal and the teleological, "prospective" function which Jung postulates in the psyche. Furthermore, the archetype has developed over time, phylogenetically, in response to the experience of actual children of their mothers (among other things). Hence the child is attuned to his environment as he arrives in the mother's arms; the "drive"-like archetype *already* contains a relational aspect. This is why Jung and others have compared the archetype theory with ethology, where instincts also are intimately bound together with their objects, called "releasers" in that theory.

Finally, I suggest that a more fundamental antinomy than that of drive and relationship is to be found in the leeway between drive *and* relationship on one side and the self (or Self) on the other. This issue is treated only in passing by Greenberg and Mitchell, which explains why their readings of Winnicott and Kohut, while superficially accurate, lack depth and sympathy. The point is that a unified, cohesive self, in *both* kinds of theories, tends to exist in *opposition* to the environment; this is a good thing for drive theories and bad for relational theories. Self theories, on the other hand, like Jung's, Winnicott's, and Kohut's, see a deep, fundamental kinship between the self—as an organized, central, conscious principle—and the world. This is expressed in varying terms as "synchronicity," "transitional realm," and "self/selfobject configuration."

Within its limits, then (dictated by the interactional orientation of the authors), this is a wonderful book. It succeeds in cutting deeply into the heart of one fundamental psychoanalytic paradox, that of drive versus relationship. If it goes overboard slightly in pushing its point and ignores other equally or more fundamental issues, this is a small price to pay for its achievements.

*Announcing . . .*

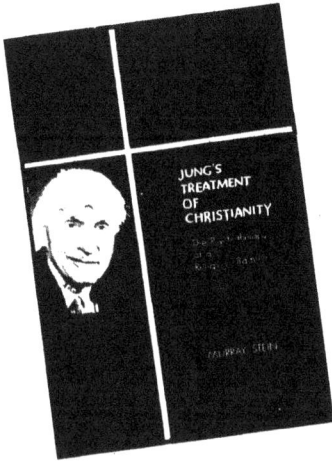

# Jung's Treatment of Christianity: The Psychotherapy of a Religious Tradition

### by Murray Stein

C. G. Jung wrote extensively on Christian themes during the last 20 years of his life. In this innovative study of those writings, Murray Stein, Ph.D., describes how Jung, the great doctor of souls, took modern Christianity under his psychotherapeutic care. By analyzing Jung's writings on the Trinity, the Mass, alchemy, the Bible, and various biblical figures, Stein demonstrates how Jung's writings represented a psychotherapeutic effort to help Christianity evolve into its next stage of development.

Jung's childhood, his father and other Christian ancestors, his relationship with Freud and psychoanalysis are all part of the drama that unfolds, with Jung the doctor at the center.

> "Stein's design of Jung as therapist of Christianity works extremely well. All this is used brilliantly. . . . I couldn't stop reading, didn't want to, am glad I didn't, learned a lot."
>
> — Eugene Gendlin, Ph.D., Professor,
> University of Chicago, author of *Focusing*

Murray Stein is a member of the Chicago Society of Jungian Analysts and has a private practice in Wilmette, Illinois. A graduate of Yale University, the C. G. Jung Institute of Zurich, and the University of Chicago, Stein is the editor of *Jungian Analysis* (1982) and the author of *In Midlife* (1983).

ISBN: 0-933029-00-4
Cloth: $24.95

ORDER FROM:
Chiron Publications
400 Linden Avenue
Wilmette, Illinois 60091

# PSYCHOLOGICAL
## PERSPECTIVES

A Semi-Annual Review of Jungian Thought
including articles, essays, poetry,
fiction, book, and film reviews

**FUTURE SPECIAL ISSUES:**
Women's Mysteries: In Art,
History, and Literature
Men

**SUBSCRIBE FOR**
1 year:   $12.00
2 years: $22.00
3 years: $30.00
add for foreign
$2.00 per year

*Published by the C.G. Jung Institute of Los Angeles*
*10349 West Pico Boulevard, Los Angeles, California 90064*

# HARVEST

*Journal for Jungian Studies published by the*
*Analytical Psychology Club*
*LONDON*

## HARVEST No. 30, 1984

ISSN 0266-4771

----------------------------------------------------------------

**ORDERS**

Cheques payable to:
Analytical Psychology Club (Harvest), Harvest Secretary,
26 Sutherland Avenue, London W9 2HQ, England
US $18.00    £7.50    S.Fr.27

NAME . . . . . . . . . . . . . . . . . . . . . . . . . . . . . . . . . . . . . . . . . . . . .
BLOCK LETTERS PLEASE

ADDRESS . . . . . . . . . . . . . . . . . . . . . . . . . . . . . . . . . . . . . . .

. . . . . . . . . . . . . . . . . . . . . . . . . . . . . . . . . . . . . . . . . . . . . .

. . . . . . . . . . . . . . . . . . . . . . . . . . . . . . . . . . . . . . . . . . . . . .

# Jungian Cassette Tapes

■ **John Beebe**, "The Father's Anima as a Clinical and Symbolic Problem." A probing of how fathers' inner attitudes affect the fate of their sons. 1 cassette, $10.

■ **Michael Fordham,** "Abandonment in Infancy." The role of abandonment in early childhood, with attention to a particular case. Vintage Fordham. 1 cassette, $10.

■ **Michael Fordham,** "Interview." A wide-ranging 90-minute conversation with the eminent English Jungian analyst and author. Of great interest to the student of the history of psychoanalysis and analytical psychology. Excellent for teaching. Interviewers: Nathan Schwartz-Salant and Murray Stein. 1 videocassette, $40. (Specify Beta or VHS.)

■ **Nathan Schwartz-Salant,** "Archetypal Aspects of Sexual Acting-out in Analysis." A discussion of the archetypal patterns and hidden meanings of sexual attractions and relations between therapists and their clients. 1 cassette, $10.

■ **Nathan Schwartz-Salant,** "The Borderline Personality: A Jungian Approach." Reflections on the genesis and purpose of borderline personality structures, with numerous clinical examples. Pictures included. 1 cassette and pictures, $10.

■ **Nathan Schwartz-Salant,** "Dynamics of the Analytic Relationship." A discussion of the *coniunctio,* with special reference to borderline states occurring in borderline and non-borderline personalities. Analysis of Jung's "Psychology of the Transference" and its imagery. 3 cassettes, $25.

■ **Nathan Schwartz-Salant,** "On Body Consciousness." A discussion of the integration of personality through body awareness and the somatic unconscious. 1 cassette, $10.

■ **Nathan Schwartz-Salant,** "The Self in Narcissistic Personality Disorders." A comprehensive seminar on a Jungian approach to pre-oedipal psychopathology. 2 cassettes, $17.50.

■ **Murray Stein,** "In Midlife." Seven lectures on transformation at midlife, in the companionable presence of Hermes. Includes a reading of the "Homeric Hymn to Hermes," by Roland Rude. 4 cassettes, $30.

■ **Murray Stein,** "Jungian Analysis: A Brief Introduction." A discussion of Jung's contributions to psychoanalytic technique and of the 4 stages of analysis. 1 cassette, $10.

■ **Murray Stein,** "Marriage Alchemy." A discussion of psychological intimacy in marriage and how to get there, with examples and a method. 1 cassette, $10.

Ill. residents add 7% sales tax

Order from:

Chiron Publications
400 Linden Avenue
Wilmette, Illinois 60091

Journal designed by Elaine M. Hill

www.ingramcontent.com/pod-product-compliance
Lightning Source LLC
Chambersburg PA
CBHW071349280326
41927CB00040B/2433